BLURRED BOUNDARIES

BLURRED BOUNDARIES

Feminist Essays on Twenty-First-Century Academic Labor

— EDITED BY —

Jessica Edens McCrary

AND Lynée Lewis Gaillet

THE UNIVERSITY OF SOUTH CAROLINA PRESS

Published by the University of South Carolina Press
Columbia, South Carolina 29208

uscpress.com

Printed in the United States of America

Library of Congress Cataloging-in-Publication Data
can be found at http://catalog.loc.gov/.

ISBN: 978-1-64336-585-5 (hardcover)
ISBN: 978-1-64336-649-4 (paperback)
ISBN: 978-1-64336-673-9 (ebook)

Dedicated to academic mothers

CONTENTS

LIST OF ILLUSTRATIONS

Figures

Tables

PREFACE

Lynée Lewis Gaillet

Editing a book collection always presents a challenge, with so many moving parts, contributors, reviewers, and publisher guidelines to consider and negotiate. Editing a book collection during a national pandemic was downright daunting. Initially, Jessica (Jessie) and I had a blurry vision for this project, one stemming from our own experiences and those of our colleagues and students. We recognized that women were shouldering huge burdens and unfathomable labor demands—both domestic and paid, and we wanted to capture a snapshot of this (extended) moment, a murky situation that, regardless of outcomes, immediately revealed the necessity to address systemic labor issues within the academy and beyond.

This project was dichotomous from its inception: How to encourage contributors to find time during a pandemic to write about experiences of being overworked and exhausted? How to ask a broad swath of authors to capture their engagements with family, friends, and work at the height of personal fear and frustration? How to find the required sense of equilibrium to make sense of events while standing in the middle of a rushing stream? How to collaborate amid a level of isolation that few of us have ever experienced? Early drafts didn't resemble the usual academic fare, essays that emanated from a space of contemplation and research. Instead, these pandemic survival narratives were raw and guttural, written from the heart and exuding pain and frustration; they stemmed from resentment and fear, and in some cases were penned from the precipice of breaking points. As editors, we weren't sure what to do with these submissions, how to validate the contributors' responses (some of which we shared) while shaping these simultaneously discordant reactions to recurring themes into an organized monograph. However, we immediately understood that this Call for Papers struck an important chord, one that uniquely blended the personal and the professional, the cultural and the familial while bringing to the foreground muted yet interminable labor issues.

We granted extensions (how could we not, given the focus of the collection?) and began plotting how we might provide a conduit for sharing these moving narratives and explorations of teaching, parenting, researching, mentoring, publishing, caring, leading, and surviving during this moment—one accompanied by the recognition of decades-long unacknowledged and pent-up frustrations. While most edited collections typically include neatly arranged sections that contain chapters of similar lengths, we knew that arrangement wouldn't be the case with our compilation. To include as many voices and perspectives as possible from among the submissions, we had to be flexible, thinking outside the norm during a time that was anything but normal. As a result, readers will find multiauthored narratives that layer experiences and in-the-moment reactions nestled among traditional chapters that rely upon scholarship and praxis to suggest new approaches to labor issues, ones formulated as we learned to live with COVID-19; lessons learned during the mayhem of the pandemic that correspond to ideas for embracing work–life balance in concrete ways; raw stories of survival merged with historical explorations of ways in which women have had to negotiate the triumvirate of duties characterizing academic labor. Each contribution, written *in situ*, now includes a coda or a set of takeaways that authors added later—once the fog began to clear, as we faced a new normal and began to make sense of 2020 and beyond. The resulting set of materials holds significance for readers working across ranks and institutional settings, including readers who identify with the shared stories, coworkers who didn't share these experiences yet sought understanding to create more equitable workspaces, administrators in positions to affect change, and intergenerational readers seeking paths of empathy for bridging ballooning alienation. Ultimately, you hold in your hands an honest set of pandemic survival narratives that embody cultural, feminist, and labor scholarship.

The (Dis)organization of This Collection

Contributors ask critical questions about the nature of academic work, past and future but especially about possibilities moving forward. Paired with the importance of documenting an historical moment, the opportunity to consider the future of academic work becomes a critical exigency for this collection. The mid-2020s timing of this work's publication provides a source of momentum, an opportunity to bring intentional decision making toward better-supported, sustainable, ethically managed academic labor practices. The chapters ask how institutions can do better, how we might harness networked institutional change to "rethink the nature of work" (hooks, 54) through the personal—often emotional and vulnerable—narratives that form the key sources of evidence.

Attempting to organize the ideas of our contributors was incredibly challenging, as recurrent themes kept cropping up across chapters, even among those pieces we assumed would not align. Structuring these essays into a coherent collection felt especially challenging given the nature of the evidence and the blurred lines between identities and the multiple "work roles" presented throughout. For example, how do we put "mothering" in a category as if parenting represents a distinct act, one separated from our professional lives? A key premise of this collection asserts that Parent and Academic are two identities worn simultaneously, without easy distinction, for many scholars. We decided a section addressing "mothering" was far too limiting and would include too many of these chapters to demarcate a meaningful distinction. Instead, you will see the varied experiences of being both parent and scholar woven throughout all sections.

Indicative of the title, *Blurred Boundaries* intentionally challenges the parameters of what a collection should or can do, as represented in variation among chapters, including themes that don't fit neatly into distinct categories. The chapter arrangement we landed upon is intentional, however, and indicative of a larger claim of the collection—neat divisions between spheres and the concept of linear forward progress represent constructs that often rely on unstated and underexamined inequities. As a reviewer of this collection put it, "'Messiness' is a reality that needs to be called out and repeated until it is expected and until everyone's labor in the face of that messiness is acknowledged and rewarded rather than effaced by gendered, raced, and classed traditions." We see this departure from the edited collection norm as a key aspect for dismantling traditional approaches to scholarship; the chapter lengths are also disparate, somewhat jarring at times, intentionally. As you read this compilation, you will encounter longer chapters that introduce theory, questions, and suggestions, alongside lived experience; shorter chapters complement and illustrate the theories, suggestions, and challenges articulated in more traditional essay formats.

While we have set subject-matter parameters in the four sections of this book (to facilitate reading), the mix of shorter narratives and full-length chapters speak across and beyond those categorizations. As we initially perused the submissions to this volume (while reading other published works addressing pandemic-era work and experience), we realized that content from each composition would resonate differently with readers. Like Lindquist et al., editors of *Recollections from an Uncommon Time,* Jessie and I were struck by how our own experiences shaped our reactions to individual chapters—"Sometimes we were in agreement about the value of the work a piece would do for its readers and for the collection; sometimes one of us would find and be deeply compelled by resonances having to do with her or his own experiences (of home, family, work, etc.)" (2023, 4). The meaning we as editors ascribe and find across the sections and stories may not reflect the many ways in which our readers might relate and ascribe meaning. For some readers, therefore, our arrangement of an extraordinary set of lived experiences may seem unorthodox.

Jessie's "Introduction: The Personal Is Professional" provides an excellent overview of the moment giving rise to this collection. While titles of chapters found within each section initially may appear disparate, we grouped essays to encourage meaningful conversation across a wide range of themes and subjects. For example, part one, "Shifting Sands and Finding Balance," loosely addresses ideas of the ever-changing relationships among professional and personal lives, with the elusive goal of achieving some working combination or balance (a now heavily connoted word) that allows multiple roles and identities to coexist. Keri Carter's "The Impact of Slow Change: Feminist Perspectives on Women's Advancement in Higher Ed Post-COVID-19" delineates ongoing and interminable labor issues that complicate women's search for balance. Her chapter, in tandem with Jessie's introduction, sets the stage for considering issues recurring throughout the volume. Carter concludes her contribution by suggesting ways for leveling the playing field for working academics as higher education moves beyond the pandemic. The subsequent pieces in this section illustrate issues raised by Carter. In a shorter narrative, "Written in Sand: On Becoming a Mother During a Global Pandemic," Laura Sceniak Matravers captures the overwhelming frustrations of so many mothers who continually felt that they fell short in a world that was increasingly unrecognizable and with no end to the pandemic in sight. Ultimately, instead of applying for tenure, Matravers (temporarily) has left academia in the best interest of her family. Adopting an autoethnographic research approach, Sara Cooper, Rebecca Hallman Martini, and Michelle Miley explore motherhood and academic responsibilities from vastly differing perspectives in "Vibrations: Mothering, Carework, and the Value of Shared Story." Representing a wide range of parenting requirements (across age and locations), these collaborators ask: What do we do with our anger? What could feminist mothering look like amid and beyond a pandemic? How do we (re)define ourselves given our obstacles? What did we learn? What should we keep and what can we let go of? And where do we go from here?" This chorus of voices, delivered in three-part harmony, resonates across divides to call for shared care work among faculty members as departments move beyond pandemic confines. Rounding out this section and restating the plight of academic caregivers, Jessica Jorgenson Borchert relies upon recent scholarship by Pamela Takayoshi, Christine Tulley, and Alex Hanson to explore ways in which writing and therapy require attention to the needs of both space and time. This narrative, presented chronologically through the unfolding months of the pandemic, calls out the lack of institutional support for caregiving that was already a problem prior to COVID-19 and seeks to overturn the outdated valuation of the 24/7 workaholic academic.

The second part, "Bridging Realms," emphasizes the multiplicity of roles including mother, educator, and academic while indicating how these positions both narrow and expand during a crisis, with meaningful results. The interplay of shorter and longer pieces, personal experience and scholarship, and expectations and capabilities reinforces the chaotic nature of translating academic labor to domestic spaces, while demonstrating ways the triumvirate of institutional responsibilities merged and truncated when overlaid with personal obligations. In "Schooling the Public: Empathy in K–12 Teachers' Social Media Posts During the COVID-19 Pandemic," Danielle De Arment-Donohue adopts Lisa Blankenship's research on domestic laborers and rhetorical empathy to suggest that the pandemic spotlighted already-strained public school systems, creating a kairotic opportunity to listen to often-neglected teacher voices in hopes of improving educational systems. Analyzing 80 public social media posts from K–12 teachers on Facebook and Twitter, she asks: (1) How has the pandemic laid bare and exacerbated the challenges women teachers face? and (2) What changes could lead to higher teacher retention rates? Examining another set of challenges when scholar-parents' parallel worlds collide, Ashley Holmes provides a modern application of domestic space and labor scholarship in "Virtual Kindergarten on My Couch: A Reflection on the Reconstruction of Domestic Space." Recalling Paula Mathieu's *Tactics of Hope*, which draws on the work of Michel de Certeau, Holmes introduces strategies for accommodating a divergent range of work and school operations occurring in one collapsed space. She tried to order the ensuing chaos by seeking "calculated actions that emanate from and depend upon 'proper' (as in propertied) spaces, like corporations, state agencies, and educational institutions . . . the goal of a strategy is to create a stable, spatial nexus that . . . minimize[s] temporal uncertainty" (this volume). Holmes shares charts, tweets, and cartoons to elucidate these strategies, concluding with a list of hopeful suggestions for addressing issues that became more pronounced during the pandemic. Also exploring collapsed time and space, Meaghan Brewer in "'It's Not Like I Have Anything Better to Do!': Rhetorics of Abundant Time During the COVID-19 Pandemic" interrogates language and interpretations of time. Referencing time as a norming device, she draws on discussions of non-normative conceptions of time from a range of disciplines. Brewer relies upon Margaret Price and Tara Wood's interdisciplinary conceptions of "crip time" to note the various ways in which university processes create rigid structures around time. Price defines crip time as referring to "a flexible approach to normative time frames," and Brewer aligns this notion with the concept of *kairos,* which, in contrast to *chronos* (normative, linear time) provides "a more subjective dimension of time" in which the savvy rhetor might identify the timing that feels right for action. Brewer understands time as having a metaphorical, subjective dimension, one that is, as Lakoff and Johnson argue, part of a conceptual system that is in part dictated by Western culture. She applies this dramatic shift in considerations of time to academic caregivers.

Arguing that at the heart of feminist rhetorical studies lies attention to the messy relationship between material conditions, experiences of the researcher, and the questions she is asking, Elizabeth Ellis Miller next analyzes Emily Oster's newsletter *ParentData* as a case study. Miller reads Oster's pandemic newsletter through Arlie Holschild's notion of emotional labor, or "the management of feeling to create a publicly observable facial and bodily display; emotional labor is sold for a wage and therefore has exchange value" (7). Miller reminds us that feminist inquiry demands being honest about personal feelings while also considering audience expectations concerning emotion and identity. This approach provides a lens for examining the complex interplay of systematic questioning into how women and parents are supported in negotiating work and emotive demands. The final essay in this section, "Reimagined Productivity: Narratives of Academic Mothers Who Choose to Homeschool" penned by Heidi M. Williams, Laura Seroka, Abby Arnold-Patti, Nandini Deo and Ceceilia Parnther, offers first-person testimony from five diverse academic mothers who homeschooled their children both before and after the pandemic. As the world returned to some pre-pandemic conditions, not all five teachers continued to homeschool, but the collaborators universally share their renewed understanding of the inequalities of women's labor given their teaching experiences.

Part three, "Time, Tension, and Transition," examines long-embedded academic issues, concepts recurring across the decades as well as throughout this volume. In "Bringing into Focus What's Been Blurred: Rewarding Relation-Based Work," experienced teacher-administrators and long-time collaborators Lee Nickoson and Mary P. Sheridan initially looked to the year 2020 hopefully as a time of transition and reset. However, they quickly realized that reform in higher education practice is impossible without first examining who does the work of compassion and asking how the labor described in the institutional pronouncements of care is shared, recognized, and rewarded. Examining 2020's transformative possibilities from the vantage point of late 2023—focusing on the invisible, often gendered and racialized labor needed to foster a community of care, Nickoson and Sheridan now understand that promise of reform relies upon what Rowan and Cavallaro call "work before the work," or the required, slow preparatory labor often abandoned in loud demands for public outcomes.

Writing from a position of fear and anxiety, Molly E. MacLachlan in "'But He Isn't *Your* Kid': Stepparenting and Work–Life Balance, COVID-19 Edition" interrogates promotion and tenure time clocks (originally designed for male academics) in terms of the reproductive cycles of women. The dichotomy that she explores is further exacerbated by the greater responsibility for service and care work that women undertake. MacLachlan urges women to say "no" more often, to resist taking on uncredited labor characterizing entrenched standards of practice within many out-of-date and out-of-touch departments. Instead, she calls for administrators to privilege flexibility in professional advancement and teaching modalities (including increased reliance upon tenure clock pauses) and to seek fair and equitable care work assignments across faculty rank and gender. Next, relying upon the providential arrival of an artifact, a broken clock, Shannon Walters extends considerations of time and promotion in "Pandemic Writing in Crip Time: Tense Dispatches from Mid-Rank." Centering the discussion on needs of mid-level career women, she outlines challenges facing the "sandwich" generation—professionals caring for both children and parents. Ironically, during the pandemic this generation of scholars found themselves caught in the middle at work as well. As junior faculty paused work clocks and extended their time to tenure while senior faculty retired in record numbers, mid-rank faculty picked up the slack. Walters explores ways in which getting back to normal, back to a prior time leaves so many faculty even further behind. And in the final essay in this section, "Challenging Ageism Through Intergenerational Initiatives," Michael Harker moves from concerns of mid-rank professors to considerations of ageism. He asks readers to seek ways to cultivate empathy and understanding while promoting collective responsibilities among generations. Harker argues that to meet needs of faculty across the spectrum, we must engage in "the double work of acknowledging the importance of understanding aging and longevity from a biological perspective and do the difficult work of prioritizing aging as a socially constructed pressure, one that deserves the same enthusiasm, attention, and funding that we give research grounded in contemporary identity studies" (see p. 195). Identifying existing programs and departments that serve as models for retaining faculty, he provides both a justification and initial plan for stemming the post-pandemic mass exodus of long-time faculty members.

Part four, "Emotional Labor and Equity in Higher Education," highlights the pursuit of equity and recognition of emotional labor, specifically where and how it takes place within the academy. Kelli R. Gill and Angela D. Mack identify and challenge norms perpetuated in the PhD exam process in "Are We Done Yet? Disruption, Fatigue, and Reimagining Our PhD Exam Timetables." From their perspectives as PhD students, the authors narrate their personal journeys to and through their PhD exams, naming feelings associated with delay, fatigue, and perceptions of failure from their gendered and raced identities within the academy. They articulate the myth of productivity that continues to permeate expectations for faculty in higher education and examine how these constraints fail to provide room for inevitable disruption and fatigue. Relying upon a counter-story approach and engaging emotional experience as a thematic device, their experiences provide powerful evidence of the continued harm of long-established and outdated approaches to the preparation and support provided to early career scholar-teacher-administrators—offering concrete strategies for how we can do better, now.

In a pair of pointed and vulnerable essays, C.C. Hendricks and Mary Lourdes Silva extend Gill and Mack's critique of academic systems that require demanding structures of productivity/success at the expense of both equity and sustainability. In "Burnt Out Before I Began: Finding, and Failing to Find, a Work–Life Balance amid the Pandemic," Hendricks narrates her experiences as a new assistant professor, Writing Program Administrator (WPA), and mom during a pandemic and discusses the impossibility of achieving a "work-life" balance given an impossible imaginary standard of success. She implores the necessity for scholarly disciplines to create platforms for women and gendered laborers to share their experiences, especially those marginalized and excluded in academic contexts. Hendricks also acknowledges how so many of the issues that the profession currently faces cannot be solved at individual or even departmental levels, as they are rooted in systemic and inequitable design. In direct critique of these structures, Silva's "My Shame Story: Gendered Ethnic Inequities of Student Evaluation of Teaching" takes the Student Evaluation of Teaching (SET) to task, as a problematic, biased, and inequitable source for evaluating instructor efficacy. She discusses a silver lining of the pandemic, the pausing of SET as a means for course and instructor evaluation, and what this break meant for the mental burden she normally faced at her predominantly white institution as a Latina woman. Through both personal experience of the negative effects of SET and rigorous scholarly work to support her claims, she suggests it is time for administrators to do the hard and essential work of expanding how and by what means institutions evaluate (and thus advance) instructors. Addressing only a few systemic issues characterizing higher education at this moment, these authors illustrate how we must first recognize and then ameliorate the gendered and raced ways that labor has been tagged, silenced, and penalized in the academy.

The last two chapters in part four, also urging academia to acknowledge and reform deeply rooted inequities in labor distribution, care expectations, and productivity standards, take different tactics and locales to ultimately advocate for a reimagined academic environment that values difference, sustainability and individual well-being. Nancy Myers and Heather Brook Adams in "Pursuing 20/20 Vision: Learning the Labor of Activist Editors" foreground the often-unseen labor of editing and our complex embodied relationship to larger forces. Centering their experience of editing a collection (*Inclusive Aims: Rhetoric's Role in Reproductive Justice*, 2024) during a global pandemic, Myers and Adams suggest the need for more equitable and continually responsive publishing of edited collections, along with the expanded visibility of compilations as crucial scholarly locations. Based on both their experiences *in situ* and upon subsequent reflection, they arrived at the (highly meta) recognition of the "feminist inventive art of the edited collection" (see p. 241) as a means of activism. They ruminate on the process of recalibrating editorial responsibilities with attention to supporting a collection, accommodating individuals within that larger whole, and expressly centering inclusivity and recognizing labor. Amidst many key lessons, their foregrounding of the embodied experience of laboring on a project of such scale, with so many messy aspects about the extrinsic goals of scholarly work set against global calamity, puts words to the feelings and experiences across this edited collection. Taylor Paige Winfield, then, echoes these questions, with a narrower focus, on her experience creating and leading an online mental and spiritual health resource through its successes and eventual sunsetting in "Empowering Rhetorics: Writing and Reading Stories as a Feminist and Spiritual Tool." Rounding out the collection's focus on care work, Winfield found herself taking on additional mentoring through this online initiative, partnering with therapists and spiritual counselors to provide an important service at the expense of her own personal and professional well-being. Notably, Winfield's narrative changed drastically from her initial proposal, as the work she was doing continued to evolve as the pandemic unfolded across months and years. She reflects on the heavily gendered expectations she felt about her care work, as a "good" woman caring for others during such an acute emergency, and the complicated internal and external pressure she felt to "do something" in response. Ultimately, her contribution to *Blurred Boundaries* became a profound location to process the successes and failures, meaning and value in both labor and in stepping away from it. Because so many aspects of what it means "to care" are embedded in culturally imbued moral and gendered expectations, the authors' considerations in this section add essential complexity to the larger themes of this collection.

Finally, Jessica Enoch reflects upon this collection in the "Afterword," characterizing this project as an "Archive, Heuristic, Argument." We are grateful for her insights and empathy, the women's labor expertise she brings to this project, her recognition of the issues that contributors struggle to articulate and untangle, and her willingness to locate herself within these collective experiences.

A Note on an Alternate Table of Contents

As in any book collection, the essays might be collated or encountered differently from the template described above, offering various reading experiences and yielding divergent foci. Many of the essays in *Blurred Boundaries* inevitably discuss parenting and care work (Matravers, Cooper et al., Borchert, Holmes, Williams et al., Walters, MacLachlan, Miller, Brewer); yet, we do not lump all those readings together. Instead, we tease out related themes that may privilege familial responsibilities but intersect with larger issues. For instance, readers interested in domestic workspaces could read contributions by Holmes, Williams et al., Matravers, Walters, and Borchert in tandem. Pieces focused on identity and academic struggles include essays crafted by De Arment-Donohue, MacLachlan, Silva, and Gill and Mack. Several of the chapters rely heavily on research and academic deliverables (Myers and Adams, Walters,

Nickoson and Sheridan); while others incorporate public perception and opinion (De Arment-Donohue, Miller). And intergenerational issues arise in pieces by Harker as well as Gill and Mack. Several essays address building support networks (Winfield, Miller, Borchert, Matravers), as well as the experiences of administrators (Hendricks, Nickoson and Sheridan, Holmes). Finally, we find a glimmer of hope in studying the codas and takeaways found at the conclusion of each chapter. Read together as separate entities, these observations and suggestions offer ways to negotiate systemic labor imbalances, discrimination, and entrenched practices.

Creating a Community Archive

At its core, the collective eyewitness commentary on the pandemic found in this collection, written from the perspective of academic, in-the-moment observers, serves as a historical reminder as well as a call to action for labor reform. We envision these collected pieces as a community archive, one that reminds us that gendered, racial, and cultural labor issues recur, circle, and resurface in times of crises—without resolution once we return to "business as usual." The year 2020 represented an unfathomable set of circumstances and threats; it's time to collectively address the concomitant labor issues before we sweep this global crisis under the rug and move on (as humans inevitably do)—particularly as we now face the next set of "unprecedented" labor challenges. Recorded narratives, ground up archives, and in-the-moment collecting and collating provide ways to instantiate experiences of a community, particularly one in crises. We see this collection serving that function, much like the need in 2016 and 2017 for feminists to capture and represent their experiences participating in women's marches—through gathering oral histories, collecting and preserving associated ephemera, and recording speeches and reactions to political policies designed to retract existing legislation. Likewise, contributions to *Blurred Boundaries: Feminist Essays on Twenty-First-Century Academic Labor* serve as in-the-moment archiving that embodies and extends ongoing archival theories and trends, illustrated in contributions to David Gold and Jessica Enoch's *Women at Work: Rhetorics of Gender and Labor;* Tarez Graban and Wendy Hayden's *Teaching through the Archives: Text, Collaboration, and Activism;* Gesa Kirsch et al.'s *Unsettling Archival Research: Engaging Critical, Communal, and Digital Archives;* and the living *Digital Archive of Literacy Narratives* (DALN) project—to name but a few.

Archivists Diana K. Wakimoto, Christine Bruce, and Helen Partridge define community archives as materials "that have been created, maintained, and controlled by community members within their communities (295)." Quoting Flinn Stevens et al., they explain that "the defining characteristic of community archives is the involvement of members of the community whose records are in the archives in collecting and accessing their history *"on their own terms"* (p. 60, emphasis in original)" (Wakimoto et al. 2013, 295). The (often raw and moving) voices in this volume do indeed speak on their own terms, finding authority to depart from the usual academic treatment of institutional issues within the frustration, fear, and exhaustion of the long 2020. This reliance upon a "multiplicity of voices and competing narratives in the archives as we work to break down unfair power relations in the archives, which silence certain sectors" illustrates another form of archival unsettling. And in the process these stories and explorations "challenge injustice and discrimination in order to create a more inclusive and just environment" within academia, and beyond (Wakimoto et al. 295).

We know that this volume only begins to scratch the surface in terms of representation of academic voices and experiences. We have attempted to curate and document a snapshot from the submissions we received, from those whom we recognize to be in privileged positions that allowed for participation during the overwhelming years central to this discussion. And yet, we hope that this collection moves beyond memorializing one moment in time (recalling elements of Samuel Pepys' diary or Daniel Defoe's fictionalized *A Journal of the Plague Year*) to serve both as a testament and challenge to address glaringly obvious differences in gendered expectations and responsibilities. Additional work is required, particularly as we emerge from the depths of the pandemic and concretize plans for addressing ongoing work inadequacies and injustices, including work–life balance anxieties, promotion and tenure issues, administration responsibilities, pressures to publish, hiring concerns, inclusion of all stakeholders' voices, and a multitude of other interminable labor worries that (re)surfaced in 2020.

Bibliography

Digital Archive of Literacy Narratives. The Ohio State University and Georgia State University. https://www.thedaln.org/.

Gold, David, and Jessica Enoch, eds. *Women at Work: Rhetorics of Gender and Labor.* University of Pittsburgh Press, 2019.

Graban, Tarez Samra, and Wendy Hayden, eds. *Teaching Through the Archives: Text, Collaboration, and Activism.* Southern Illinois University Press, 2022.

hooks, bell. *Feminism Is for Everybody.* 2nd ed. Routledge, 2014.

Kirsch, Gesa E., Romeo García, Caitlin Burns Allen, and Walker P. Smith, eds. *Unsettling Archival Research: Engaging Critical, Communal, and Digital Archives.* Southern Illinois University Press, 2023.

Lindquist, Julie, Bree Straayer, and Bump Halbritter, eds. *Recollections from an Uncommon Time: 4C20 Documentarian Tales.* National Council of Teachers of English; The WAC Clearinghouse, 2023. https://wac.colostate.edu/books/swr/documentarian/.

Wakimoto, Diana K., Christine Bruce, and Helen Partridge. "Archivist as Activist: Lessons from Three Queer Community Archives in California." *Archival Science* 13 (2013): 293–316.

Introduction

The Personal Is Professional

Jessica Edens McCrary

This volume explores how the conflation of events in 2020 played out in the lives of women and reflects on what we, collectively and individually, might do differently as laborers in the 2020s and beyond. Our initial Call for Papers generated a wide range of submissions—personal and scholarly, political and social, embodied and observational; proposers spoke eloquently from the heart. In subsequent revisions, however, contributors began to ground the extraordinary experiences and repercussions of the pandemic within bone- and soul-crushing labor issues—ones that seem interminable. In 2020, women were exposed as the glue holding the US economy afloat (Tappe et al.; Bateman and Ross; "Examining"). Women juggled professional careers (inside and outside the home), childcare and education, caregiving for older family members, unpaid household labor in addition to negotiating ramifications of a global pandemic, social justice movements, and the tumult residing at the very core of American democracy.

Yet, "juggling" is too polite a term for the kinds of pressures women faced and the decisions women made, willingly or not, in 2020. By 2021, *Forbes* estimated women had lost jobs disproportionate to men (especially Black and Latina women) with media reporting nearly three million women leaving the formal labor force by February 2021 (McGrath; Cerullo). By 2023, reports showed how the pandemic was having long-term residual effects specifically on women's relationship to labor and work and the US Bureau of Labor Statistics suggests even with returns to pre-pandemic employment rates, COVID-19 had an outsized impact on women (Weber; Morrone; Carrazana). As time has worn on, many have returned to the workforce, though some in changed or shifted work. For some, across and beyond academia, the trajectory of their careers have been forever altered (some, like our contributor Laura Sceniak Matravers left academia—at least temporarily, deciding based on the realities of her family). We also know that despite employment numbers that are back to pre-pandemic numbers, employment conditions informed by entrenched systemic issues continue to influence women's career progress (Morrone). In other words, despite numbers suggesting return to pre-pandemic employment levels, realities are changed and continue to present precarity. Based on all that we[1] know and in anticipation of what we do not yet understand about the upheaval of a global crisis that shifted—at least temporarily—the way all of us performed and thought about *work,* this collection takes up Hallenbeck and Smith's exigency, first in 2015 and again in 2024, to examine times when work is "in flux." While the full picture of the impact of COVID-19 on women's lives, especially their professional careers, will take years to develop, this collection captures a snapshot of the early assessment of what we (collectively) know and how we (academic laborers) might improve obvious and ongoing problems with the structure of university labor specifically.

What else can we learn about women and work if we consider "important moments when the home was under debate and reconstruction," Jessica Enoch asks (178). If World War II was a historical turning point for women and work, as Enoch explores in *Domestic Occupations,* the upheaval of the early 2020s is certainly another of those galvanizing moments in history. During and since the COVID-19 pandemic, women's spatial relationship to both work and home has been upended; our contributors share about those experiences in the chapters that follow. The work of this collection then, is to expand what has begun through projects that deeply consider the nature of work (like Gold and Enoch's edited collection *Women at Work*), or what Smith and Hallenbeck name as "an exigence crystallized by the pandemic: the simultaneously material and rhetorical nature of work, including the settings and material contexts in which it occurs, the values we assign to it, the ways our mind-bodies are conditioned by it, and the possibilities for how it might be otherwise." What does the COVID-19 pandemic, and the cultural events we witnessed in 2020, mean for the future of women and work? What did our experiences show us about how we might labor differently? What have institutions done (or not done, but *could do*) to improve labor conditions?

From my vantage point in 2021, I could not ignore the recurrent thought that our present moment was not only important to document for posterity but that our experiences likely contain valuable insights for how *work* and *home* might be redefined due to the upheaval, creativity, and chaos that the early years of the decade wrought. As a mid-thirties woman in a large urban area, I saw friends drop out of the workforce, defer starting businesses they had long dreamed of, switch or pause careers. Beyond my city, in my extended online community, the story was the same—women looking at their realities and knowing something had to give, and often professional aspirations and goals were that thing.

That women would set aside goals, promotions, new business ventures, and professional endeavors when faced with upheaval is neither new nor surprising. Since the US economic system is based in separation of public and private sphere (and indeed, rarely counts the private sphere as a place of economic productivity), women remain caught between their "aspirations to balance personal autonomy with caring for others" (Gerson, 8). This dichotomy seems to be exacerbated during times of social or economic upheaval, as Enoch and others have shown (Wu and Standridge; Hallenbeck and Smith; Cox and Reidner; Cardel et al.). Lynée and I saw so many women in our academic contexts struggling under the tension, exacerbated by the pandemic and myriad crises since 2020, whose personal experiences could go beyond easy, flattened narratives of this historic era.

This collection focuses on the lived and scholarly experiences of academic women during a time of incredible uncertainty and ground-shifting changes to our daily lives. Lynée and I observed throughlines across shared academic experiences of a transformative year in world and American history and asked how we might leverage lessons learned in 2020 to make changes immediately, in coming years, and even decades from now. We see this collection as part salve—*I was not going through this alone, even if it felt that way*; part historical record—capturing a moment of intense and monumental upheaval in our patterned lives; and part foundational guidance—advice we might look to for meaningful change in the practices and policies of academic labor.

The "can we have it all" impossibility remains evergreen; long before the pandemic women were acutely aware of the limits of our time set against our many obligations. But the pandemic exacerbated these tensions, throwing many women right off the razor-thin edge they walked trying to balance professional careers and education, childcare and homeschooling, caregiving responsibilities for older family members, mental and physical health, and unpaid household labor. The stories of scholars included herein illustrate those challenges and offer insight into what might happen next. As an early reviewer of this manuscript remarked, "The new considerations, scenarios, and practices that have emerged with the pandemic and [are] documented in this collection provide original and valuable insights into the long-documented and seemingly intractable power of oppressive, gendered frameworks that influence work in the U.S., and work in the U.S. academy specifically." Each contributor has considered their experience within these gendered frameworks and reflects on how academic labor might be, as a reviewer of this collection put it, "better supported, more sustainable, more ethically evaluated or managed, or more freely, safely, and livably navigated."

Twenty-twenty was a year that was at once the same experience and unique to every person. Challenges to gendered labor norms and calls for real change in equity and diversity work in higher education that occurred early in the pandemic and in the years since illustrate the core issues in Cheryl Glenn's observation that "the personal may be political, but the difficulties for women that feel personal are actually systemic" (73). In *Rhetorical Feminism and This Thing Called Hope,* Glenn illustrates that we know our difficulties are systemic, based on social structures and expectations for women, but that feminists *also* recognize the power potential in forms of resistance and embodiment. In other words, we have at our disposal the tools of rhetorical feminism—of embracing emotion, of being feminist and feminine, of the unabashedly empathetic embodied *woman,* and perhaps this is the moment in time when those powers can be used (and appreciated) to harness meaningful change in our working lives. The contributors to this collection affirm this hope, drawing on their personal and professional experiences during and beyond 2020 to illustrate what we can do better, collectively, in a post-2020 world.

Several themes are so woven across our contributors' experiences they create the bedrock of this collection. First, the collection takes up the crucial challenge to both document and understand the early 2020s in terms of contributors' relationships to labor. Second, the chapters of this collection engage the theme of blurred boundaries and identities. Many of the contributors ask the rhetorical question of whether the boundaries of their professional and personal lives, of their roles as parent and caregiver, head of household, sister, partner, or homeschooling parent were ever distinct from their role as scholar, teacher, administrator, writer. And, if they were never so discreet as social structures suggested them to be, then how do we move forward productively with that altered vantage point toward some kind of livable way to be, and do, our *blurred* identities? This theme will be clear no matter which order you read these chapters, and was so extensive throughout, it gave the collection its title—*Blurred Boundaries.*

The third emerging theme addresses the notion of outdated expectations, within and beyond academia, for the people employed to conduct the work of higher education. As is often noted, "help" at home is no longer a given, the idea of the singular male scholar with ample time to research and write having long-ago expired. From contexts as distinct as homeschooling children (Williams and Seroka et al.) to navigating identity as a stepparent (MacLachlan) to the continued prejudices experience by faculty of color and women in student evaluations of teaching (Silva) or the pressures and labor assumptions on graduate students completing their PhD exams (Gill and Mack), across this collection it is clear that societal and cultural expectations have not been working for most, for a long time. These tensions are not limited to women, or faculty of color—though they are often acutely felt by those holding such identities.

The sustainable viability of *work* in academia is an important question without a clear answer, but one this collection takes up with hope. Universities face mounting budget pressure, many operating under neoliberal policies that continue to discount humanities disciplines and ask its leaders and scholars to do more work with fewer resources, year after year. Tenure-track positions and long-term contract positions become harder to obtain, throwing many faculty into uncertainty as they try to establish and maintain viable careers in contract positions for lower wages and less institutional support, some leaving the field altogether. Publish-or-perish pressures continue to be a source of anxiety for those fortunate enough to land those hard-to-get jobs (see Walters; Jorgensen Borchert; Hendricks, this collection). If the way we have been laboring is unsustainable, and if economic pressures on universities continue as they have been, how do we reimagine work so that it sustains and invigorates, leaving mental and physical space for lives beyond work? Authors across this collection ask how we might continue to find joy in the scholarship and teaching and administration of our university identities, without leaching joy away from the reasons why we work—to invest in our loved ones, communities, rest, minds, and non-monetary activities.

These questions are being asked within and beyond our scholarly communities. We take up the calls of our colleagues in higher education to think deeply about what meaningful advancement on these subjects, and answers to these questions, could look like. In two special issues of the *Journal of Multimodal Rhetorics* (Summer and Fall 2022), writing studies scholars created an archive, comprising dozens of lived experiences that stands as testament to "the invisible labor and composition done by so many of us during the COVID-19 pandemic" (Manivannan). Writing about laboring during a pandemic, they illustrate the challenges that have always existed, of trying to write—to do scholarship—alongside daily, weekly, and monthly obligations to our own health and others'—and how the pandemic made it clear our pace wasn't sustainable. "Writing is never easy, and disability, grief, trauma, and carework commitments jumble our processes further," writes Vyshali Manivannan, one of the collections' editors.

Documentarians who were initially recruited to document the experience of attending the Conference on College Composition and Communication (CCCC) in March 2020 instead documented those same days in their homes, navigating an upturned world. These captured days, thoughts, and feelings became the 2023 *Recollections from an Uncommon Time: 4C20 Documentarian Tales*, edited by the team who had been at the helm of the Documentarian project (Lindquist et al.). Contributors reflect on and arrive at many themes which overlap with *Blurred Boundaries*—concepts of time and productivity, parenting, grief, contingent living and working, privileges surrounding race and class. These narratives illustrate the machinations of work during the early 2020s and are compelling and comforting to read, offering evidence that we were experiencing so many shared anxieties and exigencies, even while physically isolated.

Where we see *Blurred Boundaries* advancing the conversations of work beyond 2020 is in our documentation—reflections and personal experience as evidence written *in situ* during the pandemic—as well as contributors' reflections and suggestions with the benefit of distance. Across eighteen chapters that introduce experiences as varied as forming a service for online counseling to managing a residents' association to editing a collection, our contributors engage academic labor alongside many other forms of labor (Winfield; Harker, Myers and Adams, respectively). The blurred boundaries within and across their identities, labor roles, and experiences were set in relief during crisis, which lead each of them to ask questions about the nature of their professional work and identities. Taken collectively, the disparate voices included here suggest that distinct and collective experiences can illuminate areas for small and large adjustment that might begin to shift the ground toward feminist-informed practices and policies in our professional, academic institutions.

Blurred Boundaries takes up the call Anicca Cox and Rachel Riedner suggest in their 2023 article "Persistence, Coalition and Power: Institutional Citizenship and the Feminist WPA," to use personal experience as a site of knowledge creation. Theory-framed and dialogic, their conversations allowed them "to uncover some of the commonalities of our own experience about gendered labor by telling our work stories together and to further locate them in larger institutional and political discourses to map moments of agentive potential" (n.p.). We as editors and contributors also resist the expectation that we have tidy answers to enormous problems. However, our writing provides valuable insight into the individual's experience of enormous problems. Our writing invites these experiences as another form of scholarly evidence, to more deeply understand and consider where we go from here.

A Critical Juncture

In "Renewing Feminist Perspectives on Women WPAs' Service and Leadership," Hui Wu and Emily Standridge situate the twenty-first century as a meaningful time for reevaluating the service of writing program administrators, especially the woman-identifying WPAs. Importantly, they note the comparison to another key *kairotic* moment in higher education history, post WWII when college enrollment was surging, and faculty and administrators found themselves with new sets of challenges. Scholars of higher education history and pedagogy look back on that era now to consider the implications of post-war college admission, access, and policies (see Mendenhall). We in higher education stand at another critical juncture—in decades to come, we will learn from the pandemic and post-pandemic eras about how we continued to push, using feminist practices, against the unsustainable practices within higher education, and especially against persistent gendered labor and inequities.

For example, Wu and Standridge acknowledge the overrepresentation of women in WPA roles, citing a sense of civic duty and passion for how their work teaching writing and directing writing programs can have direct application to the citizenry. They note that "women WPAs bear the majority responsibility of transforming the structure of academia. Only after the structure is changed can the academic culture, style of thinking, and labor division change" (216). In fact, they suggest, women's "unusual career paths" in the academy might be precisely what better prepares them for the leadership and decision-making roles that could bring real, systemic change in higher education labor practices. The skills and perspectives academic women develop "through jobs on the periphery of institutions" end up being immensely helpful in eventual roles as department chairs, deans, or other middle and high-level administrative roles, especially because so many who end up in those leadership roles see writing and writing programs as a central tenant to a strong institution (Wu and Standridge quoting Maimon, 216). They posit, across evidence of women

WPAs moving into upper and central administration in college and universities, that "women WPAs' leadership roles . . . are likely to change the landscape of the university and the paradigm of English studies in the near future" (217).

While this volume stands alongside diverse scholarship on gendered labor in the academy, it advances the conversation by striking at the right moment, in the wake of upheaval in our educational system, with the hope that a kairotic moment has arrived. Many of our contributors serve in administrative roles within their institutions and have experience and perspective enabling them to advocate for changed practices and policies, even if incrementally. Lynée and I hope this collection will wind up in the hands of WPAs, department chairs, and administrators who are in those positions of power, and in positions to speak *to* power, toward meaningful shifts in equitable labor practices.

Our contributors' voices add to a historical narrative of women's work that continues to challenge relationships to our employers, our families, our cultural contexts, to economic and financial demands and limits. *Blurred Boundaries* extends conversations on the "rhetorical complexity of women's work experiences" (Enoch, 180) put forth by numerous feminist rhetorical scholars (see Hallenbeck and Smith; Hallenbeck; Smith; Gold and Enoch; Gaillet and Bailey; hooks) but with our sights focused on the "unprecedented" pandemic event experienced by the collective planet. How to write about something that has already been written about in every media space from every possible angle? Jennifer Marlow answers, "Of course I've been wanting to write about the experience of the pandemic, but everyone else is already doing that . . . what more can I possibly add?" ("Am I all right?", n.p.). Writing in her composing process journal in March 2020, Marlow articulates how many of us felt at the time, or perhaps since. What else is there to say, and aren't we all, by this point, majorly fatigued by writing or reading anything more about those years?

In some ways, just a few years later, the US looks very different—in the same months of the rise of COVID-19, we observed and participated in rallies, protests, and demands for action in the wake of more deaths of Black Americans via systems of white supremacy; continued political polarization heightened tension in families and communities; we watched in horror while the Capitol was overrun while Congress attempted to confirm the 2020 election results on January 6, 2021. In Georgia, where Lynée and I live, January 6 marked a different historic landmark—in a narrow run-off election, the state had elected our second Democratic senator, Reverend Raphael Warnock, defeating appointed incumbent Republican Kelly Loeffler. Democrats in the state were jubilant to have "turned Georgia blue," with electoral votes for Joe Biden, in addition to sending two progressive Democrats to represent the state in Washington, DC. A day that began with so much hope by its end looked like the demise of democracy—with its central tenants of peaceful transition of power and free and fair election processes—happening before our eyes. Even those events now feel far away, and so much has happened since, not least of which include a largescale backlash against diversity, equity, and inclusion efforts at universities and the Supreme Court's decision to overturn affirmative action in 2023.

The collective trauma we have all experienced in such a compressed amount of time feels overwhelming. Yet, important, long overdue discussions and moves to improve systemic shortfalls could finally occur. Perhaps the way time shifted brought conversations about white supremacy, social injustices, raced and gendered and classes inequities to the fore. Did the pandemic leave more space for these concerns? Did unsustainable systems and procedures that had been ignored for far too long finally reach a breaking point, when we were all pressed to bursting? On top of so much death, uncertainty, violence and distrust, was there any room left for shared humanity? Again and again in the strange year 2020 (and into 2021 and 2022 and . . .) the answers have been sometimes yes, and other times no. And on top of the turmoil, we were somehow still carrying all the mundanities of lives lived—raising children, managing financial decisions, maintaining marriages, partnerships, and friendships, figuring out what to cook for dinner, scrolling social media, exploring our outdoor spaces in new ways, trying to do our jobs with technologies many of us rarely used before 2020.

The first years of the 2020s felt both very fast and *incredibly* slow to live through. By "very fast" I mean, that it feels surreal to read the narratives from our colleagues in the summer and fall 2022 special issues of *The Journal of Multimodal Rhetorics,* to relive the specific and strange minutiae of March 2020 compared to June and compared to October of 2020. As the vaccine arrived in the spring of 2021, we hoped this might usher in resolution, but instead new variants Omicron and Delta arrived. In 2021 these new strains of coronavirus paired with social and political events left folks across the US arguing over everything from mask policies to the future of the country. These events feel at once like ages ago and just last year. The time between the start of the pandemic and my first COVID-19 vaccine were almost exactly twelve months apart; twelve months that felt both endless and shockingly compressed. As I write in 2023, we observe relatively low cases of COVID-19, my team stopped wearing masks in meetings one unceremonious Wednesday in March 2023, and now it feels like we never stopped serving food at indoor events. But COVID-19 continues to mutate, and disease and public health experts suggest lingering effects will be with us for the long run; we continue to learn new things about how the disease impacts our bodies.

All to say that time was very strange these past few years, and even if we're still very much *in situ*—observe, for example, the regressive policies coming out of state legislatures in 2023, attacking the hard-fought rights of trans and female bodies, LGBTQ+ marriages, academic freedom, reversal of affirmative action, and the ability to run strong, resourced diversity, equity, and inclusion programs at schools and organizations across the country—academic women have abundant collective knowledge that is worth documenting and considering, now and in the future. As we live through history, scholars will continue to write about and discuss, come to terms with and seek to understand this decade, one that already feels to have spanned a quarter century. Just as the editors and contributors of *Journal of Multimodal Rhetorics* special issues began, and *Recollections from an Uncommon Time* continued, we will continue to have smart, unsettled conversations about professional and creative labor that happens alongside care work. Set against the urge to *write* about what we were experiencing, was the troubling *expectation* that we continue to write, despite the global catastrophe playing out on the news and in our neighborhoods and among our communities. Mudiwa Pettus minces no words in her assessment of that first summer, after surviving a semester like no other:

> Yet, even amid this devastation, I found myself haunted by academia's troubling expectations regarding productivity. During what seemed to be the dawning of a viral-induced apocalypse and the decline of my mental health, I still could not shake the feeling that I should have been using my summer 'break' to write as much as possible. But I did not possess the capacity to do so. My ability to focus and my belief that I could write anything worthwhile, words that would prove meaningful in the face of global catastrophe, had vanished. Writing, and even attempting to write, became another source of dread. (Zoom Chat, n.p.)

And rather than provide a neat, cozy narrative about how the formation of a Black women writers group led her to this imagined form of success, Pettus shares that the group instead reminded her of her humanity, that even (especially) as academic laborers we can measure ourselves far beyond meeting research goals. The community provided a continual reminder for her that "compulsory individualism does not have to be the compass by which we are guided through our professional and personal lives" (Pettus, n.p.). Instead, the audacious act of creating/claiming a space first dedicated to mutual aid and group well-being gave its members the essential "conditions for [their] survival" (n.p.). Conscious reclamation of space, played out against the parameters of academic expectations and the unending slough of late-stage capitalism, have always rooted feminist principles, and are specifically central in Black feminist principles (Hersey). This collection also rejects patriarchal expectations for how we manage time and resists a notion of "productivity" that centers individual work and concepts of self-improvement over mutual aid and collective care (see Ahmed; Schuller; Hamad). Contributors drafted collaboratively, responding to one another in text, often from locales far apart. Some came together in Facebook groups based on shared community needs or interests, others through graduate programs. While we as editors and contributing authors are collectively only a small representation of labor in the academy, Lynée and I believe that listening to and sharing our struggles with one another is a valuable feminist practice that *can* lead to real action. Although the experiences documented here may not have tidy resolutions to their narrative, the authors share their personal experience as evidence and reflect, in the time since these experiences, on how academic labor might be made more sustainable, more livably navigated. Our resistance to neatly "solve" all the complexities in the authors' experiences is evident in the working title this project held for years—*Interminable*. The *endless* themes and pressures addressed across theory and narrative in this book suggest they are not new, and that many continue beyond the setbacks and advancements made within the shakeups since 2020.

Backlash from state lawmakers and even college and university leadership to reverse financial and labor investment into diversity, equity, and inclusion (DEI) and antiracism initiatives, many of which began in earnest in 2020, illustrate the continued resistance of those in power to any real move to shift and share power structures. Systems built to exclude continue to work as intended. We observe that even with many faculty and administrators dedicated to antiracist practices and dismantling inequitable systems, what felt so possible in 2020 is looking now to be possible is fits and spurts, in selective states, and with many limits imposed. Some of the advances we enjoyed briefly in work flexibility and DEI measures seem to be deteriorating before our eyes. So, while this book may center the experiences of 2020, with reflection on what they mean for us moving forward, we can already see the potential we had slipping away—and thus the ideas and experiences captured here remain relevant years later. It is important to capture exactly the kind of energy and uncertainty—the hope and despair—that first year of the pandemic entailed—not only for those who will look back on this era in the future, but especially so that we might use the evidence to enact meaningful shifts in our departments, scholarly work, institutions, and communities right now.

Academic Labor

Themes affecting many industries, communities, and personal and professional lives emerge through stories, experiences, and lessons of laborers in the academy. Scholarship recounts that social expectations for men and women are arranged around gendered moral obligation, and despite some advancement, ongoing inequalities "continue to pose dilemmas, especially for those who aspire to integrate home and work in a balanced, egalitarian way" (Gerson, 25). The narratives in *Blurred Boundaries* demonstrate the dilemma of gendered expectations in both professional spaces of the academy and private spaces of the home, and how lived realities can fall short of the intended ideal.

In exposing the way gaps in data collection or interpretation negatively impact women in all aspects of life, Caroline Criado Perez specifically calls out academia for its gender bias. Women are asked to do more undervalued administrative work, not only formalized program admin but social and "housekeeping" tasks such as notetaking, collecting donations for a coworker, organizing a birthday gathering, and cleaning up after everyone. Themes of administrative and emotional labor recur across the chapters (see Brewer; Daniel; Cooper, Martini, and Miley, this volume). For example, students are more likely to approach female professors with personal crises, sometimes called the "professor mom" effect, and they're also more likely to evaluate female professors lower than male counterparts (see Silva, this volume). Such gender bias undergirds a public assumption that "research done by men is associated with 'greater scientific quality,' [which] could be a product of pure sexism, but it could also be a result of the mode of thinking that sees male as universal and female as niche" (Perez). This bias, widely acknowledged in feminist scholarship across academic disciplines, highlights the continued lack of feminist rhetorical theories grounding "mainstream" rhetorical theory. Not only are feminist ideas—across all disciplines—too rarely recognized as theories, but they also still too often remain relegated to feminist collections (Glenn, 202–3). Our challenge remains to engage feminist theories and methods not in niche contexts, but across what we do professionally and personally. We know the experiences and needs of women are not singular, that in fact the decisions, labor, and power (or sometimes lack of it) women wield affects the lives of our children, partners, coworkers, communities, and political structures.

The data we *do* have shows the disparity in publishing, citations, and tenure; if women have more obligations distracting them from publishing, then their potential for tenure is diminished. We saw women in 2020 pausing the tenure clock to turn their focus to the immediate needs of their families, students, and communities; slowing down the pace of their scholarly work (Kasymova et al.; Breuning et al.; Flaherty; McMillen); and delaying progression in graduate programs (McCaughey). Stacked atop the institutional burden of invisible labor performed by women in normal conditions, as academic laborers we saw ourselves and colleagues taking on the emotional labor required by our students as they navigated their education during global uncertainty (Berheide et al.; Shalaby et al.). Shalaby et al. note "the demand for women's service and mentorship efforts often increases during times of crises and uncertainties" and COVID-19 has been no exception (n.p.). Meanwhile, many men were ironically afforded even more time to produce scholarship, causing men to leap ever further ahead (Cardel et al.). The kinds of short-term, stop-gap decisions made in 2020 to allow for more time and flexibility will affect women's academic careers for years to come. Our collection extends conversations happening across scholarly disciplines on the effects the pandemic had on academic labor, and especially on gendered inequalities that persist (Pereira). As personal narratives across this volume show, we are only just beginning to make sense of what worked, what did not, and what is overdue for renovation in our academic jobs.

This collection addresses labor within higher education. We recognize the immense privileges academic work provided during a time of upheaval. During the most intense COVID-19 uncertainty, many academic laborers had the ability to maintain income, leave, and health insurance from the relative safety of our homes or secluded office spaces while so many in our economic system risked their safety to maintain the same (or less). We do not compare ourselves and our work to that of frontline and essential workers who kept the world turning. Instead, we highlight that even with such privilege, women in academia struggled, failed, were not OKAY. We got up every day to carework (our families, our students, our institutions, our communities, ourselves) that felt impossible, at times *was* impossible. Rather than compare our field and work to others, we contend that our stories of academic labor/ing are valuable to consider as we continue to navigate the future of work.

Embodiment and Experience as Method

For each of us laboring in academic spaces, intersectional identities play an important role of our embodied selves. Important conversations on how bodies existing beyond the bounds of heteronormative white male threaten the patriarchal power structures we inhabit. In *Our Body of Work* Melissa Nicolas and Anna Sicari note how this reality often silences the important conversations we should be having about how our bodies experience laboring, especially in the academy. They stress "the importance of having open exchanges about embodied experiences in the academy in order to have more complicated and nuanced conversations about intersectionality and identity and how racism, sexism, colonialism, classism, and ableism (among many other isms) stem from patriarchal systems of power," explaining that "too often, we do not have these conversations for fear they are too personal, not academic or professional, because of the shame associated with having certain bodies and/or the knowledge that no one will listen" (4).

Too much of our real, honest conversation about embodiment still happens in the margins, rather than in scholarship, because "stories about our corporeal realities are still coded as too personal, too messy, or even just too anecdotal" (5). Our contributors deliberately engage personal research, drawing on lived experience—mess—as evidence for their scholarly claims. The embodied work throughout this collection advances the same challenge, advocating further for embodied scholarly work. Aligned with our vision and goals for this collection, Nicolas and Sicari and the contributors writing boldly and vulnerably in their respective works highlight "how personal research can be and how important embodied research is for enacting any type of institutional change" (13). There were times while editing this collection that we encountered the critique of the "value" of personal narrative, as writing that lies outside the bounds of what "counts" in academic writing. But as Vyshali Manivannan, in the *Journal of Multimodal Rhetorics* special issue (Part I), asks, "The things that earn us promotion are, traditionally, not the creative, artistic, informal things we might create and publish. But shouldn't they be? As writing that preserves, reflects on, and analyzes the effect, discourse, experiences of writing and carework during the pandemic, writing that will act as referents for future authors who need to justify to the institution similar forms of writing, shouldn't all this count? As publication lines with academic merit? As service to the field? As labor? As proof of the social, economic, and medical inequities that inform many of our lives?" (Manivannan, "First, An Opening," n.p.).

Our goal extends the constructive agenda of these two interwoven ideas—that personal narrative and finding comfort in shared experience *can* positively influence standards and practices in academia. Not only does personal experience "count" as evidence, but it should also not be relegated to secondary or less-than other forms of primary material and evidence. In the chapters that follow, you will observe this truth as it plays out for our colleagues, yielding vulnerable, nonlinear, and valuable perspectives on the current and future realities of laboring in academia. How do we carry on when obligations and expectations do not align, and when the world feels every day as if it is less habitable (bringing ever more crises in environmental, social, and political contexts) to the "fleshy bodies" each of us inhabits (Nicolas and Sicari)? We suggest refuge in the company of another's story as a time-tested salve.

By the nature of this project, there are voices missing. Jenna Morton-Aiken and Dani DeVasto note the very pressure and often impossibility of responding to calls *about the limits of their labor* (such as this collection) precisely because they were at the limits of their labor. They note how not being able to respond to calls *about* the challenges of working during the pandemic exacerbated the sneaking feeling of "failure," and the panic that not being able to submit might be something "we'll pay for that forever" in the publish or perish space (n.p.). Lynée and I leave ample space for response to this collection; we mourn the stories not included here because of very real limits on our colleagues throughout the past several years. We hope the present volume encourages more academics to add their voices to this ongoing conversation.

Note

1. Throughout this collection, the editors and contributors include all women-identifying individuals in the collective "women." In this introduction, Lynée and I sometimes use the collective "we" to refer to all women and to include ourselves, rather than discuss women as a removed "they," since she and I cannot be removed from that group.

Bibliography

Ahmed, Sara. "A Phenomenology of Whiteness." *Feminist Theory* 8, no. 2 (2007): 149–68. https://doi.org/10.1177/1464700107078139.

Bateman, Nicole, and Martha Ross. "Why Has COVID-19 Been Especially Harmful for Working Women?" *Brookings Institution.* October 2020. https://www.brookings.edu/.

Berheide, Catherine White, Megan A. Carpenter and David A. Cotter. "Teaching

College in the Time of COVID-19: Gender and Race Differences in Faculty Emotional Labor." *Sex Roles* 86 (2022): 441–55.

Breuning, Marijke, Christina Fattore, Jennifer Ramos, and Jamie Scalera. 2020. "Gender, Parenting, and Scholarly Productivity during the Global Pandemic." *APSA Preprints,* July 21. Working paper. https://preprints.apsanet.org/engage/apsa/article-details/5f16 fc5660b4ad001212f977.

Board of Governors of the Federal Reserve System. "Examining the Pandemic's Economic Effects on Women." Consumer and Community Context series. November 12, 2021. https://www.federalreserve.gov/.

Cardel, Michelle I., Emily Dhurandhar, Ceren Yarar-Fisher, et al. "Turning Chutes into Ladders for Women Faculty: A Review and Roadmap for Equity in Academia." *Journal of Women's Health* 29, no. 5 (May 2020): 721–33. http://doi.org/10.1089 /jwh.2019.8027.

Carrazana, Charbeli. "The Women's Recession is Officially Over—But Not Everyone Has Recovered Equally." *The 19th News,* September 1, 2023. https://19thnews .org/2023/09/women-back-to-work-pre-covid-employment-levels-surge/.

Cedillo, Christina V., ed. "'Invisible' Has Always Proven a Useful Verb." *Journal of Multimodal Rhetorics* 4, no. 2 (2021). http://journalofmultimodalrhetorics.com /issue-4-2.

Cerullo, Megan. "Nearly 3 Million U.S. Women Have Dropped Out of the Labor Force in the Last Year." *CBS News.* February 5, 2021. https://www.cbsnews.com/news /covid-crisis-3-million-women-labor-force/.

Cox, Anicca, and Rachel Reidner. "Persistence, Coalition and Power: Institutional Citizenship and the Feminist WPA." *Peitho* 25, no. 2 (Winter 2023). https://cfshrc.org /article/persistence-coalition-and-power-institutional-citizenship-and-the-feminist -wpa/.

Enoch, Jessica. *Domestic Occupations: Spatial Rhetorics and Women's Work.* Southern Illinois University Press, 2019.

Flaherty, Colleen. "Women Are Falling Behind: Large Scale Study Backs Up Other Research Showing Relative Declines in Women's Research Productivity During COVID-19." *Inside Higher Ed.* October 19, 2020. https://www.insidehighered.com/.

Gaillet, Lynée Lewis, and Helen Gaillet Bailey, eds. *Remembering Women Differently: Refiguring Rhetorical Work.* University of South Carolina Press, 2019.

Gerson, Kathleen. "Moral Dilemmas, Moral Strategies, and the Transformation of Gender: Lessons from Two Generations of Work and Family Change." *Gender and Society* 16, no. 1 (Feb. 2002): 8–28.

Glenn, Cheryl. *Rhetorical Feminism and This Thing Called Hope.* Southern Illinois University Press, 2018.

Gold, David, and Jessica Enoch, eds. *Women at Work: Rhetorics of Gender and Labor.* University of Pittsburgh Press, 2018.

Hallenbeck, Sarah, and Michelle Smith. "Mapping Topoi in the Rhetorical Gendering of Work." *Peitho* 17, no. 2 (2015): 200–25.

Hallenbeck, Sarah. "Inventing Feminine Ingenuity: The Gendered Tropes of Space, Motive, Training, and Scope." *Rhetoric Review* 37, no. 3 (2018): 259–72.

Hamad, Ruby. *White Tears/Brown Scars: How White Feminism Betrays Women of Color.* Catapult, 2020.

Herrera, Kylie. "Woman the ~~Gatherer, Writer,~~ Pandemic Survivor (2020)." *Journal of Multimodal Rhetorics* 6, no. 2 (Summer 2022). https://journalofmultimodalrhetorics .com/6-2-herrera.

Hersey, Tricia. *Rest is Resistance: A Manifesto.* Little Brown Spark, 2022.

Holmes, Ashley J., and Elise Verzosa Hurley. *Learning from the Mess: Method/ological Praxis in Rhetoric and Writing Studies.* The WAC Clearinghouse. University Press of Colorado, 2024. https://doi.org/10.37514/PER-B.2024.2180.

hooks, bell. *Feminism is for Everybody.* 5th ed. Routledge, 2014.

Kasymova, Salima, Jean Marie S. Place, Deborah L. Billings, and Jesus D. Aldape. "Impacts of the COVID-19 Pandemic on the Productivity of Academics Who Mother." *Gender, Work & Organization* 28 (2021): 419–33.

Lindquist, Julie, Bree Straayer, and Bump Halbritter. *Recollections from an Uncommon Time: 4C20 Documentarian Tales.* National Council of Teachers of English; The WAC Clearinghouse, January 25, 2023. https://wac.colostate.edu/books/swr /documentarian/.

Malisch, Jessica L., Breanna N. Harris, Shanen M. Sherrer, et al. "Opinion: In the Wake of COVID-19, Academia Needs New Solutions to Ensure Gender Equity," *Proceedings of the National Academy of Sciences of the United States of America,* 117, no. 27 (June 17, 2020). www.pnas.org/cgi/doi/10.1073/pnas.2010636117.

Manivannan, Vyshali. "First, an Opening: 'What Counts' as Academic Writing & Disrupting Academic Norms." *Journal of Multimodal Rhetorics* 6, no. 2 (Summer 2022). http://journalofmultimodalrhetorics.com/6-2-issue-intro.

Marlow, Jennifer. "Q: Am I All Right? Am I Not All Right? A: Both/And." *Journal of Multimodal Rhetorics* 6, no. 2 (Summer 2022). http://journalofmultimodalrhetorics .com/6-2-marlowe.

McCaughey, Jessica. "'This Seismic Life Change': Graduate Students Parenting and Writing During a Pandemic." *Peitho* 24, no. 2 (Winter 2022). https://cfshrc.org /article/this-seismic-life-change-graduate-students-parenting-and-writing-during -a-pandemic/.

McGrath, Maggie. "American Women Lost More than 5 million Jobs in 2020," *Forbes.* January 12, 2021. https://www.forbes.com/.

McMillen, Liz. "The Pandemic Hit Female Academics Hardest: What Are Colleges Doing to Do About It?" *Chronicle of Higher Education,* July 27, 2021. https://www .chronicle.com/.

Mendenhall, Annie S. *Desegregation State: College Writing Programs after the Civil Rights Movement.* Utah State University Press, 2022.

Morrone, Megan. "Women are Returning to Work, But There's More to the Story." Worklife. *BBC,* September 14, 2023. https://www.bbc.com/.

Morton-Aiken, Jenna and Dani DeVasto. "'Any Chance You Want to Work on This Together? I mean, Taking on More Seems Like a Poor Choice, But This Looks Cool.'" *Journal of Multimodal Rhetorics* 6, no 2 (Summer 2022). http://journalofmultimodal rhetorics.com/6-2-morton-aiken-and-devasto.

Nicolas, Melissa, and Anna Sicari, eds. *Our Body of Work: Embodied Administration and Teaching.* Utah State University Press, 2022.

Pettus, Mudiwa. "Zoom chat." *Journal of Multimodal Rhetorics* 6, no. 2 (Summer 2022). https://journalofmultimodalrhetorics.com/6-2-pettus

Silva, Mary Lourdes. "I Am Not Okay." *Journal of Multimodal Rhetorics* 6, no 2 (Summer 2022). http://journalofmultimodalrhetorics.com/6-2-silva.

Smith, Michelle and Sarah Hallenbeck. "Introduction: Feminist Imperatives and the Rhetoricity of Work." *Peitho* 25, no. 2 (Winter 2024). https://cfshrc.org/article /introduction-feminist-imperatives-and-the-rhetoricity-of-work/

Pereira, Maria do Mar. "Researching Gender Inequalities in Academic Labor During the COVID-19 Pandemic: Avoiding Common Problems and Asking Different Questions." *Gender, Work & Organization* 28, no. S2, Supplement: Feminist Frontiers (July 2021): 498–509. https://doi.org/10.1111/gwao.12618.

Perez, Caroline Criado. *Invisible Women: Exposing Data Bias in a World Design for Men.* Abrams Press, 2019.

Schuller, Kyla. "Leaning in or squadding up." *The Trouble with White Women: A Counterhistory of Feminism,* 219–43. Bold Type Books, 2021.

Shalaby, Marwa, Nermin Allam, and Gail Buttorff. "Gender, COVID and Faculty Service." *Inside Higher Ed.* December 17, 2020. https://www.insidehighered.com /advice/2020/12/18/increasingly-disproportionate-service-burden-female-faculty -bear-will-have/.

Smith, Michelle. *Utopian Genderscapes: Rhetorics of Women's Work in the Early Industrial Age.* Southern Illinois University Press, 2021.

Tappe, Anneken, Clare Duffy, and Tal Yellin. "These 5 Charts Show the Pandemic's Devastating Effect on Working Women." *CNN.* December 17, 2020. https://www.cnn .com/.

US Census Bureau. "The Disproportionate Impact of the COVID-19 Pandemic on Women in the Workforce." Webinar. February 14, 2023. https://www.census.gov/.

Weber, Lauren. "Millions of Women Left Work During the Pandemic. Where Are They Now?" podcast. *Wall Street Journal.* March 30, 2023l.

Wu, Hui, and Emily Standridge. "Renewing Feminist Perspectives on Women WPAs' Service and Leadership," In *Women's Ways of Making* edited by Maureen Daly Goggin and Shirley K. Rose. University Press of Colorado, 2021.

PART I

Shifting Sands and Finding Balance

CHAPTER 1

The Impact of Slow Change

Feminist Perspectives on Women's Advancement in Higher Education Post-COVID-19

Keri Carter

Women in the workforce experienced a whirlwind during the pandemic. Burdened with the illusion of choice, many women "opted out" of their careers to stay home with ailing family members or children; if they would not become the caretaker and schoolteacher, then who? Other women faced overburdened endless days, shifting into a new life as we knew it. I, like many other women, tried to do it all (acting a mother, wife, caretaker, full-time employee), which was tough even before the pandemic. On one day, I would feel like a good mother but a bad employee. If I felt like an outstanding employee, feelings of being a bad mom would arise. It was a delicate (im)balance that never felt even keeled. As the pandemic reared its ugly head, women's roles expanded. I also became a substitute teacher for my children, helping them learn things like second- and first-grade math, and as a college English instructor, none of this work was in my repertoire. These career issues were not new; they were just exacerbated by the pandemic. Higher education was no exception.

In fact, the pandemic crisis spotlighted issues known to hinder the careers of university women. My experiences, the experiences of women I knew, and the information I was reading about women in the workforce led me to question the past, present, and future of women's labor in higher education. I began to question what prior conditions in higher education led women to the decisions they made during the pandemic, ones that could negatively affect them later in their careers. I also explored the alternative ideas and work cultures in some corners of higher education that could help women counteract detrimental impacts of the pandemic, and in doing so, suggest policies and work culture changes higher education administrators can institute to finally make progress in leveling the playing field for women of academe.

To find out how we got here, we need to explore exactly how the enduring patriarchal and bureaucratic structures in higher education impacted women during the COVID-19 pandemic and its aftermath. I begin this process, first, by explaining persistent practices, such as gendered hiring practices, standardized male work norms, and the exclusion of women in power positions and social networks. Then, I share how the pandemic worsened the conditions for women in academia as examined through in-the-moment perspectives and experiences. In considering these negative experiences as well as those instances where women experienced atypical, more positive actions by administrators, I imagine a new world post-COVID-19 where higher education catches up to policy and practice that elevates women. This chapter, therefore, sheds light on how higher education institutions' pre-pandemic policies impacted women's experiences during the pandemic and then proposes explicit goals for institutions to consider to lessen the impact of gender-labor imbalances on women in higher education including long after the pandemic. I discuss women in STEM, barriers to tenure, time-off policies, childcare, gender bias, and tenure stop-the-clock policies. Overall, the pandemic has illuminated the impact of higher education's slow reaction to change, and this historical event has clarified the need for policy transformations to secure better, more equitable futures for women working in higher education.

The Impact of COVID-19 on Women Workers and Women in Academia

The broader coverage in the press and in subsequent reports suggest that the pandemic led to negative economic and domestic impacts for women. For example, the United Nations noted how the pandemic exposed ongoing social, political, and economic inequalities while also intensifying their effects on women, such as women bearing the brunt of any new work-life arrangements ("Policy Brief"). In fact, in recognition of the need for greater gender equality, UN Women issued a statement concerning gender equality and the importance of establishing a better future for women workers, noting that the pandemic deepened inequalities for women and minorities ("Gender Equality"). As the pandemic shut down the economy, the Bureau of Labor Statistics reported that women represented as high as a 16.2 percent unemployment rate in April 2020 as compared to a 13.5 percent rate for men ("Monthly Unemployment Rate of Men"). The trend continued throughout the year even when the economy began to reopen, and women as of July 2020 comprised 10.6 percent of the unemployed compared to 9.8 percent of men (Bureau of Labor Statistics, "Monthly Unemployment Rate of Women"). Ewing-Nelson of the National Women's Law Center, for example, reported that women were four times more likely to leave their jobs compared to men. When women are primary caregivers, they face increased obstacles. For example, Vesoulis noted that of secondary students during the 2019–2020 school year, over half attended via virtual learning. Additionally, in July 2020, at least 40 percent of childcare facilities were closed because of a lack of government assistance (Vesoulis). Women were forced to leave their work when faced with burdens created by the pandemic, and as a result, the pandemic caused what economists labeled a "she-cession," meaning that caring for children at home and balancing work with domestic labor may cause women to reduce hours or opt out of careers (Gupta; McCue).

During the pandemic, women described their time working from home as overburdened and too demanding as they orchestrated online learning for children, served a full day's set of meals to dependents, and performed domestic tasks often while working full-time; in short, the stay-home career mom was "maxed out" (McCue). Zachorowska-Mazurkiewicz explained, though, that women have historically completed more invisible and unpaid labor. Whether employed or not, women are often responsible for this labor, which increased even more during the pandemic. For women who left the workforce, the impact on the rest of their career may be irrevocable—leaving many women locked in lower-level positions and unable to seize leadership opportunities as well as serving a detrimental blow to a woman's lifetime potential earnings.

In narrowing this scope to higher education, interdisciplinary scholar Kathleen Manning noted that universities are inherent social institutions that create, recreate, and maintain gender differences and processes through curriculum choices, power dynamics, and workplace practices (92). The university structure stems from long-held bureaucratic traditions with limited flexibility and a slow reaction to change. Moreover, Manning explained how universities could benefit from a shift in organizational structure to that of a web, a metaphor that Helgensen used to describe a feminist, women-centered approach to organizational structure for greater participation and greater exposure of talents for all (92–93). This reconfiguration challenges the traditional hierarchical organization that colleges and universities have retained. Before the pandemic, universities already needed to remedy inequitable power structures. What, then, is the fate of women in higher education *after* the pandemic considering that their professional careers are more likely to hold uncertainty and job insecurity (Manning, 98)? Because the pandemic has pushed some women in academia further behind or to the brink of exhaustion, the advancement of women must be at the forefront of future changes in policy and practice. While the university cannot control the labor force beyond its own walls, it can lead the way in adapting policies that accommodate all workers.

Equity issues have arisen in work-from-home policies created during the pandemic. Women faculty may have chosen to utilize stop-the-clock career advancement policies, for example, in order to care for children or elderly family members. On one hand, utilizing a stopped clock allows a temporary reprieve from the often high-stakes tenure track timeline. However, the results of accepting a stopped tenure clock during non-pandemic times lead to salary penalties and risk of leaving the position (Manchester et al.; Khamis-Dakwar and Hiller; Quinn). Women academics may also feel a heavier burden concerning their workload. Bonevski explained that women, in general, tend to have larger teaching loads in comparison to male academics; workloads may increase further in shifting to online course modes, such as during the pandemic. Kitchener told us the opposite is often true of men in academia who utilize a stopped clock; they come away from the experience advancing professionally more often than women.

So, why do women academics not demand a more balanced load with their life partners? Claudia Goldin explains this situation as a problem of "greedy work," in which one partner is "on call" and must be ready to deal with life's problems at a moment's notice, such as dealing with childcare issues, whereas the other partner can remain focused on work. With greedy work prioritized, couple equity is abandoned for family stability. Therefore, gender norms become reinforced. In considering higher education, Bonevski noted that women academics in STEM, for example, describe what she sees as a vicious cycle for male-female partnerships—male partners tend to earn more; therefore, it is in the family's best financial interest to give priority to his work. When women continuously sacrifice their careers for financial safety, they may never recover and will continue to be the ones who need to make sacrifices. In the pandemic aftermath, Buckee et al. feared the vast issues faced by women academics, particularly those in crucial male-dominated fields, would create a "haemorrhaging of women from academia" (n.p.).

Reports indicate that the pandemic may have compounded challenges women already face in the workplace. Cardel et al. described these setbacks "chutes" that negatively affect women's careers, such as experiencing gender bias reports in teaching (see Silva, this volume) or perceptions that women produce less quality work. Furthermore, Buckee et al. explained that women are more likely to be doing the menial work in academia, such as operational tasks instead of writing papers or grants, and they attribute this reality, as well as increased domestic obligations, to women's decreased publishing rates.

One of the most complex gender discrepancies concerning work during the pandemic should be monitored through trends in academic publishing. Early in the pandemic, Kitchener, for example, painted a vastly different picture of male and female academic work-from-home perspectives by providing one male faculty member's description of quarantine as "helpful" because it allowed him even more time for writing. As one female academic put it, tenure review committee members might think, "Why weren't you writing?" (Kitchener). Andersen found in medical academic publishing that articles listing a woman as first author were down 19% compared to papers in the same journals for 2019, and the numbers for March and April 2020 showed a dearth of women listed as first authors, suggesting that women's academic research may have been affected more than that of men. Dolan and Lawless also found that for women submitting to the political science journal *American Journal of Political Science* during the pandemic, there was less of a gender gap; however, they noted that this trend does not mean women academics did not suffer during the pandemic. Women's submissions comprised only eight of 46 single-author papers. The journal *Comparative Political Studies* received the same number of submissions from women during the pandemic compared to the year prior, yet men's submissions increased by over 50 percent (Kitchener).

These early reports, however, do not necessarily paint the full scope of the pandemic's effect on publishing, which may not be fully known for some time. The lengthy process of research, writing, and peer-reviewed publication timelines means that we have not yet seen the extent of these outcomes. Authorship and academic discipline must also be considered. More recent reports on academic publishing reflect this complexity. For instance, Jemielniak et al.'s study noted discipline as a factor, where even in disciplines with higher rates of female authorship, fewer female single-authored pieces exist. They also agree that their results are limited, considering datasets were not available past a partial view of 2021. Further, another factor they mention beyond gender that may affect publications is parenthood. Liu et al. agree that the results are not fully clear on gender and academic publishing. They found that general gender gaps in the sciences widened. While both male and female authorships increased in their study, male authorships grew more. Additionally, women as first-author decreased, which, in turn, meant a decrease in women as lead researchers. The publication and authorship problems are especially concerning given the setbacks facing women in higher education described by Cardel et al. and the assumption that women are less competent in a variety of ways. The pandemic's effect on publishing and gender gaps in publishing should continue to be studied as more data becomes available.

The Effect of Traditions in Higher Education on Women

The issues surfacing for women academics during the pandemic are rooted in traditions of higher education. Liberal feminism administrative theory highlights what Manning called "two shifts" that women are forced into—domestic and public; any struggles to maintain high standards in either realm are seen as personal problems rather than ones created by dominating organizational gender norms (96). As Acker explained, clear negative assumptions exist about workers who divide their time, as women often do; therefore, they are considered lower in rank and less naturally suited to the work ("Hierarchies," 149). Women are devalued if they cannot conform to traditionally masculine job demands. As professional positions demand more "face time" and long hours, men are perceived as more willing to place work above familial obligations (Jacobs and Gerson). Recent research show that women perform more domestic work than men, even in couples in which both work in academia (Andersen). Women face tough choices. For instance, Hannum and Muhly noted how studies have shown that both men and women are abandoning desired parenthood instead of compromising career goals, but the results in the workforce are not equal. For top-level higher education leaders, the majority of men have children and 89% are married. Only 71% of women presidents have children compared to 93% of male presidents (67). Similarly, Teague found that among high-achieving Harvard alumni, career paths greatly differed between genders, noting that goal-achievement decrease was connected to childrearing expectations and an entrenched cultural message that women's careers need to slow while men's careers may soar ahead.

Furthermore, social construction feminist theory pushes back against concepts of gender neutrality in the workforce by recognizing that societal concepts of masculinity and femininity bleed into organizations and hiring practices. The perceived "two shifts" of women has certainly hurt women in hiring practices, especially in positions of power. With the slowdown of hiring during the pandemic and thereafter, women may be trapped in current positions or become less likely to be hired when openings occur post-pandemic—and they may not be promoted. Past hiring practices studied by Van der Brink and Benschop show us, for example, that male committee members recognize the burden of women as two pronged, which may seem positive at first ("Slaying," 79–80). However, male members may feel the need to "protect" female candidates from gendered work burdens, thereby not assigning them new appointments. Here, the assumption exists that a woman cannot manage the workload. Male candidates are seen as qualified; women are seen as risky (Van der Brink and Benschop, "Gender," 478).

These practices culminate in sheer numerical underrepresentation including in positions of authority (Manning, 95). Acker explained the lack of women at the top perpetuates difficulty for women of lower ranks ("From Glass Ceiling," 200). In fact, Van den Brink and Benschop described this situation as "an unbeatable seven-headed dragon that has a multitude of faces in academic life. One of these 'heads' of gender inequality resulting in the underrepresentation of women is biased decision-making in academic appointments" ("Slaying," 71). Socialist feminist theory labels this situation "inequality regimes," where organizations create and maintain systematic disparities in power positions resulting in fewer resources, fewer opportunities for promotion, and lower pay for those not in power (Acker, "Inequality," 444–47). Maranto and Griffin concede that the gender imbalance cycle in higher education is likely a cause as well as a reflection of underrepresentation across the board (140). As a result, little hope of improvement exists in the years following the pandemic, without intervention. Women struggling to maintain pre-pandemic workloads and making tough choices to lessen their work-life burdens may lose opportunities for advancement.

The disparity in low and high-power positions warrants further exploration. Women comprise over half of contingent faculty positions, with this number continuing to grow (Manning, 98). Bonevski additionally noted that university women are considered 1.5 times more likely to be job insecure. Top management in higher education reveals unsettling gender power dynamics as well. Ely and Meyerson found that when women *are* managers, they are more likely to complete less thrilling, quiet organizational tasks to keep the organization functioning, which leaves men time to problem solve more dramatic, attention-grabbing issues. Growth of women leaders in academia made some progress prior to the pandemic, but women still clearly have far to go to catch up to male counterparts (Nidiffer). The pandemic has tested the strides in women's advancement in higher education.

Why does imbalance persist, and how might leaders improve conditions in the 2020s and beyond? Maranto and Griffin called the exclusion in academia for women a "chilly climate" where a lack of networking and a scarcity of interconnected mentoring appear to be major obstacles. Acker also noted that gender and racial inequalities begin through social networks in the hiring process ("Inequality," 450). Van der Brink and Benschop explain that contacts within academic networks impact whether a candidate is seriously considered for a position ("Gender," 82–83). In fact, Van der Brink and Benschop note that women candidates in a range of disciplines express a lack of access to patriarchal support networks ("Slaying," 83). Other times, purely decorative hiring procedures yield a preferred candidate who is already known, as established through an internal network (Van der Brink and Benschop, "Transparency," 1469). Informal networking exclusion and marginalization exacerbate women's place in academia (Maranto and Griffin; Hannum and Muhly), and women's lack of academic networking during the pandemic may lead to more exclusion and a lack of hiring and promotion during an already stifled and stagnant academic market long after its most disruptive years. Women who opted to work from home are physically absent and may become increasingly invisible in existing networks.

In terms of assessment and evaluation, using the poststructural feminist lens, the scope of how women workers are perceived moves beyond a binary lens in favor of gender fluidity. As Manning explained, all workers are compared against the male norm, which is the expected standard (100), and Acker noted that evaluative measures are reinforced each time assessment is performed ("Hierarchies," 148). In scientific fields, Benschop and Brouns found that women needed to be 2.5 times more productive to get the same competence score as men (204). Women are perceived as the problem while men, again, serve as the norm. However, when women try to adapt to the male norms and enact power, they infringe upon the customs of subordination to men and are labeled in undesirable ways—and aren't considered leadership material (Acker, "Inequality"; Van der Brink and Benschop, "Slaying"). Hannum and Muhly believed that while norms may be shifting, "think leader, think male" still reigns (73). In this situation, women cannot emulate this norm nor exceed this norm to be viewed as worthy of leadership or excellence. During times of hardship, like the pandemic, they fall even further behind in meeting these unachievable male norm expectations.

Moving Forward with Policy and
Practice That Supports Women in Academia

Leaders in academia can take intentional steps to adopt practices and create or improve policies that will improve higher education as a work environment, for women as well as for *all* working within our departments and institutions.

Job Advertisements and Search Processes

While changing the culture of any institution takes time, universities can take small steps to invite women onto their campuses and make them feel supported, beginning with the job search process itself. Stepan-Norris and Kerrissey claim that interventions start by generating more welcoming jobs ads for women, as many advertisements reveal an uninviting culture. While higher education job advertisements routinely include an Equal Employment Opportunity Statement and campus, city, or department description, seldom do postings include clear incentives concerning work culture or descriptions of the culture, as indicated in a recent search of Higher Ed Jobs (https://www .higheredjobs.com/). There are notable exceptions. A few job advertisements, like one at the University of Denver, shares that they offer a "standard office environment" where "unexpected interruptions occur often" and "stress level is moderate to high." On the other hand, the University of Arkansas notes that they offer "a vibrant work environment and a workplace culture that promotes a healthy work–life balance," providing at least an opening question for a job candidate to ask how the institution, in fact, promotes healthy work–life balance. Adams State University notes, "We recognize that women and people of color are often less likely to apply to a position if they don't match 100% of the job qualifications. Don't let that be the reason you miss out on this opportunity!" While this statement does not necessarily speak directly to workplace culture, the recognition of gender and racial norms in the advertisements shows a keen awareness that goes a long way in terms of gaining the trust of women and people of color.

Furthermore, women committee members frequently hold lower authority on hiring and promotion/tenure committees and, therefore, may exert less influence in hiring decisions (Van der Brink and Benschop, "Transparency," 1470). Conversely, because fewer women serve in power positions, increased appointment on committees to level gender bias may become another burden and barrier in career progression. Attempts at gender representation may overburden women, especially for those in male-dominated fields, and does not guarantee that placement of women on those committees will result in fairer hiring practices. However, Van der Brink and Benschop have seen a real desire to appoint women in underrepresented science fields ("Slaying," 85–86).

Climate Shifting

While Stepan-Norris and Kerrissey suggest developing a climate that is, in fact, welcoming to women once they are hired, post-pandemic universities should extend this concept beyond mere welcoming. They need to be explicit in creating psychologically safe spaces so that all marginalized groups benefit and flourish in this environment. With the pandemic altering work–life balances as we know it, colleges and universities have the opportunity to shift cultural climates by implementing clear, formal procedures such as incorporating training programs that educate about exclusionary practices, creating mentoring programs, holding chairs accountable for maintaining inclusive environments, and creating family and work support systems (Maranto and Griffin; Stepan-Norris and Kerrissey).

Research indicates that gender discrimination and gender bias are pervasive in workplace practices, with women being compared against masculine or gender-neutral work norms even in common, routine practices in higher education (Grossman; Parker and Funk; Malisch et al.; Manning). Post-pandemic, women faculty may experience increased backlash when applying for tenure and promotion within the institution. Title IX protects individuals from discrimination on the basis of sex (US Department of Education); however, implicit bias may still affect the outcomes for women. Colleges and universities should acknowledge and increase awareness of gender-based biases that can arise out of the COVID-19 pandemic. For one, colleges should consider requiring gender bias training for tenure committees. This tactic does create a monetary burden for the university, and as tenure committees routinely change, the departments would have the responsibility of ensuring new members undergo gender bias training. However, this policy change could have long-term, positive effects.

To promote work–life balance, higher education administrators must support initiatives such as flexible work options, similar to the required changes many higher education institutions had to make as work and life transformed during the COVID-19 pandemic. Ironically, the pandemic has proven the value and of work-life initiatives. Colleges and universities should also consider offering childcare subsidies to faculty members, an act that would communicate the institution's support of primary caregivers and help attract female job candidates, who often serve in those roles. In the long run, offering childcare incentives can help women stay in academia and move into leadership positions.

Embracing Leadership Styles

Due to a confluence of factors, higher education may be at the right historical juncture to foster increased female leadership roles. Hannum and Muhly noted that baby boomers are in the process of leaving leadership positions in higher education, providing room for new women leaders to emerge and thereby changing the male-dominated cyclical system (66). In fact, women may prove to have an advantage in the post-pandemic future of higher education concerning leadership style that may likely exhibit collaboration and sensitivity over a more dominating masculine approach (Koenig et al.; Paustian-Underdahl et al.; Ritt). As Taub noted, the pandemic has shown how a new type of leader, one who is caring and thoughtful, can redefine what it means to be a strong leader. Taub referenced New Zealand's Jacinda Ardern who addressed the nation in a sweatshirt on Facebook Live, telling viewers she just put her toddler to bed before empathizing with their fear and anxiety caused by lockdowns. In other words, women should learn to embrace elements of their leadership style versus adapting to a male norm.

Furthermore, women need leadership development programs to succeed at their institutions (Madsen, 135). Along with channels for creating networking, mentoring, and making connections, university-sponsored programming need not teach a male norm but rather encourage each woman to embrace their strengths and draw on their distinct experiences.

Tenure and Stopped Clock Policies

During the pandemic, workers may have needed time off to deal with issues and challenges created by COVID-19. In the wake of this crisis, employees may still need time to deal with health repercussions from long- COVID illnesses and mental health issues. Leaders in higher education should enact policies and practices to help faculty feel supported and normalize needing time off as life events occur both from the effects of the pandemic and beyond.

The pandemic affected all three areas of tenure—teaching, scholarship, and service ("AAUP"). Scholars who work with human subjects may not have had access to them to complete their research (Cox); beyond the issue of human subjects or even access to labs and other necessities for research, tenure-related problems, especially regarding scholarship and service, exist because of how time was impacted from pandemic-related issues such as childcare. In academia, tenure presents an image of not only personal success but also institutional success. To maintain this image, universities can set goals to reduce barriers to tenure and help faculty continue to advance in the pandemic aftermath, as well as invest time and resources in new faculty to help them successfully move through the tenure process.

Currently, faculty may be concerned about scrutiny concerning not meeting pre-pandemic requirements, affecting faculty whose tenure review will not occur until several years past the pandemic (Cox). Emerging stop-the-clock policies offering faculty an additional year to account for how the pandemic may have disrupted progress towards tenure align with the American Association of University Professors' suggestions. However, women tend to use stop-the-clock policies more overall, potentially leaving them two or more years behind compared to male faculty who may take this option. Additionally, they may not be eligible for promotions or administrative roles due to the time lag. Many institutions also noted that professors had to request, versus automatically receive, a stopped-clock pandemic year by a specific date. Institutions differ on whether a faculty member can revert to the original clock and apply for tenure on time if needs change; this is a preferential option (Radasanu et al.). Nevertheless, given gender imbalance, institutions should consider establishing future stopped clock polices as "opt-out" versus "opt-in" options. "Opt-out" stop-the-clock policies normalized the extra time often needed due to non-work delays during the pandemic and can encourage faculty to take advantage of the policy going forward.

Many institutions have not prioritized mitigating the gendered effects of the pandemic on women workers. Rather, these policies were born out of the needs of faculty overall as well as haste and simplicity of implementation, building upon existing stopped-clock policies. For example, once a board approved an additional year added onto the exiting stopped-clock year allowance, faculty could simply request and receive written approval that they were granted an extra year in their tenure timeframe. Faculty and administration were familiar with this protocol, proving to be a cost-effective option that may have saved the institution money long-term considering the pay increase that follows moving faculty up the tenure ranks. It also allowed the institution to *express* support for faculty, women in particular, without having to institute any major changes. Rather than starting from scratch and considering how special populations may be further set back, the universities prioritized the fastest and easiest solution. However, did this policy truly work to achieve the goal of supporting women workers since men typically benefit from stop-the-clock policies concerning productivity and advancement (Antecol et al., 2439)? More can be done to protect vulnerable workers. Faculty may have feared using stop-the-clock policies and worried that any time off reflected poorly on their ability to meet expectations of professorship. On one hand, faculty, especially women, benefited from flexibility, and some appreciated the support and responsiveness that stopping the clock provided, while others may have felt the policy did not do enough to support women and mitigate the gendered effects of the pandemic on women (Gomollón-Bel).

The institutions that had better original stop-the-clock policies prior to the pandemic not surprisingly revealed better COVID-19 stop-the-clock policies. At Vanderbilt University, Princeton University and the University of Chicago, parents received a one-time automatic year of stopped clock with each child (UC Hastings College of Law). In a message communicated by Vanderbilt's Lacy Paschal, the university implemented their COVID-19 stop-the-clock as an opt-out policy, a more effective and equitable practice than when considered as an opt-in policy.

Furthermore, the University of Massachusetts at Amherst stood out as a clear frontrunner in effective implementation of COVID-19 stop-the-clock policies. Mickey et al. note that the university automatically delayed all tenure and promotion reviews for all faculty. With this opt-out policy, any faculty member wanting to stay on the current track would have to ask to be reviewed at their original time, thus normalizing extra time. They instituted this policy noting that they hoped to mitigate the gendered effects on women caused by the pandemic and acknowledging that women already face gender biases during evaluations. The university also alleviated the issue of salary loss that faculty face because of stop-the-clock policies; when a faculty member gains tenure, they will receive a retroactive salary adjustment from the time they would have originally received tenure. Genuinely recognizing and addressing the disadvantage of women in higher education during the pandemic, the University of Massachusetts at Amherst also suspended traditional and often biased teacher evaluations for more holistic assessments. Their administration has been open in recognizing the increased demands both at work and in the home, especially for women caregivers, and have committed to an open dialogue between faculty and administration. Finally, the university has recognized that the effects of COVID-19 on women and minorities will extend beyond the initial pandemic and has expressed institutional memory as a priority; therefore, faculty will have the opportunity to write about COVID-19's impact on their career each year of their review until the documentation is no longer needed.

Stopping the clock to mitigate the gendered effects of COVID-19 may or may not be effective depending on the motivation behind the policy, the recognition of the problem, and the commitment to solving it. For institutions such as the University of Massachusetts at Amherst, new policies level the playing field for all faculty by authentically identifying pandemic-related issues. For institutions with traditional stop-the-clock policies, the pandemic policy will likely be small to minimal in achieving its goals and, in fact, may harm women faculty as they will have incurred the salary setbacks noted by Manchester et al. and Khamis-Dakwar and Hiller. These setbacks are multiplied if the women also stop-the-clock for the birth of a child. Therefore, while traditional stopped clock policies aim to protect workers, they do not necessarily solve the issue of setbacks for women workers during initial delays caused by the pandemic. The cost was free, but the consequences may be dire, especially if women leave the institution or delay career progression. For stop-the-clock policies to be successful in mitigating the effect of the pandemic on women workers in higher education, institutions must take additional steps such as working to reverse any effects of the stopped clock including salary penalties.

Concluding Thoughts and Looking Forward

Although the pandemic brought many working women to their breaking point, the opportunity exists in the aftermath to embrace the upheaval of "normal" to provide better, more equitable experiences for women in higher education. Research indicates that the pandemic has set into motion negative consequences for working women, and in some cases, has caused women to leave the workforce altogether. In academia, many faculty women, especially mothers, experienced a loss of productivity that can put into motion a lifetime of setbacks, lower pay, and lost opportunities for leadership. The longstanding practices of higher education to adhere to masculine work norms have closed doors for women in a multitude of ways. It is unsurprising, then, that colleges and universities have shown modest change in gender profile and makeup in areas such as leadership positions and in STEM disciplines. However, in contending with the pandemic, colleges and universities were forced to buck slow change by making quick decisions to protect workers from illness. Higher education institutions can change when desire to change exists; we have proof. The chance to embrace new culture has been left on the field's doorstep, and yet the desire to return to "normal" in procedure and practice continues to present challenges. In the years past the pandemic's onset, little progress has been made as faculty, staff, and administrators in higher education continue to struggle with many other pervasive issues including declining enrollments, financial instability, and meeting student needs and demands. While these issues require and deserve immediate attention and creative solutions, we cannot neglect the workforce problems that the pandemic highlighted. Returning to business as usual will not solve these visible and deeply felt concerns nor the more invisible but also deeply pervasive issues caused by higher education's outdated, gendered labor practices and policies.

Adjusting higher education policy can shift the academy's culture into a more inclusive one, but those in higher education leadership must fight for this new way of operating. One goal should be to retain and promote women workers in higher education, which can be achieved through small but powerful changes including creating inviting hiring practices, having women with equal voice as representation on committees, providing bias awareness training, shifting views of leadership, and offering childcare and work-life support. One of the principal policy and culture changes needed is normalizing additional time for all by reexamining the effects of stop-the-clock policies. While some may celebrate how women "did it all" during the pandemic, individuals should stop exalting pushing through standards that are designed to exclude. Women deserve better, and now is the time to reach for a future inclusive of all in higher education.

Bibliography

Acker, Joan. "From Glass Ceiling to Inequality Regimes." *Sociologie du Travail* 51, no. 2 (2009): 199–217.

Acker, Joan. "Hierarchies, Jobs, Bodies: A Theory of Gendered Organizations." *Gender & Society* 4, no. 2 (1990): 139–58.

Acker, Joan. "Inequality Regimes: Gender, Class, and Race in Organizations." *Gender & Society* 20, no. 4 (2006): 441–64.

American Association of University Professors. "AAUP Principles and Standards for the COVID-19 Crisis." https://www.aaup.org/ (site discontinued).

Andersen, Jens Peter, Mathias Wullum Nielsen, Nicole L. Simone, Resa E. Lewiss, and Reshma Jagsi. "Meta-Research: COVID-19 Medical Papers have Fewer Women First Authors than Expected." *eLife,* June 15, 2020. https://doi.org/10.7554/eLife .58807.

Antecol, Heather, Kelly Bedard, Jenna Stearns. "Equal but Inequitable: Who Benefits from Gender-Neutral Tenure Clock Stopping Policies." *American Economic Review* 108, no. 9 (2018): 2420–41. https://doi.org/10.1257/aer.20160613.

Benschop, Yvonne, and Margo Brouns. "Crumbling Ivory Towers: Academic Organizing and Its Gender Effects." *Gender, Work, & Organization* 10, no. 2 (2003): 194–212.

Bonevski, Billie. "Why We Can't Let Women's Gains Fall Victim to COVID-19." *Newcastle Herald,* June 9, 2020. https://www.newcastleherald.com.au/story/6784522/.

Buckee, Caroline, Bethany Hedt-Gauthier, Ayesha Mahmud, et al. "Women in Science are Battling Both COVID-19 and the Patriarchy." *Times Higher Education,* May 15, 2020. https://www.timeshighereducation.com/.

Bureau of Labor Statistics. "Monthly Unemployment Rate of Men in the United States from July 2019 to July 2020 (Seasonally Adjusted)" [Graph]. *Statista,* August 7, 2020. https://www.statista.com/statistics/193935/.

Bureau of Labor Statistics. "Monthly Unemployment Rate of Women in the United States from July 2019 to July 2020 (Seasonally Adjusted)" [Graph]. *Statista,* August 7, 2020. https://www.statista.com/statistics/193938/.

Cardel, Michelle I., Emily Dhurandhar, Ceren Yarar-Fisher, et al. "Turning Chutes into Ladders for Women Faculty: A Review and Roadmap for Equity in Academia." *Journal of Women's Health* 29, no. 5 (2020): 721–33. https://doi.org/10.1089/jwh.2019.8027.

Cox, Monica F. "Maintaining Tenure Goals During the COVID-19 Pandemic." *American Society for Microbiology,* May 20, 2020. https://asm.org/.

Dolan, Kathleen, and Jennifer Lawless. "It Takes a Submission: Gendered Patterns in the Pages of AJPS." *American Journal of Political Science.* April 20, 2020. https://ajps.org/.

Ely, Robin J., and Debra E. Meyerson. "Advancing Gender Equity in Organizations: The Challenge and Importance of a Gender Narrative." *Organization* 7, no. 4 (2000): 589–608. https://doi.org/10.1177/135050840074005.

Ewing-Nelson, Claire. "Four Times More Women Than Men Dropped Out of the Labor Force in September" [Fact Sheet]. *National Women's Law Center,* Oct. 2020. https://nwlc.org/wp-content/uploads/2020/10/september-jobs-fs1.pdf.

Golden, Claudia. *Career and Family: Women's Century-Long Journey Toward Equity.* Princeton University Press, 2021.

Gomollón-Bel, Fernado. "Tick Tock. Should We Stop the Tenure Clock?" *Chemical and Engineering News* 98, no. 21 (June 1, 2020). https://cen.acs.org/.

Grossman, Joanna L. "Gender Bias and the Law." *Addressing Gender Bias in Science and Technology,* edited by Samina Azad, 145–59. Washington, DC: American Chemical Society Publications, 2020. https://doi.org/10.1021/bk-2020-1354.ch009.

Gupta, Alisha. H. "Why Some Women Call This Recession a 'She-cession.'" *New York Times,* May 9, 2020. https://www.nytimes.com/.

Hannum, Kelly, and Shannon Muhly. "Women Leaders Within Higher Education in the United States: Supports, Barriers, and Experiences of Being a Senior Leader." *Advancing Women in Leadership* 35 (2015): 65–75.

Helgesen, Sally. *The Web of Inclusion: A New Architecture for Building Great Organizations.* Beard Books, 1995.

Jacobs, Jerry A., and Kathleen Gerson. *The Time Divide: Work, Family, and Gender Inequality.* Harvard University Press, 2004.

Jemielniak, Dariusz, Agnieszka Sławska, and Maciej Wilamowski. "COVID-19 Effect on the Gender Gap in Academic Publishing." *Journal of Information Science* 46, no. 6 (2022): 1587–92. https://doi.org/10.1177/01655515211068168.

Khamis-Dakwar, Reem, and Josh Hiller. "The Problems with Pausing the Tenure Clock." *Inside Higher Ed,* July 7, 2020. https://www.insidehighered.com/.

Kitchener, Caroline. "Women Academics Seem to Be Submitting Fewer Papers During Coronavirus." *The Lily,* April 24, 2020. https://www.washingtonpost.com/.

Koenig, Anne M., A. H. Eagly, A. A. Mitchell, and T. Ristikari. "Are Leader Stereotypes Masculine? A Meta-Analysis of Three Research Paradigms." *Psychological Bulletin* 137 (2011): 616–42, https://doi.org/10.1037/a0023557.

Liu, Meijun, Ning Zhang, Xiao Hu, et al. "Further Divided Gender Gaps in Research Productivity and Collaboration during the COVID-19 Pandemic: Evidence from Coronavirus-Related Literature." *Journal of Infometrics* 16, no. 2 (2022): 101295. https://doi.org/10.1016/j.joi.2022.101295.

Madsen, Susan. "Women and Leadership in Higher Education: Current Realities, Challenges, and Future Directions." *Advances in Developing Human Resources* 14, no. 2 (2011): 131–39. https://doi.org/10.1177/1523422311436299.

Malisch, Jessica L., Breanna N. Harris, Shanen M. Sherrer, et al. "In the Wake of COVID-19, Academia Needs New Solutions to Ensure Gender Equity." *Proceedings of the National Academy of Sciences of the United States of America* 117, no. 27 (June 17, 2020): 15378–81. https://doi.org/10.1073/pnas.2010636117.

Manchester, Colleen F., Lisa M. Leslie, and Amit Kramer. "Is the Clock Still Ticking? An Evaluation of the Consequences of Stopping the Tenure Clock." *Industrial and Labor Relations Review* 66, no. 1 (2013): 3–31.

Manning, Kathleen. *Organizational Theory in Higher Education.* 2nd ed. Routledge, 2018.

Maranto, Cheryl L., and Andrea E. C. Griffin. "The Antecedents of a 'Chilly Climate' for Women Faculty in Higher Education." *Human Relations* 64, no. 2 (2011): 139–59. https://doi.org/10.1177/0018726710377932.

McCue, Duncan "'I Don't Know How I'm Gonna Go Back to the Office': COVID-19 Forces Women to Rethink Careers." *Canadian Broadcasting Corporation.* May 24, 2020. https://www.cbc.ca/radio/checkup/covid19-female-professionals-rethink-careers-1.5582187.

Mickey, Ethel L., Dessie Clark, and Joya Misra. "Measures to Support Faculty During COVID-19." *Inside Higher Ed.* Sept. 4, 2020. https://www.insidehighered.com/.

Nidiffer, Janna. "Overview: Women as Leaders in Academia." *Gender and Women's Leadership: A Reference Handbook,* edited by Karen O'Connor. Sage, 2010.

Parker, Kim, and Cary Funk. "Gender Discrimination Comes in Many Forms for

Today's Working Women." *Pew Research Center,* December 14, 2017. https://www
.pewresearch.org/.

Paschal, Lacy. "Message for Tenure Track Faculty." *Vanderbilt University,* March 19,
2020. https://www.vanderbilt.edu/.

Paustian-Underdahl, Samantha. C., Lisa Slatterly Walker, and David J. Woehr. "Gender
and Perceptions of Leadership Effectiveness: A Meta-Analysis of Contextual Mod-
erators." *Journal of Applied Psychology* 99, no. 6 (2014): 1129–45. http://dx.doi
.org/10.1037/a0036751.

Quinn, Kate. "Tenure Clock Extension Policies: Who Uses Them and to What Effect?"
Journal about Women in Higher Education 3, no. 1 (2010): 185–209.

Radasanu, Andreea, Jessica Reyman, and Patty Wallace. "Reviewing Tenure Extension
Policy." *Presidential Commission on the Status of Women,* 2019, https://www.niu.edu
/president/_pdf/reviewing-tenure-extension-policy.pdf.

Ritt, Elizabeth. "Hearing the Opus: The Paradox for Women Leaders in the Postmodern
University." *Advancing Women in Leadership Journal* 17 (2004 Winter). https://doi
.org/10.21423/awlj-v16.a188.

Stepan-Norris, Judith, and Jasmine Kerrissey. "Enhancing Gender Equity in Academia:
Lessons from the ADVANCE Program." *Sociological Perspectives* 59, no. 2 (2016):
225–45. https://doi.org/10.1177/0731121415582103.

Taub, Amanda. "Why are Women-Led Nations Doing Better with COVID-19?" *New York
Times,* May 18, 2020. https://www.nytimes.com/.

Teague, Leah. "Higher Education Plays Critical Role in Society: More Women Leaders
Can Make a Difference." *Forum on Public Policy Online* 2015, no. 2 (2015). https://eric
.ed.gov/?id=EJ1091521.

UC Hastings College of Law. "Effective Policies and Programs for Retention and Advancement of Women in Academia." https://worklifelaw.org/publications/Effective
-Policies-and-Programs-for-Retention-and-Advancement-of-Women-in-Academia
.pdf.

United Nations. "Policy Brief: The Impact of COVID 19 on Women." April 9, 2020.
https://unsdg.un.org/resources/policy-brief-impact-covid-19-women.

UN Women. "Gender Equality Experts Recommend Key Actions for COVID-19 Response
and Recovery for G7 Leaders." May 14, 2020. https://www.unwomen.org/.

US Department of Education. "Sex Discrimination: Overview of the Law." 2020. https://
www2.ed.gov/policy/rights/guid/ocr/sexoverview.html.

Van den Brink, Marieke, and Yvonne Benschop. "Slaying the Seven-Headed Dragon:
The Quest for Gender Change in Academia." *Gender, Work, & Organization* 19, no. 1
(2012): 71–92.

Van den Brink, Marieke, and Yvonne Benschop. "Gender in Academic Networking: The
Role of Gatekeepers in Professorial Recruitment." *Journal of Management Studies* 51,
no. 3 (2014): 460–92. https://doi.org/10.1111/joms.12060.

Van den Brink, Marieke, Yvonne Benschop, and Willy Jansen. "Transparency in Academic Recruitment: A Problematic Tool for Gender Equality?" *Organization Studies* 31, no. 11 (2010): 1460–83. https://doi.org/10.1177/0170840610380812.

Vesoulis, Abby. "'If We Had a Panic Button, We'd Be Hitting It.' Women are Exiting the Labor Force En Masse—and That's Bad for Everyone." *Time,* Oct. 17, 2020. https://time.com/5900583/women-workforce-economy-covid/.

Zachorowska-Mazurkiewicz, Anna. "Gender, Unpaid Labour and Economics." *Folia Oeconomica* 6, no. 326 (2016): 121–32. https://doi.org/10.18778/0208-6018.326.08.

Written in Sand

On Becoming a Mother
During a Global Pandemic

Laura Sceniak Matravers

The memos I've written for myself are neither right nor wrong [. . .]
they're written in sand so that I can revise them whenever I feel, know,
imagine a truer [. . .] idea for myself. [. . .] *The goal is to surrender [. . .]*
who I just was in order to become who this next moment calls me to be.
—Glennon Doyle, *Untamed* (emphasis added)

Fall 2021

I openly admit that I struggle to make sense of my experience of the events of
2020. One fact, though, seems clear: the COVID-19 pandemic violently exacerbated fault lines in our country's social (and political) fabric. Existing divides
have been both uncovered and deepened, and the pandemic starkly exposed
how tenuously new parents emerge in a social system so fundamentally broken
that a global pandemic provides—at least for some—certain conditions that are
more favorable than during non-pandemic times.

In Fall 2019, I began my second year on the tenure track, in the community
college job I took after earning my PhD. At the time, I had spent the better part
of the previous decade teetering, at my best, on the edge of burnout—and at my
worst, trapped in its ugly throes. Mere months before learning about COVID-
19, though, I learned that I was pregnant. With this news, I resolved to finally
resist the all-consuming nature of the academic lifestyle and sought to practice
a more mindful existence moving forward. I made significant efforts to establish healthier lifestyle habits and maintain new boundaries. I soon discovered
that a clear distinction between my home and professional lives significantly

improved my overall well-being and, subsequently, my productivity. Triumphantly, I achieved balance.

Then I had a baby during the COVID-19 pandemic.

In March 2020, six months into my pregnancy and two months into creeping worry over the virus exponentially frequenting the news, my college announced a sudden shift to remote work. The next day, my husband's employer sent him home, where he and I remained for the next fourteen months. Virtually overnight, we had to learn to survive the quiet terror of uncertainty as we forged ahead to cope with the new reality unfolding around us. I quickly learned that the work–life balance I had so carefully fashioned was as simple as it was precarious, and its reliance on physical boundaries (namely, the distinction between work and home) made that balance impossible in my new material working conditions.

The tiny traumas of pandemic isolation soon piled up: supply shortages that made it difficult to prepare for our baby's arrival; the state of constant panic in which I existed because of the unknowns of the virus and its uncertain impact on my pregnant body; and the typical pregnancy experiences—birthing classes, in-person baby showers, my family getting to feel the baby kick—that were steadily stolen away as I watched the case count and death toll tick higher and higher. It was against this backdrop of an escalating global pandemic that I embarked on my journey into new motherhood. My daughter was born two months after shelter-in-place orders were called in our state, and safety precautions were rigid—only my husband, a single suitcase, and I were allowed into the hospital on the day she was born. Our families drove 200 miles to simply be in the same city as us, but they would not meet her until months or even a year later.[1] We left the hospital and returned home, newborn in tow, to our continued isolation with no clear understanding of how to be. While news of the pandemic, wildfires, police brutality, and protests trickled in from outside, we fumbled our way, alone, through severe sleep deprivation, feeding struggles, my own recovery from the traumas of childbirth, and the unshakeable sense of continually falling short in a world that was increasingly unrecognizable.

As the waning days of summer 2020 brought my husband and I closer to our returns to work, we faced a dilemma that so many American families face during pandemic and non-pandemic times alike—childcare. We had been on multiple daycare waitlists for nearly a year, but due to stringent pandemic regulations and workers (understandably) leaving their posts, fewer spots were available—and, as the pandemic raged on, worry over risk of exposure to COVID-19 mounted. When we learned that both of our employers were continuing remote work protocols, we made the call to forgo childcare. At ten weeks postpartum, I returned to work remotely, with no childcare and no hands-on help. I continued to navigate the isolation of pandemic life as I simultaneously juggled new motherhood, being a parent who worked from home, and translating my entire professional existence into a virtual setting. Instead of striving for the new impossibility of work–life balance, I worked tirelessly to maintain new boundaries to ensure our family's physical health.

Those boundaries were maintained at the high costs of mental health and emotional well-being. From August 2020 through May 2021, every waking hour of every day in our household was mapped out in a spreadsheet I painstakingly created to help establish some order to the chaos. From morning until bedtime, my husband and I were either working or taking care of our daughter; time for anything else was unscheduled and, consequently, fleeting. Ultimately, we worked seven days a week, every week, for nine monthsstraight, either for our jobs or for our household, with no reprieve and what felt like no end in sight. While I had previously enjoyed numerous healthy habits, opportunities to engage in any acts of self-preservation came at a cost I could rarely afford, such as falling even more behind on grading. Furthermore, because of differences in our employers' demands on our time, my husband needed more scheduled weekly work hours than I did. This uneven dispersal of our work time resulted in my necessarily taking on more caregiver/household duties, which had several consequences. First, the line between my professional and personal lives blurred to the point of nonexistence, as I often had no choice but to work during the times I was "off the clock" from my job. Second, my husband and I, though equal contributors to our household income, fell into traditional gendered roles—despite how hard we otherwise push back against those roles in our marriage—a pandemic experience that is not unique (Gogoi; Hsu; Nam; Gross). Finally, the complete reversal of the strides I had previously made towards work–life balance, coupled with my postpartum experience left me struggling to cope in the face of these enormous challenges.

However, these challenges of new parenthood, though undeniably exacerbated by the existence of initial uncertainties around covid-19 and, eventually, its variants, are not all unique to pandemic existence. With or without a pandemic, my husband and I would have struggled to find adequate childcare, and the multitude of impossible and often contradictory demands placed on women who have both careers and children remains unchanged. Moreover, I am reluctant to acknowledge that having a baby during a global pandemic actually afforded some allowances that my family otherwise would not have had. For example, our household pandemic isolation, though psychologically grueling, offered a solution to the dilemma of childcare, as well as ample time to work through the numerous role transitions that result from the birth of a child. I have, as have we all, lived through the unimaginable, yet cannot fathom the difficult realities of being a new mom who works outside the home in non-pandemic times—having to physically return to work after only six unpaid weeks,[2] likely with no childcare secured. My daughter's first year was impossibly difficult, and I am still recovering from the emotional fallout while I continue to adapt to ever-changing pandemic circumstances. However, I can think of no other conceivable situation that would have allowed my husband and I both to stay home with our daughter for an entire year after she was born and still maintain gainful employment and benefits, with the additional privilege of no interruption to my promotion and tenure clock.

Fall 2023

Despite it all, my daughter thrives, as does my newly minted son. I, though, grieve for the normalcy we have lost, and continue to struggle to make sense of the circumstances that have since shaped me. Returning to this narrative at this time is deeply complicated, as my life has undergone several radical transformations that have enmeshed me even further in the traditional gender roles I once so staunchly resisted. Namely—in my past life, this academic year, I would be applying for tenure—in the job I left a mere few months ago. Instead, I now care full-time for my toddler daughter and infant son, making the hands that type this coda those of a stay-at-home mom. How could this have happened?

It would be disingenuous to state that the pandemic made me do it, but I cannot deny the role my pandemic experiences played in this decision. In retrospect, my husband and I never quite found our footing in the "new normal" of our previous context. After returning to on-site work and finally enrolling our daughter in daycare, we continued to feel the strain our two full-time jobs put on our family, and agreed that, once feasible, one of us would change employment status. My most recent and inevitable professional burnout—ignited by the pandemic experiences described above, then later stoked by pandemic-related administrative decisions, which made me feel unsafe and unsupported as a worker, followed by significant institutional changes at my former college that exacerbated an already-heavy workload and negatively impacted the general workplace environment—incited me to step away from the academic workforce, at least for the time being. Simultaneously, the recent sudden death of a close family member cemented a difficult lesson the pandemic had already taught us—our time together is not guaranteed. In a whirlwind, we learned that I was pregnant again, my husband found a job that allowed us to relocate close to family, and I made plans to resign.

These decisions were incredibly difficult to make, and this past year—while borne from the many privileges of mobility—became another nearly impossible year (I managed our relocation, while working, while growing a human, while caring for a toddler). Stepping away from the career to which I have devoted my entire adult life continues, unsurprisingly, to be a choice I struggle with, though I recognize the extreme privilege of being in circumstances that allow this to be a choice I *can* make. Several months into my new role, I both cherish the limitless time I get with my children and feel ambivalence about my decision to not resume working for a paycheck after my son was born. I miss my job (at times) and worry constantly about the roles my husband and I are modeling for our children. However. *However.* Once again, I cannot fathom doing *this*—mothering a brand-new baby, this time alongside a toddler—while also handling the demands of being employed outside the home. As the world continues hurtling on past the events of 2020, I am struck by how little seems to have fundamentally changed for families in response. Ultimately, the COVID-19 pandemic showed us many things about ourselves, including just how quickly we move on. As a nation, we experienced a collective trauma—though even that's not entirely true, given how easily reality fragments along the lines of media consumption—followed by no meaningful or lasting response, no steps toward substantial systemic change in how we treat our childcare workers, the kinds of support available to mothers of all employment varieties, the number of hours of life workers are expected to give their employers. Nothing, collectively, came of it. After a year of pandemic life, we all—my household included—carried on, went back to our jobs and complained about the cost of childcare (if we could find it) and how hard it is stay afloat while balancing the impossible demands of our professional and personal lives, as if living through the collapse of the boundaries between those roles hadn't given us any inkling that there is something unsustainable with the status quo.

Fall 2024

It is disorienting to return to this piece now and review these snapshots of myself over the past three years. Since my last run-in with this narrative, the shifts have been more subtle, like puzzle pieces slowly settling themselves into place (but actually through my own excruciating toil)—I have found my sea legs as a stay-at-home mother of two, returned to my former college as a remote adjunct instructor, and made peace with my decision to resign months before I would have gone up for tenure (despite how loudly my former doctoral-candidate-on-the-job-market-self surely still protests). I realize, in retrospect, that my ambivalence about my decision to resign came out of the grief I felt for the professional life I surrendered. However, I recognize now that I have merely been rewriting my conception of that life, as well as my understanding of who I am with—or without—it.

Notes

1. My daughter was deemed high-risk at birth, and no visitors were allowed during her first two months. When she was old enough, visitors were allowed, but only if they tested and quarantined first. Visits were rare due to the level of coordination required because of our distance from family and the limited availability of COVID-19 tests at the time. She did not meet everyone in her extended family until her first birthday.

2. Because of sheer happenstance, I gave birth at the beginning of my summer break (I worked on a nine-month contract, and teaching summer classes was optional), a week after the spring semester ended and ten weeks before the following semester began. As such, I was lucky enough to not only not have to take any official leave, but to also get an additional month without work responsibilities.

Bibliography

Gogoi, Pallavi. "Stuck-At-Home Moms: The Pandemic's Devastating Toll on Women." *NPR*, October 28, 2020. https://www.npr.org/2020/10/28/928253674.

Gross, Terry. "Almost A Year into the Pandemic, Working Moms Feel 'Forgotten.'" *NPR*, February 18, 2021. https://www.npr.org/2021/02/18/968930085.

Hsu, Andrea. "Even the Most Successful Women Pay a Big Price." *NPR*, October 20, 2020. https://www.npr.org/2020/10/20/924566058.

Nam, Rafael. "'I Come Up Short Every Day': Couples Under Strain as Families Are Stuck at Home." *NPR*, November 12, 2020. https://www.npr.org/2020/11/12/929551120.

Vibrations

Mothering, Carework, and the Value of Shared Story

*Sara Cooper, Rebecca Hallman Martini,
and Michelle Miley*

We seem to know that the important thing is to swim together—to send
out our vibrations, our stories, so that no one gets lost.
—Sue Monk Kidd

Sue Monk Kidd (1996), whose words begin our story, compares women's movement through the world to whale breaching, which is believed to be a means of communicating "when the seas get high and wild" (2). The vibrations caused by these intense physical gestures are not unlike, she says, women telling their stories. They keep us all from getting lost. They do so through the body.[1]

We write our stories as mothers who are also academics[2] navigating the unruly seas of our pandemic living. Nearly every time we talk (via Zoom, text, or email), we tell stories about how these moments in which we are living (and have been living since March 2020) bring to the surface often raging and unavoidable problems and ways of thinking that existed long before the pandemic began. Analysis of our personal stories is necessary to understand not only what our experiences are and have been, but also what they should and might be. Using an autoethnographic approach, we weave our stories together to connect and communicate with a larger culture of those who do the mothering, the nurturing, the care work within our institutions.[3]

Our text works from Rebecca Jackson and Jackie Grutsch McKinney's four definitions of autoethnography in writing studies: (1) we write from personal experience; (2) we use an inductive, qualitative approach for project design, data collection, and analysis; (3) we write in conversation with other texts; and (4) we write back to intervene in a cultural narrative (11). In autoethnography, researchers situate themselves first in their own stories, moving inward and then outward to understand how their story fits into the greater cultural narrative (Adams, Jones, and Ellis, 49). We have shaped our narrative with this inward-outward rhythm in mind; our inward narratives are foregrounded, woven together as the main text, and our outward analysis, explanation, and academic citations are incorporated primarily through footnotes.

We are in three very different phases in our own mothering experiences. When the pandemic began, Becky was pregnant with her second daughter, mothering a toddler, and navigating a new university. Sara, a single mom to a four-year-old, had developed a good support system of women within her community, one from which she was suddenly isolated when the pandemic hit. Michelle had sent her oldest off to college and was asking questions about what it meant to do care work as her mothering identity shifted. We realized we had all experienced invisibility, isolation, and devaluing of the mother work we were doing both at home and within our institutions over the eighteen months navigating COVID-19. At the same time, we acknowledged the powerful ways our identities as mothers informed this work. We write to remain "attuned to both the promise and peril of maternal rhetorics" (Buchanan, 23). We write to honor and value our mother work.

We consider our stories to be in process—partial, unfinished, and in the midst. Even still, we are in the process of theorizing our experiences. And yet, as challenging as this emotional labor feels (and it has been emotional), we find value in writing from within this experience. In both our telling and our method, this project's shape is "not the exclamation point, but the question mark" (Bochner, 77). It enables us to ask questions beyond "what happened?," questions such as—What do we do with our anger? What could feminist mothering look like during and beyond a pandemic? How do we (re)define ourselves given our obstacles? What did we learn? What should we keep and what can we let go of? Where do we go from here?

We realize there are no immediate answers. As with the early conversations that led to this chapter, what is important, here and now, is coming together to tell our stories through dialogue. And by writing together, we advocate for shared care work—for ourselves, for each other, and for our communities. We are putting our vibrations out into the world, keeping track of one another so none of us strays too far. And by doing so, we commit to the creative work that is mother work.

Write From the Body (Sara)

It is a Wednesday morning in the fall of 2021. I want to tell a story about caregiving during the pandemic but am unsure how to begin. I have been reading Dorothy Smith who tells me inquiry, from women's standpoint, is "always and necessarily from sites of bodily being" (23). I ask myself, what did you experience in your body? I check in with my body (how often do we do this as academics?) and realize I am hungry. I haven't eaten breakfast, have become accustomed to beginning my day by opening my laptop. I write at the top of the page "write from the body" and head to the kitchen. I'm going to cook a real breakfast—bacon, sweet potato hash.[4]

I am chopping onions and broccoli, pouring olive oil into the pan. Doing the work women have always done, though rarely solely for themselves. My attention is on the sizzling, the feel of the knife pressing into the thick skin of a sweet potato. I take a bite of the bacon moments after I've removed it from the stove. A pleasure. This return to the senses is also a return to memory. I begin typing, from the kitchen, while the hash continues to cook, pausing to crumble the remaining strips of bacon into the pan. I wash the grease from my hands.

The Single Flash of My Pregnant Belly (Becky)

Being pregnant during the pandemic was a strange experience. While in many ways my pregnant body was feeling increasingly crowded, I also felt very much alone. So much so, that on one occasion, I stood up in the middle of zooming with my composition theory and pedagogy graduate students to show them my pregnant belly that they otherwise could not see and had not seen. We were discussing embodiment and identity, so I figured if this wasn't the right time, when would be? I was desperate to show my eight-month pregnant belly to someone at my institution, as if to say, *See all of this that I'm carrying around? I'm tired, and I may not have all my thoughts together, but I'm showing up and I'm doing the best I can.*

It's not surprising to me, nor was it by mistake, that the single visual flash of my pregnant belly in all of ten months' time happened with my graduate students, all of whom were women. They were a special bunch, all so very committed and engaged in our course material focusing on inclusivity and accessibility in the teaching of writing. Honestly admitting to one another when they were feeling run down, making space in our class for venting and community and discussing our failures as well as our successes helped us all. I'm not sure I would have made it through the third trimester without them, to be honest. On the first day of class in January, I told them that our class was sure to get dicey around April 13, as I was due to have a baby then. Given that our university had no parental leave policy, I would be giving birth near the end of our semester, not sure when, and doing the best I could to wrap our course up fairly. To say they were shocked and angry on my behalf would be an understatement.

Besides a few friends in my department and my department Chair, no one else knew I was pregnant.[5] Since I was relatively new to the university, no one knew me that well and no one could tell I was pregnant when I only Zoomed from the chest up. It's surprising how few opportunities there were for casual niceties among colleagues, a staple in the South. Despite being a private person, by the time I was in my final trimester, I was ready to let everyone know I was pregnant. I waited to hear "so, how are you doing?" or "what's new?" so I could share the news. No one ever seemed to ask.

To complicate matters, I was going up for my preliminary tenure vote in Spring 2021, scheduled for exactly a week before my baby was due. In fact, I was asked to provide tenure and promotion materials for external reviewers while I was literally in labor. *I imagine by now you've welcomed a new one into your family.* And then, reminded to do this again, less than 24 hours after my child was born. *Making sure you received this.* From my hospital bed, I write: *I just had the baby and am still in the hospital. Would it be okay if I get back to you in the next couple days?*

Separated from the Body (Michelle)

In June 2019, my daughter graduated from high school. We spent the summer celebrating her accomplishments and excitedly getting ready for her college years. In August 2019, we packed up the car, drove the three hours to her university, unloaded all her belongings into her dorm room, took her to buy last minute supplies, had one last family dinner, and then drove away. When I got home, I sat down in the middle of her room, surrounded by all the belongings she had left behind—memories of her childhood—and sobbed. For eighteen years, my mothering identity had been strong. From the moment she was born, I cared for her—physically, emotionally, socially. Because her father and I divorced when she was four, and because I had moved away with her and my son, that care work fell solely on me. Single mothering combined with what

Ennis calls the "patriarchal institution" meant that most often I had the sole responsibility of making sure my children were not only cared for but that they flourished.

Pervasive to the white, upper middle-class culture I grew up in is the belief that the sole responsibility of care work belongs to the mother. Westervelt connects this belief, termed "intensive mothering," to patriarchal, neoliberal valuing of the individual. "One of the more unusual aspects of white American motherhood," she argues, "is the cultural tendency to place more importance on the individual . . . than on the collective good" (13). The message mothers receive to "take care of your children" comes with the second message—if the children are harmed or if they fail in any way, you, too, have failed. Intensive mothering is not the only model available to us, however. Dani McClain writes of the power of community as women support one another and mother together in *We Live for the We: The Political Power of Black Motherhood.*

Despite my mind resisting, my body feels the force of intensive mothering.[6] I love nurturing my children; I love caring for them. And, even while developing an identity beyond my mother identity,[7] the priority in my life since my daughter's birth has been my children's care.[8] Still I often have felt the guilt of having failed my children because I was not available to them—could not be available to them—twenty-four/seven. How could I not feel the guilt? Cultural forces are strong.

Now my daughter was beginning a new chapter of her life, one in which I would not be daily, physically present. I could not cook her dinners, making sure she had the nutrients she needed. I could not drive her to the places she needed to go. I could not take her in my arms after a long or difficult day. What was my new identity to be? I still was "mother," but my mother work was no longer physically visible. Separated from the body. What if she failed? What if she wasn't ok?

In March 2020, I drove back to her university, packed her up, and drove her home again.

One Space Where I Felt a Mothering Community (Becky)

In some ways, I was glad no one could see my belly and no one knew, as I wasn't sure whether a mothering identity would work for or against me. I did already have one child, but I don't think many people even knew that. As an untenured, young, female faculty member, I didn't see many spaces for my mothering identity, so I tended not to acknowledge it at work. This wasn't very hard to do when I could, in some ways wonderfully, forget my mothering identity when at work and forget my work identity while at home.[9] I loved putting in a full day of work at the office and then not doing any work on nights and weekends, something I worked hard to do post-graduate school. Yet being pregnant during the pandemic made the work/home split impossible—I was always working from home, and I could never forget that I was literally carrying one of my babies with me at all times. Sometimes, I craved a break from my body, but that never occurred, even when I was only confronted with my image via Zoom from the chest up.

There was one space where I felt a mothering community during each of my two pregnancies. During the first, it was at a prenatal yoga class where it was humbling to be surrounded by so many other pregnant bodies even if for only one hour per week. During this second pregnancy, it was as a silent, virtual lurker on a local, online group for mothers. Although I don't know its exact history, the group was formed decades ago, likely due to the need for such space and community in a town so strongly shaped by its connection to the university, where there was no formal recognition of even the most heightened parts of mothering—pregnancy, childbirth, raising an infant, losing a baby.

As I listened to people post, never once posting myself, I heard many stories of mothers struggling to make it through the year. Mother-teachers who could get no approval to offer online courses, despite their child's extreme vulnerability to COVID-19, mothers who lost babies late in pregnancy and then required to finish the semester face-to-face because there was no longer a reason to be online, mothers who were like me—pregnant and scared about how to make it through both the academic year and the pandemic, as well as the academic year in a pandemic. As I heard these stories, I watched the community fold itself around each telling. I saw a space where status and rank and age did not seem to matter, but identity as mother did. I watched mothers bravely move their personal private stories from this inner-sphere outward, to the wider public. I felt like if I needed a place to go, I had one, and I went there, even if quietly present. This is what I did when I felt too alone.

Insisting on the Body in this Disembodied Space (Sara)

It is one of the first department meetings post-campus shutdown in the spring of 2020. We are, of course, meeting via Zoom. My four-year-old daughter, dressed as Elsa, is wrapping her costume's long shimmering train around my body—my shoulders, head, neck. Her daycare has been closed for more than a month. I am adamant about keeping my camera on, want to make visible the care work I am doing while also doing my job. I realize this is not what I'm supposed to do as a pre-tenure faculty member. I don't care. I am angry that I've been asked to do what feels impossible as a single mother with no family nearby suddenly cut off from all childcare and the community of mothers who supported me through my first two years on my own in this rural town. I am insisting on the body in this disembodied space[10]—this Zoom meeting, but also the university itself. (Should we pretend the body was ever welcomed, even when we were "face to face"?) Several colleagues write post-sign-off to say my daughter's antics were the best part of the meeting. That we should always have children present. I think: *we should.* I think: *we do.*

Take Care of Your Students (Michelle)

Though frightened about our impending future, frightened for our physical selves, I felt some sense of relief. She was coming home, and at home, I could make sure she was well. If she wasn't, I could intervene. At home, my world slowed down. My children (my son a freshman in high school) were safely at home. They were old enough to shift into online school without much guidance from me. In the evenings, we gathered for dinner and often a television show. The pandemic gave me extra time with my children; I felt lucky.

But at work, the anxiety rose. As the Director of the Writing Center, I was moving our tutoring sessions and course partnerships online, figuring out what remote work looked like for our office staff, figuring out how to continue tutor education—or not. Logistically, this was a nightmare. And I also knew that everyone—staff and tutors—was experiencing major disruptions in their lives. I saw on my screen and heard in their stories how the lockdown affected people in different ways. Undergraduate tutors in lockdown who had gone home spoke of the complexities of living again within their parents' homes. For many, there was some relief in the safety of home; for others, there was added stress and anxiety. Those who stayed in apartments spoke of the fear of getting sick, of roommates not following quarantine guidelines, of small living spaces during a time when we had no escape to school or workspaces. Others who lived alone talked of feeling isolated, separated from their communities of support. Some of my staff had young children. Their children, like Sara's daughter, made appearances during our meetings.

I shifted my senior capstone class online. How did I guide these students through the culmination of their college careers? How could we celebrate their accomplishments (a celebration that seemed even more important now that they would have no graduation ceremony), and ease their anxiety about what it meant to graduate and start their new chapters in the middle of a global pandemic? This was my primary work. And I had to do it virtually. Disembodied care work.

Juggling all of this, I heard one directive coming down from above—"Take care of your students." I reacted to these emails with anger. My blood rose. My ears rang. What else did they think I would be doing? What else have I ever done? Who was going to help me take care of all these people? Who was taking care of me?

"Take care of your students." I have previously written about the need for valuing nurture in our institutions.[11] Here was a moment when "care" seemed to be the priority. And yet, just as for mothers in America, the directive came with an unstated message—the work of care was mine, and mine alone. If anyone was not cared for, I was to blame. The work of care was—is—an individual, isolated experience.

Take Care of Yourself (Becky)

Between listening and learning that there was, indeed, a mothering community at my university, I became more aware of how I too was doing mother work and care work. I just called it "mentoring," literally, in my tenure and promotion narrative, as this is an acceptable way for a professional to spend their time as they worked towards tenure. While not entirely valued, mentoring is somewhat of an expectation. Yet, there was quite a bit of "unofficial mentorship," that didn't make it into the narrative. It was the moments in those conversations with graduate students, both as a class and individually, where students began to share parts of themselves and stories about pain in the academy that they hadn't really found space for before. It was the moments when I listened to female graduate students explaining discomfort they felt from a male supervisor who had made me feel the same discomfort. It was the moments I shared my own most painful memory with my students, through tears and out of concern for their well-being, as a plea—try to take care of yourself.[12]

This Is How My Daughter and I Get by Each Day (Sara)

I wake up at 5 am, long before she is up. I work. When she wakes up, I fix her breakfast (usually cereal and strawberries). I find the tablet so we can Facetime "Grammy and Papa." This will go on for at least four hours while I work—another seeming impossibility, though (as I find myself thinking so often during the pandemic) this, too, is reality. My mom works full time and can't be on as often, but my stepdad, who is recovering from an illness, puts in the time.

They make faces, tell stories, role play . . . he watches her play with her lovies. (They have grown incredibly close, in part from caring for one another during the pandemic.)

Every day, in the afternoon, we bike together to our mostly deserted campus. We park ourselves under a tree and do what we call "acroyoga." This mostly involves me balancing her on my feet, sometimes flipping her on my knees, from my feet to my hands, over my head. I am certain other parents would be horrified by what we get up to in these sessions. We both trust our bodies, perhaps more than we should. But like so much of life during the pandemic, this is dangerous. Difficult to keep balanced. Always the threat of a fall.

In the evenings she watches movies for several hours while I teach my graduate classes. My students remember how she would yell from the other room for snacks in the middle of class, her voice extra loud because she is wearing headphones. Often enough at issue was an incorrect raisin-to-goldfish ratio. I would tuck her into bed an hour past bedtime, frazzled by the lack of any kind of boundary between my work and home selves.[13] No quiet before class to collect my thoughts. No drive home to transition back in.[14]

Finding the Places of Care That She Can, Apart from Me (Michelle)

In August 2020, both my and my daughter's universities reopened. I drove her back to her campus again. At home, I prayed for her safety, once again unable to directly care for her physical needs, unable to create the web of relationships she needs. I still feel the anxiety of her not being physically present. I ache for her as she negotiates mask mandates, socially-distanced and online classes, canceled community events, semesters of take-out food. This is not the college experience I wanted for her. But I cannot be the sole caregiver. I never could be. She must move into her own adulthood, finding the places of care that she can, apart from me.

The Writing Center reopened, too. My staff and I focused on creating spaces for socially distanced, masked, ventilated in-person connection— community, relationship, care for one another. For our students, community and connection are important. I heard this from my own daughter who insisted she needed to return to her own campus. I heard it from our writing center tutors who communicated over and over how much they missed being together.

Felten and Lambert argue that nurturing relationships are at the core of a successful college experience. They argue that "the key is not tasking each student with identifying a single mentor who will meet all of their needs, but rather creating a relationship-rich environment where students will have frequent opportunities to connect with many peers, faculty, staff, and others on and off campus" (6). And yet the task of building an environment of nurture and care cannot exist if we isolate nurture, isolate care work to individuals. Care work must belong to us all, and we must care for one another as well as for the students. Anything less creates an environment in which care is devalued and the work of nurturing is made invisible.

We Decide to Center Story (Sara)

At work, I am taking a different kind of risk from what my daughter and I do on our abandoned campus. As a member of the executive committee of an unofficial women's faculty group on campus, I have written a set of recommendations for supporting faculty caregivers during the pandemic. Like many such documents written at campuses across the nation, ours is a response to the myriad articles and studies about women faculty shouldering the majority of the burden of care work during the pandemic, resulting in their decreased productivity and opportunity as compared to their male counterparts (Minello, Martucci, and Manzo). More, though, it is a response to our own experiences of these inequities. Many of us in the group are mothers ourselves. We are asking for increased flexibility for teaching and office hours, clearer policies on taking leave, retroactive raises for faculty who would be financially impacted by delayed tenure and promotion, a public acknowledgement of the burden caregivers are experiencing.

The other officers of the group and I meet regularly to refine our recommendations and develop a plan for sharing them. This is work. It takes time. We are aware of the irony of caregivers working to lessen caregiving work. This is also emotional labor. After many conversations about how to approach our meetings with administrators, we decided to center story. At three meetings, including one with our president and provost, several of us open by telling our stories of caregiving during the pandemic. We want to take back the narrative by centering our own. We want to take up space with our experiences before they can take it up with opinions and digressions and placating. Telling my story, I feel like I did during the department meeting as my daughter wrapped me in fabric. We were insisting on our bodies—our lived experiences—in this administrative space where bodies have no place.

Hesitating to Share (Becky)

After Maya was born, my partner and I talked about what to do. Should we share a birth announcement and a photo with the department, even though most people didn't even know I had been pregnant? Wouldn't it be weirder to just show up with a baby, having not said anything? I hesitated to share. Of course, the graduate students in my course and the writing center staff already knew. They helped carry me through the semester, with their kindness and grit. We decided to announce Maya's birth, even though it felt like a risk. Even though, I wasn't so sure. My preliminary tenure vote had already passed through, so why not? I felt some shame for not finding a way to mention my pregnancy earlier, for feeling the pressure to hide it. Was it me? Or was it the culture of academia? How was it ever going to change without insisting on, without celebrating, the presence of our children? I am choosing not to hide this part of me anymore.

I Unmute to Ask (Sara)

I wish there was a different end to this story. I find myself asking—*At what point does someone say, 'wow, this has been hard. Let us help you.'* Instead, the answer is always, "We can't do this because . . ." or "but look at all we've already given you." A colleague and friend told me recently that the reason we were so easy to ignore is because most perceive us as just a bunch of moms worrying about our kids. When has this demographic ever been one whose voices are encouraged, within the academy or outside of it?

At a recent meeting of the women's faculty group, one member brings up organizing in response to Texas's recent ban on abortion. She has been active in other forms of protest, significantly against the confederate monument in our town square. She says, though, that she is considering an "online march" because of fears about COVID-19 spread and backlash from our conservative community. I unmute to ask, "What does an online march look like? Isn't protest about asserting our bodies into a space?" I hadn't realized, until voicing it, how present this question had been for me throughout our caregiver advocacy work, nor had it occurred to me what we were doing was a form of online protest. We were tired from insisting on our bodies in spaces where they were traditionally erased. "Yes," she said, "but I don't feel safe asserting my body into this space."

I think of my daughter balanced on my feet on a university campus where our bodies are not welcome. I think of how easy it would be for us both to collapse. This is dangerous.

I also think of my email to my graduate students the week we were all sent home from campuses. It is several paragraphs long, focused on the importance of caring for one another. I end by quoting Anna in *Frozen II* (a prominent figure in my pandemic life from one of the only texts I was analyzing): "Do the next right thing." It feels trite on the one hand. On the other, it comes from my daughter's world, a world that cannot be erased despite not "belonging," a world where sisters can push back against a patriarchy that says there is no room for their particular kind of magic.

A friend and I who were leading the women's faculty group in fall 2021 met at the start of the school year to discuss how to pick back up with this work when we were all so tired, so discouraged. We kept asking, *where can we actually affect change*? If not through institutional policy, where? While we have no clear answer, we do have the sense that the answer is, in part, finding direct ways to support one another, locally and specifically, while we continue the work. This colleague is a painter. I am a writer. We also decide, together, that we needed a new question—"What can we make? What can we build?"

We Create Together (Michelle)

During the early days of the lockdown, I read Robin Wall Kimmerer's *Braiding Sweetgrass.* In her chapter titled *A Mother's Work,* she writes of her own transition when her daughters moved away to college: "I have shed tears . . . when I thought that motherhood would end. But . . . being a good mother doesn't end with creating a home where just my children can flourish. A good mother grows into a richly eutrophic old woman, knowing that her work doesn't end until she creates a home where all of life's beings can flourish. There are grandchildren to nurture, and frog children, nestlings, goslings, seedlings, and spores, and I still want to be a good mother" (97). And there are students, colleagues, young mothers beginning their own journey. As I transition into a new stage of mothering, my work of nurture is not done. Every time I work for my tutors, my staff, my students, I imagine someone doing the same for my daughter. I commit to the work of creation, of community, of shared care work. I commit to "take care of my students." But I cannot do it alone. None of us can.

And so, we embrace the shape of the question mark—curved like a pregnant belly, cautiously expectant. Where do we go from here? What can we bring into the world? What do we want? Adrienne Rich reminds us, drawing from Audre Lorde's poem, "The question of what do we want beyond a 'safe space' is crucial to the differences between the individualistic telling with no place to go and a collective movement to empower women" (xxviii).

We want our care work—care of our children, our students, our coworkers, our selves—recognized and valued. And we want to care for one another as well. Our care work at home and at work has shifted as we have moved past the lockdown of the pandemic. All of us have had our worlds disrupted, and the effects are real. We all feel the anxiety of the last few years. But we have learned from the pandemic how to come together and care for one another, even by seeking out environments like the one we've created through the writing of this text. In these environments we both give *and* receive care. These environments, virtual or face-to-face, give us strength to continue to advocate for the value of care work within our institutions.

We know to insist on our embodied experiences, take up space (in our advocacy work, through our teaching and administrative roles, on the page), even when that is complicated by distance—a daughter many miles away, a screen-mediated interaction, an institution that attempts to mute our stories. We know that nurture work, to be sustained, must be collaborative. This is how we keep our experiences, our labor, from being erased.

In one sense, not much has changed in our institutions since the pandemic despite all the resolve to learn from the experience. Our advocacy for care work might be seen as ineffective. Despite the pandemic tales of how much time teaching began to take, not just because of the move online but because of the additional care students needed, the call for care work—take care of your students—without the valuing of the time or labor continues. Now that we are back on campus, we see the strain on faculty faces, in their bodies, particularly those who do that care work. We hear the weariness.

And yet, change has happened.

Sara's women's faculty group has taken the form of amplifying one another's successes, bringing one another meals, organizing events that center women's stories, and adding at least one additional happy hour to our yearly events. Further, in the spring of 2022, her department drew on the group's caregiver recommendations to revise departmental policies with an emphasis on supporting faculty caregivers and those with disabilities and/or health challenges. The revisions, now approved by department vote, support temporary shifts in course delivery mode when circumstances require it. They also allow the department to consider caregiving, disability status, and health challenges when evaluating requests for sabbatical and reassigned time. While the department's power is limited without the support of larger institutional policies, there is also value in changing what we can at the local level and increasing equity through policy. The women's faculty group is now sharing this work, as a model, with departments across campus. Since receiving tenure, Becky has worked hard to reprioritize her work commitments to keep what serves her and let go of the rest, She has found care and community through writing this piece and strengthening connections with friends and colleagues who share her values (such as the editorial team at the WAC Clearinghouse) rather than pushing for locally bound, institutionally recognized support. The good in these caring communities has trickled into her work with graduate students, several of whom have read versions of this piece in progress. In Michelle's new role as Associate Dean of her College, she is able to plant seeds to build community amongst new faculty and across departments through both formal and informal networks of care. And those seeds grow. Faculty begin to care for one another. We continue to press on, knowing that our ad hoc communities can-will-must eventually make their ways into our institutional structures.

One final story—we create together. We are sitting around a table at Spelman College at the Feminisms and Rhetorics conference revisiting this piece. This is the first time we've gathered face-to-face since before the pandemic. Since arriving in Atlanta, we have been sharing meals—gyros from the conference food trucks, naan and palak paneer from a neighborhood restaurant—and sharing new stories. Becky is feeling the pressure of working full time—teaching, directing a writing center, and collecting data for her second book—while caring for a toddler and a kindergartner. Michelle has just sent her second child off to college and is feeling the emptiness (and fullness) of the nest while taking on a new leadership role at her institution. Sara, recently tenured, is navigating shared custody and the complex feelings that accompany weekends apart from her daughter since her daughter's father moved closer. None of us feel things have gotten exceptionally easier. The pandemic, as many have recognized, illuminated inequities that have always been present. What continues to grow, however, is the urgency we feel to connect and share. We all have absorbed Tamika Carey's 2023 keynote on *The Usages of Fatigue* where she invites us to think of fatigue as an invitation to listen. We are fatigued, all of us, but we are renewed.

For our conference roundtable, we open by asking all twenty participants to introduce themselves with their professional *and* personal titles (cat mama, sister, partner, child). After reading excerpts from this chapter aloud, we invite attendees to participate in a story circle, sharing their narratives about care work. We find intimacy in sharing these private stories that have belonged only to us so far with others gathered here—and in hearing this room full of strangers, colleagues, and friends, one by one, without interruption, share their own stories. This experience illustrates what it looks like to value care work, to refuse the divide between professional and personal, mind and body, caregiving and care receiving, to shift the narrative and in turn begin to shift institutional structures.

While there is a world of work outside of this space, in this room we send our stories out, sharing together, so that none of us get lost. We know that generations of women support us—and generations to come, who are listening. Our identities as mothers can help us both advocate for the importance of nurture in the academy—often devalued and relegated to women—and for the resources such nurturing requires. As we share our stories, as we send our vibrations out into this unruly sea, as we come to know that by doing so, we keep from getting lost. And by doing so, we care for one another. We create together.

Notes

1. This chapter is dedicated to our children—Abby, Matt, Ayla, Esme, and Maya. You, too, keep us from getting lost.

2. Though "academic mothers" is the phrase more commonly used, we choose to make primary our identities as mothers.

3. Disability justice activist Leah Lakshmi Piepzna-Samarasinha (2018) defines care work as a form of justice that emphasizes "a collective responsibility that's maybe even deeply joyful" rather than "an individual chore, an unfortunate cost of having an unfortunate body" (33). We work from a similar concept of care work.

4. A month before the pandemic my body stopped digesting food correctly. In response, I cut out sugar, dairy, coffee, alcohol, legumes, and grains. I've become practiced at depriving my body.

5. My department chair did know, as she had to sign off on my ADA request so that I could teach online in Spring 2021.

6. Judith Warner talks about the pressures from intensive mothering pervasive in American culture in *Perfect Madness: Motherhood in the Age of Anxiety.*

7. In my work, I have written how feminist mothering theory has been an important framework for me personally and professionally. In *Feminist Mothering*, Andrea O'Reilley writes, "A theory of feminist mothering begins with the recognition that mothers *and children* benefit when the mother lives her life, and practices mothering, from a position of agency, authority, authenticity, and autonomy. . . . A feminist theory on motherhood also foregrounds maternal power and confers value to mothering.

Mothering, thus, from a feminist perspective and practice, redefines motherwork as a social and political act. In contrast to patriarchal motherhood that limits mothering to privatized care undertaken in the domestic sphere, feminist mothering regards itself as explicitly and profoundly political and social" (11).

8. After I got the official word that I had been promoted to associate professor and had received tenure, I came home one evening to a small gift and note my daughter had placed on my pillow. She wrote of the importance of seeing me work to reach this milestone, and of how proud she was of me. I treasure that note.

9. Dorothy Smith talks about this split in *Institutional Ethnography.* She writes: "My experiences uncovered radical differences between home and academy in how they were situated, and how they situated me, in the society. Home was organized around the particularities of my children's bodies, faces, movements, the sounds of their voices, the smell of their hair, the arguments, the play, the evening rituals of reading, the stress of getting them off to school in the morning, cooking and serving meals, and the multitudes of the everyday . . . . My first act on arriving in the department office . . . was to open my mail and thus to enter a world of action in texts. I knew a practice of subjectivity in the university that excluded the local and bodily from its field" (12).

10. Mothering does not "require self-erasure" (O'Reilly, qtd. in Kinser, 125).

11. In "Bringing Feminist Theory Home," a chapter in *Theories and Methods of Writing Center Studies: A Practical Guide,* edited by Joanna Mackiewicz and Rebecca Babcock (2020), I argue for valuing nurture and care work within rhetoric and writing studies. My argument is like that of Shari Stenberg's (2015) who argues for the valuing of feminine characteristics in our neoliberal institutions.

12. This most painful memory has been published as a chapter in "When Things Fall Apart," in Rebecca Jackson and Jackie Grutsch McKinney's *Self+Culture+Writing: Autoethnography for/as Writing Studies.*

13. Amber Kinser calls feminist mothering "irresolvably messy," pointing to "a mother's struggle to reconcile, to reconcile herself to, the blurriness of boundaries that delineate her various selves and the relational and identity tensions that emerge in mother work" (123).

14. I asked my chair if we could eliminate peer teaching observations during the Spring 2020 semester. It was not that I was worried so much about teaching quality (though that had inevitably suffered). I just couldn't fathom having my attention further divided, nor did I want to invite my colleagues into my parenting life in this way. Feeding my child while teaching my class, both forms of caregiving, felt different than listening in on a department meeting. This was personal.

Bibliography

Adams, Tony E., Stacy Holman Jones, and Carolyn Ellis. *Autoethnography: Understanding Qualitative Research.* Oxford University Press, 2015.

Bochner, Arthur. "Heart of the Matter: A Mini-Manifesto for Autoethnography." *International Review of Qualitative Research* 10, no.1 (2017): 67–80. https://journals .sagepub.com/doi/10.1525/irqr.2017.10.1.67https://doi.org/.

Buchanan, Lindal. *Rhetorics of Motherhood.* Southern Illinois University Press, 2013.

Carey, Tamika K. "The Uses of Fatigue: Investments and Invitations." Keynote at Feminisms and Rhetorics Conference, Spelman College, October 1, 2023.

Ennis, Linda Rose, ed. *Intensive Mothering: The Cultural Contradictions of Modern Motherhood.* Demeter Press, 2014.

Felten, Peter, and Leo M. Lambert. *Relationship-Rich Education: How Human Connections Drive Success in College.* Johns Hopkins University Press, 2020.

Jackson, Rebecca, and Jackie Grutsch McKinney. "Critical Introduction." Introduction to *Self+Culture+Writing: Autoethnography for/as Writing Studies,* edited by Rebecca Jackson and Jackie Grutsch McKinney. Utah State University Press, 2021. https:// muse.jhu.edu/book/97460.

Kidd, Sue Monk. *The Dance of the Dissident Daughter.* HarperOne, 1996

Kinser, Amber E. "Mothering as Relational Consciousness." In *Feminist Mothering,* edited by Andrea O'Reilly, SUNY Press, 2008.

McClain, Dani. *We Live for the We: The Political Power of Black Motherhood."* Bold Type Books, 2019.

Miley, Michelle. "Feminist Mothering: A Theory/Practice for Writing Center Administration." *WLN: A Journal of Writing Center Scholarship* 29, no.1 (2016): 17–24. https:// wac.colostate.edu/docs/wln/v41n1/miley.pdfhttps://doi.org/.

Miley, Michelle. "Bringing Feminist Theory Home." In *Theories and Methods of Writing Center Studies: A Practical Guide,* edited by Joanna Mackiewicz and Rebecca Babcock. Routledge, 2020.

Minello, Alessandro, Sara Martucci, and Lidia K.C. Manzo. "The Pandemic and the Academic Mothers: Present Hardships and Future Perspectives." *European Societies* 23, 1 (2021): S82–S94. https://doi.org/10.1080/14616696.2020.1809690.

Monk Kidd, Sue. *The Dance of the Dissident Daughter: A Woman's Journey from Christian Tradition to the Sacred Feminine.* HarperCollins, 1996.

O'Reilly. Andrea. "Feminist Mothering." In *Maternal Theory: Essential Readings,* edited by Andrea O'Reilly. Ontario: Demeter Press, 2007.

O'Reilly, Andrea. Introduction to *Feminist Mothering,* edited by Andrea O'Reilly. SUNY Press, 2008.

Piepzna-Samarasinha, Leah Lakshni. *Carework: Dreaming Disability Justice.* Arsenal Pulp Press, 2018.

Rich, Adrienne. *Of Woman Born: Motherhood as Experience and Institution.* W. W. Norton & Company, 2021.

Smith, Dorothy. *Institutional Ethnography: A Sociology for People.* AltaMira Press, 2005.

Stenberg, Shari J. *Repurposing Composition: Feminist Interventions for a Neoliberal Age.* University Press of Colorado, 2015.

Wall Kimmerer, Robin. *Braiding Sweetgrass: Indigenous Wisdom, Scientific Knowledge, and the Teachings of Plants.* Milkweed Editions, 2013.

Warner, Judith. *Perfect Madness: Motherhood in the Age of Anxiety.* New York: Penguin, 2006.

Westervelt, Amy. *Forget "Having it All:" How America Messed Up Motherhood-and How to Fix It.* Seal Press, 2018.

CHAPTER 4

Writing and Therapy

Writing as an Academic Caregiver During the COVID-19 Pandemic

Jessica Jorgenson Borchert

I contribute this chapter as a tenured Associate Professor of English at a regional, comprehensive state university in the Midwest, but what I document here occurred prior to my tenure and promotion in spring of 2021.[1] The events of this chapter cover my fourth year as an Assistant Professor, Writing Across the Curriculum administrator, and a mother to identical twins, who at the time of the start of the COVID-19 pandemic were two and a half years old. My identity positions as a recently tenured and promoted academic and a mother to twin girls who are now six remain two identity positions that operate in a state of conflict, as scholarship and motherhood both demand large moments of time, and being a parent sometimes means time is never your own. Despite the conflict in these positions, I still must believe that personal identities shape and support professional ones. I have to believe in this dichotomy of conflict as how am I to be a good mother or a successful scholar otherwise? After all, our identity positions not only shape our writing processes, but also influence the things we choose to write about.

As an academic who teaches writing, I have always encouraged my students to examine their writing process and be up front about how their lives and identities affect their writing. As Pamela Takayoshi argues, "If teachers of writing are to effectively help writers learn to be effective and productive in contemporary academic and non-academic contexts, then [they] need to know what composing demands writers must negotiate" and these demands include lived, personal identities (573). Christine Tulley's work has acknowledged that the need to unpack the writing processes through gender is necessary in understanding how the writing process is navigated by individuals who have caregiving duties. Alongside Tulley, Alex Hanson's scholarship has explored how single caregivers navigate academic experiences in spaces that are not always supportive toward the needs of single caregivers. As an academic mother, further examining the rhetoric of productivity within the writing process (or sometimes lack thereof) is crucial to understanding ways of supporting academic caregivers.

This chapter shares how the pandemic affected my writing process as an academic caregiver. Like many others during the pandemic, I lost the structure of my office where I did most of my writing and had to move to writing during brief available moments. As Deryugina, Shurchkov, and Stearns argued, female academics were often disproportionately affected by the COVID-19 pandemic when compared to their male academic counterparts due to the demands of family life while trying to still maintain a work structure at home; my narrative follows in a similar pattern. Most of my writing takes place in social spaces, like coffee shops, and sometimes those social spaces pattern a chaotic blending of responsibilities, like writing from home. Such a structure allowed me to further observe the dual roles facing academic caregivers (Guy and Arthur); therefore, I also use this chapter to examine writing and therapy as a *process.* Writing and therapy require attention to the needs of space and time. When that space or time collapses, as it did during the pandemic, then that process must change or become adapted. I was familiar with the writing process, but parenting twin toddlers presented challenges. Time became broken, fractured, which was similar to the spaces of time I committed to therapy. Therapy itself became a fractured narrative, finding space and opportunity for it where I could. My writing time was somewhat similar. I'd take on a task, only to have a toddler in a meltdown seconds later. A Facebook post I made in July 2020 echoes how my work time and childcare time were intertwined.

I could not work from home without simultaneously caring for children, and the weight of doing both was notable. My contribution begins during the lockdown of spring and summer 2020 and continues into December 2020 when I chose to seek therapy, after many months of sleeplessness and anxiety. To better combine the processes of therapy and the processes of writing, I'll organize my narrative chronologically, while also recognizing the writing process and the therapeutic process, like the learning process, is messy. This means I will include interruptions, or intercalary notes, framed as italics, within my narrative to share feelings that demonstrate struggling mental health. What you read may appear messy, or sound messy because it does not transition seamlessly and at times includes incomplete sentences, but these interruptions help to give a form to what at the time felt formless. My contribution concludes with a Coda with the goal to establish a call to universities, professional organizations, and faculty to continue to find ways to support academic caregivers beyond the pandemic.

Spring 2020

At first the pandemic seemed so distant, but on a day in March after I had finished teaching a class, I received an email from my department chair asking for COVID plans in case our in-person classes moved to remote learning. It wasn't until the next week we learned that we likely would end up teaching remotely for the remainder of the semester.

Panic of how and where. How was I going to parent and teach in a pandemic from home? Where would I find a workspace? A blur of boundaries. A collapse of time.

My university gave us a week to prepare our classes for remote delivery. For students, this was an extended spring break, but for instructors this extended time was the furthest thing from a break. I went into my office each day of our week off to prepare for remote instruction not just because I needed that time to prepare, but because I needed that time to write and revise scholarship I had in process and get as much administrative planning for helping instructors who teach writing-intensive classes to move their course content online. In other words, I was helping others move their classes online before I was working on my own courses.

When classes resumed online, I tried teaching synchronously, mostly because it seemed as if something our administration was demanding, but with my schedule overlapping with mealtimes and nap times, and my two-year old twins knowing I was home, synchronous teaching became impossible. Synchronous classes were also challenging to my students who were struggling with more demanding work schedules and instructors asking for synchronous attendance, and so I moved everything to asynchronous delivery.

While moving to asynchronous teaching was on the surface easier to structure, my work time had collapsed into compact doses of time. I planned to work primarily in the morning, for two hours, while my partner could watch the kids. I would try to get some writing done, but found myself grading and giving feedback on papers, emailing, and making short videos and other course content. When I was with the kids all afternoon, I used my mobile Canvas app and the Outlook email app[2] for work tasks. The Canvas mobile app allowed me to grade shorter tasks, like discussion posts and quizzes, while the email app helped me to respond to student questions and needs from faculty and staff in a timely manner.

But everything was overlapping and folding onto and into itself and I had no feeling of time.

I finished the semester and gave myself space to finish by deleting the final writing assignment from each class and allowing students to revise any previous assignments. Students shared how they were grateful for this change in our course and a few students did turn in revised assignments. At the end of that semester, I turned in final grades. I do not remember much about the end of the semester, but I have records that remind me it happened.

Summer 2020

I wanted to write over the summer, but with the continued pandemic and no outside childcare, summer proved to be equally challenging. My kids were toddlers, requiring a lot of attention, and email communications from work continued over the summer. With my administrative duties for Writing Across the Curriculum, I also needed to create professional development for faculty training over the summer months, along with completing my promotion and tenure dossier.

Work and caregiving continued in a collapsing, conflicting time. I remember often spending time in my living room, surrounded by my kids' toys, jotting down research notes for a project or putting together documents for promotion and tenure. I would often try to strategize and work in moments my kids seemed occupied, only to have time interrupted by a crying child or having to complete a daily task, such as meal preparation, for my kids. Instead of long bursts of time, something I had not had in months by this time, I worked in brief intervals, precariously scaffolding my work time. When I managed longer periods for writing, it was often after bedtime and focused mainly on my materials for promotion and tenure, for which I needed longer bursts of time. Overall, not much writing was getting done. It seemed as if the writing goals I had pre-pandemic were unattainable.

The blank page. Blank. Blink of the curser. Blink. Blank. Blink. Blank.

Fall 2020 and Spring 2021

My campus chose to return to in-person work fall semester, which gave me back my office and structured writing time, which I needed to complete my tenure and promotion dossier. But after so much lack of structure, after so many interruptions within a collapsing of time, I had to create new habits. I had become attuned to a lack of structure, and now that I was free to plan my time, I admittedly felt lost.

Unstructured/ruptured.

To create structure, I set up a research accountability spreadsheet in an Excel to document weekly goals and track how each goal was met. I signed up for a Writing Group through the Association of Writing Across the Curriculum, which matched us up with a group of other academics to help us create space for writing and accountability for our writing goals. My group consists of myself and two other academics[3] who meet each week for one hour on Zoom to devote time to writing.

Changes to my writing process began after I found ways to create accountability. I balanced work between the confines of home and the valuable space of my office. I also had a course release to pursue research during the spring semester, an opportunity provided to faculty in my department on a rotating basis. While the irony of having research time as a parent during a pandemic wasn't lost on me, I committed to using time through the support of the writing group, and my weekly goal setting in the accountability document.[4]

Am I getting it together? Am I finally together?

Despite having some structured time back for writing, my mental health had not recovered. I started realizing the grasp of the pandemic on my mental health after too many sleepless nights where I felt anxious about work events that would not be happening for weeks or months. One morning I shared a Facebook post asking for advice for sleeping, sharing how I was having trouble staying asleep at night. I was desperate for a solution so I could keep functioning during the day where I had to care for children and meet academic deadlines. After posting this question, I received a lot of advice that filtered around having a solid bedtime routine and doing things like burning lavender incense or using lavender essential oils to get to sleep. I did take some of the recommendations—I got a weighted blanket. I burned lavender incense. I developed a better bedtime routine. But when I was thinking about the sleep issue, I started to think about why I couldn't sleep. I chose to reach out to someone. I found a local therapist who worked with patients who had anxiety. I began working to understand the reasons for my anxiety and process my anxious behaviors. I would meet my therapist each Friday afternoon, working on goals of processing my behaviors, which also led to going back to instances of childhood trauma that included themes of abandonment and abuse. I learned that a lot of my anxiety grew out of those abusive instances. Admittedly, these are things I am still working through on a daily basis as prior pieces of my life unfold and become exposed. Therapy is a process, like the writing process, and it's a continuously unfolding one. I've learned useful strategies since beginning therapy, but anxiety is something I continue to manage daily.

Coda, or a Call to Action for Further Support of Academic Caregivers

As I reflect on my 2020 story in 2022 and 2023, I realize my narrative is similar to the stories of many other academic caregivers during pandemic teaching; many of us felt the way I did because of a lack of institutional support for caregiving, which was a problem that existed prior to COVID-19. Academic spaces value the 24/7 workaholic, but this picture fails to grasp the realities that many academic caregivers face as they balance the demands of academia with the needs of their family. Ward and Wolf-Wendel highlighted the lives of caregivers in academic research institutions, and these narratives remain relatively unchanged and unchallenged. This raises the question of what more can be done to support academic caregivers who are navigating the dual demands of an academic career and parenthood?

Institutions of higher education need to examine policies and procedures to see what can be changed to give academic caregivers space to thrive professionally. Policies should be flexible, allowing for time to work from home to support caregiving responsibilities. Pamela Takayoshi argues for an examination of composing practices that provide universities data about how faculty find time to write. Such a study would be beneficial to academic caregivers who, as Tulley has noted, often carve up writing time in carefully constructed ways, such as during a T-ball game or while a child naps. I will admit I have done similar things and have even written notes for an upcoming article on my phone while my kids played at our local public library.

Universities should also provide mental health support for faculty, beyond the standard employee assistance programs, and develop policies and procedures that support faculty and staff in seeking help for handling mental health challenges. Advertising local and regional mental health resources is also paramount in supporting mental health needs, especially considering the National Education Association's study on the higher rates of depression and anxiety among college and university faculty. Academic jobs are incredibly demanding because they often require active research agendas, teaching loads, and service requirements, all of which can add up to what may feel like insurmountable tasks leading to unmet mental health needs. As Lashuel noted in their own experiences as an early career scientist in a faculty position, sharing their own mental health struggles was challenging as few supports were in place. Because many academics relocate to new areas due to academic career trajectories, they may not always be aware of the resources available to them to support mental health needs. Having universities add mental health support and awareness to new faculty orientation programs or to Human Resource orientation meetings would raise faculty awareness of mental health support that may be available to them and their children or dependents.

Along with universities, professional organizations also need to find ways of supporting academic caregivers. Many conferences, such as the Conference on College Composition and Communication (CCCC), have created spaces to support the needs of academic caregivers. The Mothers in Rhetoric and Composition Special Interest Group (SIG) is one example that provides a space to discuss the varied needs of academic caregivers and an arena where academic caregivers can support one another. The pandemic also resulted in many professional organizations allowing for the creation of virtual or hybrid conference attendance. This shift in conference attendance provides another crucial way to support academic caregivers who may be unable to travel to an academic conference, a requirement for many faculty members including those who do not have research responsibilities. We need to remain aware of current trends and scholarship in our fields to teach our content area effectively.

Giving academic caregivers supportive and inclusive spaces to accomplish writing and research goals is necessary for academic caregivers to be academically successful. Creating writing groups on campus that meet regularly to support one another's writing time and goals facilitates this goal, as my writing group has done for me. Not only do writing groups create a space and structure for writing, but they may also help form a supportive and inclusive community to other scholars in pursuing their own writing and research goals. Alex Hanson's dissertation suggests other ways to build structures that support academic caregivers and writing time.

It is especially important to note that academic caregivers who are multiply marginalized face greater challenges in seeking support for caregiving needs than those who identify as white, cisgendered, heteronormative academics. All our university colleagues need to work together to find ways of creating supportive structures, networks, and institutional policies that are flexible for all academic caregivers and their families. I encourage academic caregivers to support one another to create inclusive spaces for academic productivity within institutional contexts.

Notes

1. Since writing this manuscript, I have moved to a non-tenure track position at a large state institution.

2. The email app turned out to become a source of anxiety and during therapy my therapist advised me to delete the app. The app was interfering with family time, as I would be trying to respond to emails when I should be listening to my partner or my children. No longer do I have email apps on my phone.

3. I need to give a shoutout to my WAC Writing Group—Kat O'Meara and Clare Birmingham. This essay exists in part because of you both!

4. I recognize the privilege I have as a tenure-stream faculty member who has opportunity for course releases allowing research and writing time.

Bibliography

Deryugina, Tatyana, Olga Shurchkov, and Jenna E. Stearns. "COVID-19 Disruptions Disproportionately Affect Female Academics." *AEA Papers and Proceedings* 111 (2021): 164–68.

Guy, Batsheva, and Brittany Arthur. "Academic Motherhood during COVID-19: Navigating Our Dual Roles as Educators and Mothers." *Gender, Work & Organization* 27, no. 5 (2020): 887–99.

Hanson, Alex. "Making Space for What Lies in the Interstices: The Composing Practices of Single Moms." *Writers: Craft and Context* 2, no. 1 (2020): 31–39.

Lashuel, Hilal A. "Mental Health in Academia: What about faculty?" *Elife,* January 8, 2020. doi.org/10.7554/eLife.54551.

Takayoshi, Pamela. "Writing in the Social Worlds: An Argument for Researching Composing Practices." *College Composition and Communication* 69, no. 4 (2018): 550–80.

Tulley, Christine. *How Writing Faculty Write: Strategies for Process, Product, and Productivity.* University Press of Colorado, 2018.

Ward, Kelly, and Lisa Wolf-Wendel, "Academic Motherhood: Managing Complex Roles in Research Universities." *The Review of Higher Education* 27, no. 2 (2004): 233–57.

PART II

Bridging Realms

Schooling the Public

Empathy in K–12 Teachers' Social Media Posts During the COVID-19 Pandemic

Danielle De Arment-Donohue

The summer of 2020 was emotionally charged as the United States inched closer to a presidential election, faced outrage in the wake of Breonna Taylor's and George Floyd's killings, and dealt with an ongoing pandemic. Evident in news coverage and social media, the initial public support for teachers who blossomed during the early spring days of the COVID-19 pandemic quickly deteriorated as debates rippled across the nation about whether to open schools in the fall. Frustrations were pointed at state officials, local school boards, unions, and even teachers like my colleagues and me in our small rural district. Yet, teachers were dealing with the same difficulties as other families along with increasingly taxing work environments. Virtual and hybrid instructional models blurred conceptions of the private and public spheres as teachers collapsed boundaries between home and work, creating new pressures.

Examining the historically feminized field, spatial boundary collapse, and drawing parallels to Lisa Blankenship's work on domestic laborers and rhetorical empathy, I suggest the pandemic has put a spotlight on strained public schools and the difficulties working mothers encounter, creating a crisis but also a kairotic opportunity to listen to often-neglected teacher voices in hopes of improving working conditions leading to ongoing teacher shortages that continue to plague districts at the time of this writing. According to The Learning Policy Institute, of the over 3.2 million teachers in the United States, over 40,000 positions were unfilled leading into the 2024–2025 school year, and over 360,000 positions were filled with individuals who were not fully certified for their teaching assignments (Tan et al., 2024). Shortages are most common in schools with higher populations of students of color, exacerbating inequities (US Department of Education). To illuminate the lives behind such statistics and study this unprecedented time's effects on women teachers, especially those who are mothers, I present the results of a discourse analysis of 80 public social media posts from K–12 teachers on Facebook and Twitter to discover *How has the pandemic impacted teachers who are mothers?* and *What changes could lead to teacher retention?* I find teachers' didactic[1] language seeks to dispute inaccurate assumptions and unreasonable expectations by asserting their humanity and calling for empathy amid a pandemic that laid bare and exacerbated challenges facing teachers who are mothers.

For many of my colleagues and me, that summer's respite was short, and unease grew as we prepared for in-person learning. We received word that a co-worker was put on a ventilator. He would eventually recover but retire from teaching. Then, unexpectedly, our school board decided the high school would begin virtually. We had two weeks to prepare. Over the 2020–2021 school year, we would experience virtual teaching from our building; a hybrid model starting in November with two groups of students attending on alternating days; a new schedule in April allowing more in-person attendance; and in the midst of it all, an Internet firewall deficiency that kicked us offline several times a day for two months. I used my phone's hotspot to stay on with virtual students, figured out which masks worked best for reading Alice Walker and Seamus Heaney aloud, and became skilled at walking around my classroom holding my laptop on my hip like I had carried my kids as toddlers. I learned not to watch school board meetings or visit local groups' social media to avoid dispiriting comments. I wondered—Didn't people realize how hard we were working to rethink and revise every aspect of instruction? That we needed parents to be allies instead of adversaries? That we, too, were struggling to ensure our children were taken care of in these bizarre times?

While I dealt with these questions personally as a white teacher in a rural district, I took note of the national public sentiments toward teachers, documented by headlines such as "Has the Public Turned on Teachers? At First Deemed Pandemic Heroes, Some Now Feel Like Villains" from *Education Week* (Will). The unfiltered world of social media abounded with messages such as this tweet from celebrity Adam Carolla—"We're now saying teachers are heroes while cops are villains. We live in a world where the people who are actually brave enough to go do their job are the bad guys" (Carolla). Another from the account OpenSchoolsChicago questions teachers' collective work ethic—"The heroes are the parents at home, giving up income and opportunity and their sanity to do both their jobs and a hell of a lot of teachers' jobs, too" (Open Schools Chicago).

Condemnatory rhetoric likely stemmed from the upheaval families experienced due to increased unemployment and implications of closures, which required rethinking work, childcare, schooling, and divisions of labor. Women have been disproportionately affected in the job market, especially the fifteen million singlemother households (Tertilt et al. 16). Of course, many of the nation's teachers have faced similar struggles. As of 2020, 77 percent of K–12 teachers were women (National Center, "Teachers"), and while there is no clear data about how many are mothers, we know 40 percent of working mothers hold jobs in education, health care, and social services (Christnacht and Sullivan).

In 2020, sociology and education researchers Greg Wiggan, Delphia Smith, and Marcia J Watson-Vandiver predicted teacher shortages, citing teaching's low status as a factor, which they attribute to its perceived disconnection from the economy. School closures' economic, social, and physical discomforts have challenged that assumption and brought attention—positive and negative—to the education field. Teacher-mothers' social media posts during the height of the pandemic expose how the fraught legacy of feminized careers continues to haunt women in workplaces, as they experience the effects of reduced professionalization; negative public sentiment; and expectations that set them up to struggle to work, raise a family, and attend to their own mental and physical health. But my examination also reveals that teachers are seeking to engage others and communicate across differences by employing rhetorical empathy to share intimate aspects of their struggles and call attention to issues related to their well-being, a topic that has been absent from most conversations about the education field. Implications of this analysis include the need for encouraging teachers to communicate their experiences and struggles as a way of increasing public understanding and partnership and guiding policy decisions that accommodate teachers with families, promote teacher well-being, and improve teacher retention.

The Feminization of the Teaching Profession

Gender and women's studies scholar Elizabeth Boyle argues that understanding the perception of teachers in the United States requires examining the feminization of the career field. From 1800–1850, teaching allowed women to work outside of the home "while still being examples of purity and nurturance," exhibiting the "cult of domesticity and true womanhood" ideals of the era. By 1900, improving opportunities for men and the lower cost of women teachers rendered the profession "essentially female" (Boyle).

Until 1950, women were typically required to leave the profession upon marriage, and single women's wages remained low. Increasing entrance requirements dissuaded young men, who viewed teaching as a temporary job. And, as teaching became more standardized, women often reported to male administrators. In 1888, while 67 percent of teachers were women, only 4 percent of administrators were female (Grumet, 38). Today, gains have been made at the school administrator level. In 2020, 56 percent of principals were female; however, an imbalance persists at the superintendent level where district decisions are made (National Center, "Principals"). As of 2020, a mere 27 percent of superintendents were women (AASA). The gender breakdown of those at the helm is roughly the inverse of the teacher population, 77 percent of whom are women.

There were ramifications for this historical imbalance as there are for its persistence. Michael Sedlak and Steven Schlossman explain, "the prevalence of women in teaching has contributed to pressure to strengthen bureaucratic controls over teacher behavior and to 'deskill' the profession" (28). Boyle writes, women teachers did the "'dirty work' for a society that did not respect them or allow them to make decisions." While men gradually reentered the field from 1900 until the present, the profession remains feminized and continues to battle deprofessionalization.

Education scholar Morwenna Griffiths moves beyond the imbalanced numbers in the field to study the feminized culture. She argues that management styles rooted in hegemonic masculinity have created a problematic culture that perpetuates lower status and prevents the filed from attracting a diverse workforce. Other education researchers have similarly focused on the culture and what perpetuates it. For instance, Sally Campbell Galman found a hidden curriculum in university education programs that reinforces norms associated with western femininity and rewards students for quiet compliance, training teachers to do the same.

In many ways the field is publicly regarded and advertised to women as a good career choice. Discussing the current era, Boyle states what many assume—"The teaching hours and part-year schedule are well suited to women with children, making the profession fit easily into traditional women's lives, but this has further contributed to the feminization of the profession, leading to lower salaries and prestige." While there are certainly benefits to the schedule, most teachers would point out they have little flexibility, work well beyond contract hours, bring work home, have difficulty finding childcare during pre-service weeks and teacher workdays, and pursue recertification over the summer. Boyle points out, "Little research has been done on female teachers' views on their jobs and how they view their subordinate status in the educational field." Herein lies the problem—without bringing teachers' voices to bear in the research, we are left to look at larger trends and rely on assumptions.

Examining Teachers' Voices

Writing about post-secondary composition instructors in "M[other]: Lives on the Outside," Lil Brannon asserts that the lack of attention paid to the gender disparity in her field suggests "we must still search for some alternative ground for action against social structures that subjugate women as women, silence their 'voices,' and deny even the reality let alone the value of their differentiated 'experience'" (457). One possible path toward these goals lies in Robert V. Bullough, Jr.'s compelling argument for conducting research about teachers' lives that centers their voices by linking their day-to-day troubles to larger public social issues. His approach emphasizes "the human dimension of institutional change" rather than top-down reform initiatives (20). Bullough concludes, "there may be no more important task before us than championing the cause of teachers and making clear the ineluctable connection between their well-being and the well-being of children" (23). In this continuing crisis—and perhaps watershed—moment, listening to how teachers have been struggling and/or coping provides insights about how to support them.

Given these goals and the current political divides that often preclude open dialogue, Blankenship's work on rhetorical empathy provides a profitable lens through which we can consider teachers' voices. In particular, her examination of strategic empathy in Jane Addams' domestic labor reform efforts and Joyce Fernandes' activist work on social media to draw attention to Brazilian house cleaners' dehumanization reveals how women can bring "attention to the very real, personal stories of people caught up in exploitative systems" (Blankenship, 63). I rely on Blankenship's definition of rhetorical empathy as signifying "an immersion in an Other's experience through verbal and visual artistic expression" and "as coming alongside or feeling with the experiences of an Other rather than feeling for or displacing an Other" (5, 6). Social media in particular offers space for participation and circulation of ideas that can foster empathy when authors invite others into their own intimate experience of a shared social phenomenon many relate to in some capacity.

Studies from disciplines such as linguistics, rhetoric, and sociology have found evidence of larger social phenomena by studying language in social media posts. Methods include quantitative, qualitative, and mixed-methods approaches; and data-gathering and analysis can be done manually or involve specifically designed software to aid with very large datasets (Tannen and Trester; Cotter and Perrin; Rüdiger and Dayter). Studies typically view datasets of gathered posts as a unified corpus that reflects social and cultural phenomena across individual posts, which also helps account for ethical issues. Even when users have chosen to make their posts public, treating them as a corpus rather than citing individual authors' names or handles provides a layer of anonymity for those who have not consented to participation even though consent is not required for public posts (Stenberg). These practices, which align with the Association of Internet Researchers' ethical guidelines, informed my methods and helped mitigate risk for individuals (franzke et al.).

For my study, public posts provided a readily available corpus that captured teachers' voices from across the nation and reflected the boundary collapse between public and private that happens when work takes place at home. I searched public posts from Facebook and Twitter (now known as X) from March 2020 to April 2021, focusing on women K–12 teachers in the United States with a particular interest in teachers who mention motherhood. I selected posts that demonstrate the professional and/or personal demands teachers faced over this year-long period. Posts were often networked with a variety of hashtags, which I employed both to find more relevant posts and narrow the search process. These included:

#teachersmatter	#teacherproblems
#valueteachers	#teachersarentexpendible
#protectteachers	#teachershavefamiliestoo
#pandemicteaching	#teachermom
#teachingfromhome	#listentoteachers
#supportteachers	#hearmyteachervoice

Because of its intersections with the Black Lives Matter (BLM) social justice movement, another relevant hashtag I followed, #teacherlivesmatter, requires a more nuanced treatment, which I discuss below. Though inherent in many issues teachers address, I do not explore the complex politics at play in a concerted specific way because these issues vary widely by state and district, and the search did not preclude or target any specific geographic areas. With few limitations on the search, the corpus organically includes posts from a diverse group of women from many areas of the United States; however, demographics are unavailable since it would be problematic to make assumptions about how authors identify in terms of race or ethnicity based on inferences from a picture or profile.

The total corpus includes 80 posts: 51 from Facebook and 29 from Twitter. Facebook posts tend to be longer with more material to analyze; however, tweets often contain extra text as images or memes. Most of the posts are text-based, but several employ pictures of workspaces and children, or narrated videos. I was most interested in text, so I excluded posts from highly visual platforms such as Instagram or TikTok though their content may be linked or referenced in these posts.

Analysis was managed by hand, and I engaged in an emergent coding process, developing an initial comprehensive list of features and making note of larger key themes. My codes were at first unwieldy, which I attribute to a large and diverse data set with teachers from all over the country in various situations. But clear patterns emerged that allowed me to develop broader categories with subcategories that offered detail about individuals' experiences. Revised codes were applied in a second pass of the data, resulting in minor revisions applied during a third pass.

Discourse analysis proved fitting to explore themes and tactics in this casual, stream-of-consciousness writing. Because of these characteristics as well as the varying lengths of and subjects tackled in many posts, I used nonexclusive coding to capture all that each post contained. If a single post contained repeated instances of the same code, I only counted that code once in the total count; however, if a post addressed multiple issues, it was coded for all relevant codes. Coding resulted in the thematic categories and subcategories shown in table 5.1.

Didactic tactics were most frequent (64.8 percent), meaning posts worked to teach in some way, often by persuading, exposing, revealing, or correcting. The second largest category relates to spatial collapse or temporal stress (26 percent). My analysis focuses on these two most predominant categories, but smaller percentages including calls to action (6.1 percent), such as pleas for mask-wearing or encouraging political participation, and those containing hopeful endings (3.1 percent) are also noteworthy. (See figure 5.1.)

TABLE 5.1. Thematic Categories and Instances

Category	Subcategory	Instances
Didactic	Safety first	31
	Concerned about own children and family	27
	Overwhelmed, struggling, exhausted	24
	Anxiety	11
	Feel undervalued	10
	Care about students	9
	Underfunded or inequity issues	8
	Defending professionalism	7
	Total	127
Spatial Collapse and Temporal Stress	Split between mothering and work	23
	Addressing the lack of time, martyr expectations, and/or need for boundaries	17
	Home now a classroom	11
	Total	51
Call to Action	Asking for support or a change in behavior	12
Hopeful Tone	Motivational closing ("I/we can do it") or hope with vaccination	6

Educators Educating

Fittingly, didactic posts demonstrate teachers doing what they do best. Yet, how they instructed the public about the nature of their jobs and struggles differed. The most common theme was safety, as 24 percent of teachers' didactic moves implored states and districts to think of safety first. One representative post implored: "I have an idea: ask TEACHERS what we need to feel safe until the vaccine is available." Of didactic tactics, 21 percent expressed concern for their families' safety, as in this example—"Today, I peacefully decline putting my life and the life of my unborn child at risk. I peacefully decline being part of the system that views our children's lives as disposable . . . Until further notice I

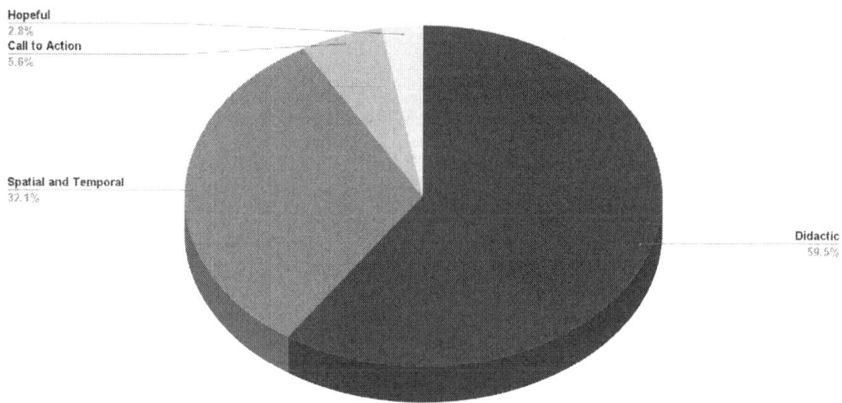

FIGURE 5.1. *Categories of teachers' social media posts*

will be teaching from the staff room . . . [M]y life is worth more!" Others expressed the idea of an impossible choice, as in this post: "Your livelihood or your life . . . That's the choice for teachers [. . .] It's either work or live." Anxiety was tied to safety and mentioned explicitly in 8.6 percent of didactic moves like this one: "I'm scared, I'm angry, I'm riddled with anxiety, I'm disillusioned, I feel like my life and health don't matter to my district, the state, and even this country. #TeachNotDie #ProtectTeachers #ProtectStudents"

Posts that addressed safety and the 6 percent that highlight underfunding overlap, as in this example:

> According to the safety guidelines recommended by the CDC, I am in need of the following items which I will have to purchase myself. I am asking for your help in acquiring these items which will contribute to the safety and wellness of myself and the students in my space. [A list including sanitizer, gloves, extra masks, and tissues follows.] I'm graciously/humbly asking for donations. #ListentoTeachers

Another trend involved correcting misconceptions (12.5 percent of didactic tactics), including the idea that teachers fearful of returning do not care about their students (7 percent insisted they do) with language such as "I still love my babies." The following examples demonstrate corrections with language defending teachers' professionalism (5 percent overtly asserted their professional identity):

> I'm tired of defending my job & my reason for not wanting to go
> back—yet. I'm tired of defending the number of hours I put into my job
> & people telling me how easy I have it. I'm tired of people telling me
> HOW to do my job when they don't teach at all.

Notable in examples above and below, 12.5 percent of didactic instances employed lists to capture the overwhelming nature of the situation and the tasks
and worries it has included. I encountered lists across every coded category. Invoking traditional rhetorical tools of Aristotelian persuasion such as repetition,
especially anaphora and epistrophe, in compelling ways connotes a speech-like
quality as in these two examples:

> This year is a lot. A lot of changes. A lot of hate. A lot of energy spent.
> A lot of screens. A lot of extra demands. [. . .] You are not a bad
> teacher if you are overwhelmed. You are not a bad teacher for setting
> boundaries. You are not a bad teacher for putting your needs first.
>
> Your child's teacher will know they have a fever long before the
> nurse. Your child's teacher will hear the cough before the nurse. Your
> child's teacher will be at high risk. Your school nurse will be high risk.
> Your child's teacher still wants to go home to their own family healthy.

Such moments layer sentiments that the audience can agree with, which aggre-
gate into a compelling argument. But, as teachers know, lecturing is only one
method of instruction. Educators frequently invited others to see their perspective by simply documenting their experiences. Readers are put in the teacher's
shoes in the following post that employs a more free-form list using asyndeton,
giving off a rushed sense of overload:

> I still needs to figure out how to use Canvas, figuring out how to use
> Edgenuity, what was Clever again? Nearpod can do what? If you use
> Peardeck you can . . . Now make sure you make them lessons engaging
> (because when the admin log into your class they wanna see them kids
> fully engaged) [. . .] Did I call parents who kids haven't [. . .] logged
> on! Do these kids go to bed, why are they emailing me this late . . .
> but let me respond don't want folks saying they called you and you
> not answering. Hold up, is there another email reminding us to do
> something else? Oh how about making sure your own kids are on
> task! Did [my own three kids] complete their work? Why is one say-
> ing his computer not working? [Two of them say their] Internet Out

Again . . . ? It's time to go, but Hold up, did you say we have a meeting
. . . let me get my mask . . . so I guess I'll have to do this when I get
home . . . but girl [. . .] who's gonna cook?? I guess me 😔, and oh
yeah them clothes not gone fold themselves and should I sweep and
mop the floor today . . . #TeacherLivesMatter

The post above is one of eighteen that used the hashtag #teacherlivesmatter.
The phrase "Black Lives Matter" permeated public discourse as Black Lives
Matter social justice protests reached a crescendo over the summer of 2020.
But, taking up this phrasing for different purposes has caused division and
detracted from the BLM movement, as exemplified by the controversial "Blue
Lives Matter" slogan.

The 2019 Teacher of the Year, Rodney Robinson, who advocates for Black
teachers and students, saw the development of this hashtag and posted, "Please
don't start a re-opening schools protest called #teacherlivesmatter. It's offensive to black people and their struggle. I agree that there are a lot of stupid
ignorant plans to open school right now but that slogan ain't it. Especially
when 80 percent of teachers are white" (Robinson). To his point, tweets such as
"Maybe if we make it a hash tag, people will care #teacherlivesmatter" read as
appropriative and flippant.

For many teachers from historically marginalized groups, the summer of
2020 included national confrontations about racially motivated police violence
and indifference toward their personal health and safety in their profession,
which may have compounded a sense of dehumanization. However, the fact
that Rodney Robinson's message was retweeted 730 times, garnered 4.1K likes,
and generated a list of alternative hashtags in the comments such as #Teacher-
sNotMartyrs, #LetTeachersLive, and #TeachersDontWannaDie, indicates there
are ways to address the crisis the pandemic caused for many teachers without
detracting from social justice efforts.

Encouraging Empathy

Citing our current divided climate, Blankenship has argued in *Changing the
Subject: A Theory of Rhetorical Empathy* that, "In our age of tremendous polarization between right and left, black and white, rural and urban, us and them,
the need for ways of connecting across difference could not be more urgent"
(4). Teachers' posts offer brief glimpses into their everyday experiences, inviting empathy from readers. Their treatment of issues is often nuanced, encouraging readers to consider others' experiences—perhaps unsurprisingly since

teachers are accustomed to thinking about others' needs—as exemplified in this post responding to a proposed opening plan:

> Selfishly, I hope [. . .] we can just put safety first and stay home. However, I realize my privilege in that statement because I can just keep my kids home with me if I'm home, they don't have [special education needs], and we have enough devices to go around with reliable internet.

This teacher noted her privilege, and the complexities other families face while sharing her own worries, making connections across difference. Most common were teachers' posts that simply expressed a desire to be seen as human and like others in ways that ask readers to connect and identify with them. Blankenship explains how such communication comes from a place of learning rather than working toward forcing a change of mind by making a point. It requires vulnerability from the communicator that can create a disarming emotional engagement for the audience wherein the rhetor becomes relatable and their plight is identifiable, resulting in empathy (Blankenship, 16).

Indeed, teachers' posts exposed their inner world and demonstrated great vulnerability. Teachers admitted to struggling and even failing at work and home in posts like this:

> It's been a long, hard year. The rules keep changing. It's like trying to hit a moving target. The kids are not thriving. This is not the kind of teaching I signed up for. I've had more than one breakdown over it in the last 12 months. I just want to be able to work with my students the way that they need me to.

Social media posts, as Anders Persson argues about Facebook, foster oversharing with limited personal sharing in response, creating "a special information state" with an "uneven distribution of knowledge" (111). The imbalance creates excellent conditions for people to develop empathy since personal accounts let readers see struggles. While the performative aspect of social media may complicate messages, posts admitting to failings seem more authentic than those presenting self-promotion or images of perfection. Blankenship reminds us of the "potential for enactments of rhetorical empathy in the multimodality of the web and its user participation," which can make social media fertile ground for reaching common ground (20). As public posts, these statements have an unknown rhetorical velocity—that is, they may be shared and spread indeterminably with those who may not have similar experiences or views, yet their content and form reveal a desire to be understood and allow outsiders to consider their difficulties behind the scenes—the opposite of the ultra-polished presentations of identity we may associate with social media.

No Room of One's Own with Spatial Collapse and Temporal Stress

Language revealing an overpacked life appeared 69 times. Several examples above illustrate difficulty fitting every responsibility into 24 hours. But spatial overcrowding has also been an issue. Efforts to turn an area of the home into a classroom space appeared in eleven posts, often accompanied by pictures or videos to document transformations. One teacher wrote:

> This is my dining room turned into a virtual teaching space. I am also supporting my own elementary school children with their learning. Today their recess time lines up with one of my lessons and they came to participate. It's a tough balance. #teachermom

This post also includes the "mom split," as I coded it, visible in 28 percent of the data set. These posts include images of teachers working with children on their lap, in the background asleep, or included in lesson planning. One mom wrote, "Working remotely while mom-ing. I might make it look easy but it's not. I'm exhausted but I'm dedicated to do both and do them well. This will pass and I will make it through. It will be a story to tell the twins." For some, the load was too heavy. Three teachers described relief that they had resigned and could stay home safely with their children.

Temporal demands, which encroached on non-contract hours well before the pandemic, were exacerbated as instructional practices were reimagined. As in many professions, work was also physically inescapable as people quarantined. German philosopher Jürgen Habermas observed that in the eighteenth century the private domain, once "devoted to the development of the inner life," had "started to dissolve into a sphere of pseudo-privacy" (157). And our reliance on school systems to handle education starting at age five aligns with Habermas' observation that teaching has been "hand[ed] over formally to the schools as family members are socialized by "extrafamilial authorities" (156). The Internet age has increased pressure on the division between public and private, and the pandemic completely collapsed the separation, changing daily routines and their physical structures.

The internet brought teachers into students' homes, disrupting divisions of labor between parents and teachers and making time and space scarce and coveted resources. Virtual learning meant teachers were occupying a space and perhaps elements of a role within the home that might typically be filled by a nanny or babysitter. While I do not equate teaching during the pandemic with domestic labor, I do suggest there is a correlation between the spatial collapse for parents and teachers and a change in perceptions and expectations of teachers.

"The Personal Is Political"

When teachers ask for empathy by letting readers into their lives and showing vulnerability, such communication can be accompanied by motivations beyond the personal. Blankenship reminds us that "[R]hetorical strategies characterized by a strategic kind of empathy are in keeping with a woman-centered and feminist political philosophy that the personal is always political." Personal stories have the power to employ pathos to show the reader that they are more alike than different (63).

In her analysis of Jane Addams' and Joyce Fernandes' advocacy work, Blankenship notes the efforts centered on showing audiences what life is like for those they employ, encouraging identification with common struggles rather than continuing to ignore the worker's life beyond their immediate usefulness to the reader. In 1893 Addams told an audience of wealthy white women, "So strongly is the employer imbued with the sanctity of her own family life that this sacrifice of the cook's family life seems to her perfectly justifiable" and suggested the cook "figured as a burnt offering" made to "the patriarchal altar" (Blankenship, 70).

Undoubtedly emotions would have been stirred by this alarming language. While it may seem over the top, consider the idea that teachers should sacrifice their lives and their family's lives for their jobs represented in posts such as this one: "You praise us when we take bullets for kids and now we have to risk our families?" The shock of this pathos-heavy post also reminds us that teachers are expected to do much more than teach content. In the county where I most recently taught, when the fire alarm rang, teachers entered the hallway first to check for an active shooter, who may have pulled the alarm to create a mass of easy targets.

More mundane daily encroachment on personal and family time takes its toll as well. Blankenship notes, "Addams invites her audience of women who employ domestic help to imagine them as fellow wives and mothers trying to run their own households" (73). We see this reminder of similarity raised by teachers who are mothers in the fifty posts that reference families and the visuals of mothers with children on their laps while they work at laptops, depicting the precarious balance with children literally positioned between them and their work.

These posts push against a history of limitations for women teachers and demand that they be seen as both mothers and teachers. Boyle documents how the history of teaching reveals that the profession was not set up for mothers, and present conditions make clear it is still not conducive to setting teachers up for professional and personal success. Writing about the feminization of composition, Lil Brannon argued the "teacher as nurturer" trope makes "teaching fully women's work," requiring "no financial compensation or reduced loads for the time that is spent. To ask for money or fewer students or 'a life' only evokes the crass masculinist values of power and self-interestedness. The nurturer, then, must remain silent and thereby deny the contributions of and reinscribe the invisibility of women's work" (460). That sounds awfully bleak, but the small shaft of light these posts demonstrate is that not all voices are silent today, and many are calling for action. Perhaps it takes a crisis and feeling that, like one teacher noted, "I am officially in the most hated career as deemed by society" to push teachers into self-advocacy. As another explained, "Advocacy is NOT synonymous with defiance, rebellion, or insubordination." Posts like this one demonstrate an empowered interest in affecting change.

How Teachers' Experiential Knowledge Can Inform Change

Teachers' posts demonstrate a desire to be understood whether through overtly persuasive language, aggressively defensive rhetoric, or—most commonly—appeals to pathos that offer a snapshot of their lives and induce empathy. This kairotic moment and these calls for empathy demonstrate we need not only to listen to teachers' voices but actively seek them out to learn how to best improve working conditions and attend to teachers' well-being. We must also seek out perspectives of teachers from marginalized minority groups to support and encourage more diversity in the field. In addition, the gender disparity at the superintendent level should instead reflect the employees in the field, so more people with similar firsthand experiences run districts. This will require deliberate efforts to recruit teachers with children—and those from historically marginalized groups—and support them in pursing administrative certification.

Of note, searches for hashtags such as #protectteachers and #valueteachers contained results from well before the pandemic, confirming many problems teachers address have been battles for decades. Calls for higher teacher pay are not new, and concern for school safety has been commonplace since the Columbine shooting in 1999. One post explains debates must be reframed because the root cause of closures is that "[t]eachers know they don't have what they need to keep kids safe," citing families without access to medical care or stable housing and buildings with lead and asbestos, plumbing and HVAC issues. She ends with, "Teachers' working conditions are student learning conditions."

The second annual Merrimack College Teacher Survey found that well-being, both for students and teachers, continues to be a large issue in public education (Merrimack College). The survey indicates that teachers who are men are more likely to be highly satisfied with their careers, and Millennial teachers are least satisfied. The study authors attribute this age disparity to the fact that Millennial teachers are the most likely to have young and school-aged children (7). The survey emphasizes that giving voice to the people behind these statistics is key to retention. When teachers were asked what graduate programs should teach future administrators about how to support teacher well-being, the top response was that leaders should learn to "understand, support, care for, value, and listen to teachers" (22). The posts gathered for this study indicate teachers know what they need to be more successful, but systems for gathering teacher voices to better inform institutional responses that would address those needs are required to get this information to those with decision-making power. Further, encouraging the kind of honesty and vulnerability evident in these social media posts and meeting it with empathy will be crucial for communication that contributes to change.

The pandemic era has emphasized the incompatibility of rigid, unsupportive workplaces and working mothers' needs and well-being. Posts from teachers who are mothers are laced with the irony of feeling they cannot meet their own children's developmental needs because the demands of meeting students' needs are overwhelming and require time beyond contract hours. Those who devote their professional lives to teaching because they so greatly believe in the project and possibilities of education should be able to support their own children, too. The more difficult we make this balance, the more we risk teacher retention.

Tertilt et al. found social norms for heteronormative families shifted with the pandemic's demands leading to fathers shouldering—at least temporarily—more childcare responsibilities. But systemic institutional changes are needed to more permanently support all families. Educators (and others) need affordable childcare and workplace flexibility, so they can meet their own children's needs instead of being pitted against their students' parents by outdated systems that do not accommodate working parents. Essentially, every level from home to school to state to nation must adjust to create conditions that will sustain teachers throughout their careers and raise the status of and outcomes for public education.

Continued scholarship on teachers' well-being, working conditions, and career decisions should include examining the effects of measures designed to support teachers during the pandemic to yield information about effective ways to respect teachers' personal and family lives, present flexible choices, allot more planning and assessment time during contract hours, provide free or low-cost daycare options, prioritize affordable health care and safety, and guarantee better compensation.

Most importantly, those at the helm of educational institutions should seek out input from those they employ. The gulf between teachers and other stakeholders becomes wider when we do not encounter one another's experiences with empathy, identifying with one another's difficulties and making personal burdens common problems to address through systemic changes that would benefit us all. The 7.5 percent of teachers' posts that end on a positive note are evidence of the hopeful attitude sustaining many teachers. Yet, a never-give-up mentality can prevent changes when teachers do not express their struggles and advocate for more manageable teaching situations. The data I gathered only represent teachers outspoken enough to make their insights public, but we must encourage input from all. As one teacher reminded readers in her post, "Just because someone carries it well doesn't mean it's not heavy."

Note

1. The word "didactic" originates from Greek and means intended to teach or instruct. Rhetorical scholar Michael Kearney (2022) notes professor of Greek and theology Philip Melanchthon first added the term to the three classical genres of rhetoric (demonstrative, judicial, and deliberative) in 1521 during the Protestant Reformation (32). Kearney points to how didactic communication emphasizes rhetoric's power to inspire change.

Bibliography

AASA (The School Superintendents Association). "AASA Releases Key Findings from American Superintendent 2020 Decennial Study." Targeted News Service. *AASA*, February 10, 2020. https://www.aasa.org/content.aspx?id=44397.
Blankenship, Lisa. *Changing the Subject: A Theory of Rhetorical Empathy.* Utah State University Press, 2019.

Boyle, Elizabeth. "The Feminization of Teaching in America." *Louis Kampf Writing Prize Essay*, Massachusetts Institute of Technology, 2004. https://stuff.mit.edu/afs/athena .mit.edu/org/w/wgs/prize/eb04.html.

Brannon, Lil. "M[other]: Lives on the Outside." *Written Communication* 10, no. 3 (1993): 457–65. https://doi.org/10.1177/0741088393010003009.

Bullough, Robert V. "The Writing of Teachers' Lives—Where Personal Troubles and Social Issues Meet." *Teacher Education Quarterly* 35, no. 4 (2008): 7–26.

Carolla, Adam (@adamcarolla). "We're now saying teachers are heroes while cops are villains. We live in a world where the people who are actually brave enough to do their job are the bad guys." Twitter (now X), July 29, 2020, 1:01 p.m. https://twitter .com/adamcarolla/status/1288520063197290497.

Christnacht, Cheridan, and Briana Sullivan. "The Choices Working Mothers Make." *The United States Census Bureau,* May 8, 2020. https://www.census.gov/library /stories/2020/05/the-choices-working-mothers-make.html.

Cotter, Colleen, and Daniel Perrin, eds. *The Routledge Handbook of Language and Media.* Taylor and Francis, 2017. https://doi.org/10.4324/9781315673134.

franzke, aline shakti, Anja Bechmann, Michael Zimmer, Charles Ess, and the Association of Internet Researchers. *Internet Research: Ethical Guidelines 3.0.* AoIR, 2020. https://aoir.org/reports/ethics3.pdf.

Galman, Sally. *Wise and Foolish Virgins: White Women at Work in the Feminized World of Primary School Teaching.* Lexington Books/Fortress Academic, 2012.

Griffiths, Morwenna. "The Feminization of Teaching and the Practice of Teaching: Threat or Opportunity?" *Educational Theory* 56, no. 4 (2006): 387–405.

Grumet, Madeleine R. *Bitter Milk: Women and Teaching.* University of Massachusetts Press, 1988.

Habermas, Jürgen. *The Structural Transformation of the Public Sphere: An Inquiry into a Category of Bourgeois Society.* MIT Press, 1991. First published 1962 by Hermann Lucterhand Veriag.

Kearney, Michael R. "Melanchthon's Didactic Genre and the Rhetoric of Reformation." *Rhetorica* 40, no. 1 (2022): 23–42.

Merrimack College. "Is Teacher Morale on the Rise: 2nd Annual Merrimack College Teacher Survey 2023 Results." EdWeek Research Center, 2023. https://www.edweek .org/products/whitepaper/is-teacher-morale-on-the-rise-results-of-the-second -annual-merrimack-college-teacher-survey.

National Center for Education Statistics. "Characteristics of Public School Principals." *NCES.* November 2023. https://nces.ed.gov/programs/coe/indicator/cls/public -school-principals.

National Center for Education Statistics. "Characteristics of Public School Teachers." *NCES.* May 2023. https://nces.ed.gov/programs/coe/indicator/clr/public-school -teachers.

Open Schools Chicago (@ChicagoOpen). "The heroes are the parents at home, giving up income and opportunity and their sanity to do both their jobs." Twitter (now X), March 10, 2020, 5:53 p.m. https://x.com/ChicagoOpen/status/1369783586593910790.

Persson, Anders. *Framing Social Interaction: Continuities and Cracks in Goffman's Frame Analysis.* New York: Taylor and Francis, 2018. https://doi.org/10.4324/9781315582931.

Robinson, Rodney (@RodRobinsonRVA). "Please don't start a re opening schools protest called #teacherlivesmatter. It's offensive to black people and their struggle. I agree that there are a lot of stupid ignorant plans to open school right now but that slogan ain't it. Especially when 80 percent of teachers are white." Twitter (now X), July 8, 2020, 1:53 p.m., https://twitter.com/rodrobinsonrva/status/1280923050645618689.

Rüdiger, Sofia, and Daria Dayter, eds. *Corpus Approaches to Social Media.* John Benjamins Publishing Company, 2020.

Sedlak, Michael, and Steven Schlossman. "Who Will Teach? Historical Perspectives on the Changing Appeal of Teaching as a Profession." *Review of Research in Education* 14 (1987): 93–131.

Stenberg, Shari J. "Tweet Me Your First Assaults: Writing Shame and the Rhetorical Work of #NotOkay." *Rhetoric Society Quarterly* 48, no. 2 (2018): 119–38. https://doi.org/10.1080/02773945.2017.1402126.

Tan, Tiffany S., Ivett Arellano, and Susan Kemper Patrick. "State Teacher Shortages 2024 Update: Teaching Positions Left Vacant or Filled by Teachers without Full Certification." *Learning Policy Institute,* July 31, 2024, https://learningpolicyinstitute.org/.

Tannen, Deborah, and Anna Marie Trester, eds. *Discourse 2.0: Language and New Media.* Georgetown University Press, 2013.

Tertilt, Michèle, Titan Alon, Jane Olmstead-Rumsey, and Matthias Doepke. "The Impact of COVID-19 on Gender Equality." *NBER Working Paper Series,* 2020. https://doi.org/10.3386/w26947.

US Department of Education. "Raise the Bar Policy Brief: Eliminating Educator Shortages through Increased Compensation, High-Quality and Affordable Educator Preparation and Teacher Leadership." *U.S. Department of Education,* July 26, 2023, https://www.ed.gov/raisethebar/eliminating-educator-shortages-compensation-preparation-leadership#_ftn5 (site discontinued).

Wiggan, Greg, Delphia Smith, and Marcia J Watson-Vandiver. "The National Teacher Shortage, Urban Education and the Cognitive Sociology of Labor." *The Urban Review* 53, no. 1 (2021): 43–75.

Will, Madeline. "Has the Public Turned on Teachers? At First Deemed Pandemic Heroes, Some Now Feel Like Villains." *Education Week,* January 25, 2020, https://www.edweek.org/.

CHAPTER 6

Virtual Kindergarten on My Couch
A Reflection on the Reconstruction of Domestic Space

Ashley J. Holmes

> We'll go on because that's what we do: We sweep up all
> our pieces and put them back together as best we can.
> —Dan Sinker, "Parents Are Not Okay"

Three bedrooms. One living room. One eat-in kitchen. Two porches. For the most intense months of working and schooling from home during the COVID-19 pandemic, my life became defined and spatially organized by the walls, layout, and square footage of these rooms in my metro-Atlanta home. Former living and dining spaces were transformed into kindergarten and fourth grade classrooms, two college professors' classrooms and offices, a tutoring center for a struggling reader, a piano practice room, a site for standardized testing, and a gymnasium, among many other things—often these disparate activities were happening concurrently in a shared space. While in the following pages I reflect on the spatial and temporal challenges my family navigated during lock down, virtual schooling, and remote work, I also acknowledge the many privileges I had that mitigated additional stressors during the pandemic, including a multiroom home with a yard, stable jobs that allowed my spouse and I to work remotely for fourteen months, a supportive partner to commiserate with and share the labor of pandemic parenting, and maintenance of good physical health within our family.

When I think back (with a bit of distance) to the details of our early pandemic experiences, I can smile at remembering the yoga mat on the front porch for online "gym" class, seeing through the window my five-year-old trying to form the poses. I remember how special it was to make hot cocoa and popcorn

FIGURE 6.1. *Screen shot of the YouTube video*
"Spell Sight Words in FortNite" by PhonicsMan.

from the teacher-mailed care package for my nine-year-old's virtual class holiday party. And I can chuckle at remembering the day I was trying to focus on reading and providing feedback on a graduate student's thesis proposal while my kindergartener worked on a sight words activity next to me that involved listening to the song "Spell Sight Words in FortNite"—a YouTube video with FortNite videogame characters dancing and PhonicsMan rapping, "B-A-L-L. Ball. Do it. Yep. G-O-O-D. Good. Do it. Yep. Let's go. Spell sight words in Fortnite. Spell sight words in FortNite. FortNite. FortNite. Spell sight words in Fortnite" (figure 6.1).

In this particular moment, I was extremely frustrated and overwhelmed by what seemed like an impossible situation—it was important that my kindergartener learn his sight words, but how could I focus on my work with this song blaring? Like many other pandemic parents, I turned to social media to highlight the absurdity of this experience, tweeting on February 9, 2021, "Update from today's concurrent work shift with virtual kindergarten: currently attempting to read a proposal on Hugh Blair's theory of taste while the 'Spell Sight Words in FortNite' song blasts from the iPad next to me. #send more coffee." I made sure to include a hyperlink to the PhonicsMan video for anyone who might want to experience a "taste" of my aural reality.

While these moments are somewhat amusing now, they also viscerally bring me back to how physically, mentally, and spatially challenging it was to be a working mother trying to balance a full-time job with supporting my elementary-age children in virtual learning, all in a shared space. The further away in time we move from the "lockdown" and months of remote work and school, the more ability I have to see the PhonicsMan incident as an isolated moment that we were able to move past, within a pandemic that would evolve and eventually result in going back to school and work. However, in February 2021, we still didn't have access to the vaccine in our state, and there was not yet a light at the end of the tunnel with regards to at-home schooling. With distance, I can see how social media became a kind of external support and community affirmation of just how difficult pandemic parenting was in that moment, but I also see how this legitimately difficult situation was framed as ironic and humorous—I remember thinking I had to poke fun and laugh about the moment, in a shared social media experience with others, to keep from bursting into tears in front of my kindergartener.

A version of this experience is likely familiar to parents in the US and internationally. Whether we had school-aged children at the time or not, we all experienced how the COVID-19 pandemic drastically altered our lives in 2020—immediately and without warning, our homes became locations for safety and lockdown. Spaces previously marked as domestic and familial had to, out of necessity, shift into workplaces and (for those of us with young kids) schoolhouses. As Jessica Enoch argues in *Domestic Occupations: Spatial Rhetorics and Women's Work:* spatial (re)construction occurs through a variety of means and agencies . . . human actors create space not only through design and material composition but also through the rules and expectations for the space, the presence or absence of bodies and objects within the space, the activities that happen within the space, and the symbolic representation of it" (10). Even though I am still trying to parse the difficulties and emotional reactions I had to the pandemic, I am beginning to see that part of what caused such dissonance, particularly as the months of telework for me and my partner and virtual, at-home schooling for my children wore on, were the ways in which my domestic and work spaces collapsed into each other and how the rules that had previously governed my engagement with these spaces had to be rewritten.

My positioning as a working mother factored prominently into the challenges of pandemic work and parenting. In October of 2020—at a time when white-collar US workers were settling into a "new normal" of teleworking and many companies resumed business as online but mostly usual—Marianne Cooper wrote in *The Atlantic:* "with work, school, and child care happening under one roof for so many families, working mothers are at unprecedented risk of experiencing a pandemic-sized motherhood penalty." Framing the tension between the "ideal worker" completely devoted to the job and the "good mother" completely devoted to her family, Cooper argues that the increased visibility of women as mothers during the pandemic—e.g., holding a child during Zoom meetings, requesting flexible meeting times to accommodate childcare—opened opportunities for unfair but research-proven bias. "Research shows," Cooper writes, drawing on a study of the motherhood penalty, "that motherhood triggers (false) assumptions that mothers are more focused on their children than their job and are therefore less competent, committed, and productive at work than fathers or employees without children"; ultimately, this bias results in career penalties such as "being paid less or being passed over in hiring and promotion decisions."

While I do not know the extent to which the pandemic may have impacted my perception as a contributing worker or how it may affect my long-term career advancement, I can say with certainty that my concerns about this negative perception impacted the way I was able to move through the pandemic. I took extra care to schedule important workshops I was leading at times when my partner could parent our kids; when we both had meetings at the same time, my children were given strict instructions to not interrupt unless it was an emergency. While I shared some of these mothering challenges with trusted colleagues, much of the time I aligned with what Cooper identifies as a common reaction—"many working mothers are trying to keep their struggles under wraps." The social media post about PhonicsMan was an anomaly, as I rarely revealed in public space the extreme challenges of pandemic parenting. As someone who truly loves my work *and* being a mother, I couldn't help but feeling like I was constantly in a double bind, without the theoretical or literal space to succeed in both roles. Because society sees the ideal worker and good mother as "ideologically incompatible," working mothers are constantly having to choose one role or the other—"You can be one or the other. There is no *space* to be both" (Cooper, emphasis mine). Teleworking combined with at-home virtual learning meant my children and I shared domestic space but for the purposes of work and school (in addition to domesticity); the constant presence of my children in our home space and the domestic activities we associate with those living spaces made it nearly impossible to separate home and work, mother and professor. How could I deny my five-year-old a couch cuddle in the middle of his virtual kindergarten class time? How could I refuse to help my dyslexic nine-year-old with a reading activity for an online assignment? The reality was that I couldn't. It wasn't until I made peace with the fact that I didn't want to entirely cut off these mothering responsibilities in the face of a pandemic that I was able to (re)orient my family's lived experiences, spatially and temporally, in a way that served each of our needs as whole persons.

While I'm not sure I fully achieved it, I strived toward a tactical approach to spatial (re)construction in our shared domestic space. As Paula Mathieu writes in *Tactics of Hope*, drawing on the work of Michel de Certeau, *strategies* are "calculated actions that emanate from and depend upon 'proper' (as in propertied) spaces, like corporations, state agencies, and educational institutions . . . the goal of a strategy is to create a stable, spatial nexus that . . . minimize[s] temporal uncertainty" (16). The pandemic took away our sense of control over our lives; for those of us educational or corporate laborers teleworking from home, our domestic spaces attempted to emulate strategic thinking and practices that thrive on stability, "measurability," and "rationality" (Mathieu, 16). However, the experience of trying to support virtual elementary school while working full time online was neither stable nor rational, even though it tried to masquerade as that. Spatial instability and temporal uncertainty were the norm. One day's problem to solve—in what space could I hold the Writing Across the Curriculum online workshop I was leading so that attendees wouldn't hear my nine-year-old's virtual piano practice scheduled at the same time? Sharing a similar experience, one graduate student mother I advise confided that she was planning to hold her virtual prospectus defense from her family's RV in their driveway to have a quiet space for presentation and Q&A. In my house, spaces previously constructed as leisurely, such as my screened-in front porch, became (re)constructed as workspaces for Zoom meetings, academic writing, and reading preparation for the graduate course I was teaching. My living room couch, where I sit to watch TV and unwind at the end of my workdays, became the site of kindergarten via Zoom—only after my five-year-old son rejected the carefully organized Ikea desk space I created for him. Who wouldn't want to attend kindergarten from the comfort of your home couch?

When I began to let go of any presumed sense of control over this absurdly challenging situation, I reflect now on the ways I was moving toward what Mathieu, via de Certeau, frames as a tactical response to the situation. Unlike strategies, *tactics* "are at one's disposal when one 'cannot count on a 'proper' (a spatial or institutional location, nor thus on a borderline distinguishing the other as a visible totality)' (xx)" (16). As Mathieu emphasizes, "tactics are available when we do not control the space," and they depend on time (16); "tactics seek rhetorically timely actions" (17)—a literal seizing of the moment and, as de Certeau writes, "a clever utilization of time, of the opportunities it presents . . . " (qtd. in Mathieu, 17). When I couldn't control the spaces and the ways the boundaries of their purposes were overlapping and collapsing, I turned to what little control I could have over managing the logistics of our time.

Each Sunday, my partner and I would map out the week's schedule—blocking off each of our synchronous teaching times and online work meetings, webinars, and office hours. Then we laid those schedules alongside our kindergarten and fourth graders' online learning schedules. Not only did we have to sort out the times we would each be in different virtual locations, but we also had to match that with the literal spaces of our home—who got the office space at what time? Who needed to hold their meeting outside on the porch—was it too cold to sit outside for one hour that day? And, importantly, which of the parents was "taking lead" at what times in supporting our elementary at-home learners who, despite assumptions made by our public school system, needed *a lot* of help to complete virtual assignments.

As figures 6.2 and 6.3 show, our children had different subjects at different times. What this schedule does not show is how our school district mandated that kindergarteners should not sit in synchronous online meetings for more than twenty minutes—which is probably a good idea; however, the effect was each block of class for Science or Math started with twenty minutes of live instruction followed by about a half hour of asynchronous practice (i.e., mom or dad helping with an iPad activity). Oh, and don't forget to log back in to this new Zoom link, with a new ID, and random password for the next class in twenty-five minutes—while also helping your fourth grader figure out if they are on Teams (which requires the Chromebook) or Zoom (which requires the iPad) for their next class: "Wait—your next class is PE. Where are your shoes? You need shoes for PE!"

As the months and months (and months) of working and schooling from home continued, our family became more tactical in using our shared domestic spaces and overlapping time commitments. We were more careful to minimize scheduling conflicts when we could control the meeting or work times. For example, my preferred research writing time is in the morning, but I had to shift to afternoons: 2:00 – 5:00 PM became (out of necessity) the most productive work hours when both my husband and I could work and not have to also support our children in learning. We developed a clearer set of delineations around who works when, who primarily parents when, and how to ask for help when we needed two parents to support virtual schooling—one with the

Daily Schedule: Kindergarten

Start	End	Monday	Tuesday	Wednesday	Thursday	Friday
7:15	8:30	Breakfast	Breakfast	Workday: No synchronous (live) lessons will be scheduled. Student Conferencing (tutoring, small groups); Parent Conferences; Professional Learning for Leaders and Teachers; Instructional and Collaborative Planning	Breakfast	Breakfast
8:30	8:45	Technology Check	Technology Check		Technology Check	Technology Check
8:45	9:00	Morning Meeting	Morning Meeting		Morning Meeting	Morning Meeting
9:00	9:40	Extended Learning Time	Extended Learning Time		Extended Learning Time	Extended Learning Time
9:45	10:30	English Language Arts	English Language Arts		English Language Arts	English Language Arts
10:30	10:40	Technology Check	Technology Check		Technology Check	Technology Check
10:40	11:25	Math	Math		Math	Math
11:25	11:35	Technology Check	Technology Check		Technology Check	Technology Check
11:35	12:20	Specials	Specials		Specials	Specials
12:20	1:05	Lunch	Lunch		Lunch	Lunch
1:05	1:50	Science	Social Studies		Science	Social Studies

FIGURE 6.2. *Daily schedule of virtual learning for my kindergartener from 8:30 AM to 1:50 PM.*

Mrs. Martin & Ms. Clary Daily Schedule

Wed.	Time	Codes for Microsoft Teams	Monday/Thursday	Tuesday/Friday
Meetings/ No Live Classes	7:45-8:30		Breakfast	
	8:30-8:45		Technology Check, Gather Materials & Login	
	8:45-8:55		School Pride, Announcements, Etc.	
	8:55-9:40		Extended Learning Time	
	9:45-10:30	Porter- ni7z4vx	Math	
	10:30-10:40		Technology Check, Gather Materials & Login	
	10:40-11:25	Pugh- dej2wom	Science (Mon./Thurs)	Social Studies (Tues./Fri)
	11:25-11:35		Technology Check, Gather Materials & Login	
	11:35-12:20	Martin- uuo1keq	Reading/ELA	
	12:20-1:05		Lunch Technology Check, Gather Materials & Login	
	1:05-1:50		Instructional Time/Specials (Mon./Thurs) Music/STEM	(Tues./Fri) P.E/Art

FIGURE 6.3. *Daily schedule of virtual learning for my fourth grader from 8:30 AM to 1:50 PM.*

kindergartener and one with the fourth grader. I also developed an intricate system of alarms on my phone (two to three minutes before the start of a scheduled meeting or online class) that helped indicate to all of us that it was time for one of us to be online somewhere (figure 6.4). To this day, I can't use the ring tone that we used for these alarms (iPhone's "Constellation" tone)—it carries too much sensory and emotional baggage. While I can easily choose a different ring tone, it's harder to change walls and rooms, the square footage of spaces.

With the many changes to how we have experienced, used, and oriented our domestic space during the COVID-19 pandemic, Enoch's work has reminded me that this is a process continuing to unfold for us personally—the (re)construction of space carries an "emotional dimension," because we have feelings about spaces and we create various "positive and negative bonds" to those spaces, especially in "the highly emotive space of the home" (Enoch). As women emerge from the pandemic, we are invited to interrogate our prior relationship with our domestic spaces and to envision new possible futures.

FIGURE 6.4. *Screenshot of the multiple alarms set on my phone to remind us of synchronous online school and work meeting times throughout the day.*

As hopeful as I want to be about these new opportunities for re-imagining our spaces and our roles, about better supporting working mothers and advancing more just and equitable childcare and child tax relief legislation, I am also having a hard time envisioning an entirely rosy picture. As I wrote revisions to this chapter, my then-first grader was sent home for ten days to quarantine from a school exposure to COVID; thankfully, we received results of a negative COVID test, and he returned to school soon. However, having him home again for virtual asynchronous learning while balancing my job once again reignited the emotional, spatial, and temporal difficulties of March 2020 through September 2021. In August of 2021, Dan Sinker wrote about the impossible decision parents faced of whether to send our children back to school prior to the release of a vaccine for kids eleven and younger—and in some cases, in schools without mask mandates—just as the Delta variant was surging. Sinker describes the physical and emotional exhaustion many parents were feeling:

> It's enough to bring a parent to tears—except that every parent I know ran out a long time ago. . . . Ran out of tears, ran out of energy, ran out of patience. . . . All this and parents are somehow expected to be okay.

> We are expected to send our kids off into God knows what, to work
> our jobs and live our lives like nothing's wrong, and to hold it all to-
> gether for months and maybe now for years without seeing a way out.
> This is not okay. Nothing is okay. No parent is okay, and I'm not sure
> how we can come back from this.

Sinker's words rang true—parents, and especially working mothers with young children, were not okay. They were not during the pandemic, and they are still today recovering from the lost time, the intense stressors, and possible mental and physical health concerns.

And, as I worked on the final pages of this chapter, attempting to think, focus, and write a closing few sentences, my quarantined first grader was watching a BrainPOP Jr. science video, blaring from the iPad next to me (figure 6.5). Since I was having trouble holding onto both an academic argument and first grade science facts about temperature, I leave you with the words of Moby the Robot for now—"The temperature tells you how hot or cold something is. You can use a thermometer to measure the temperature" (BrainPOP Jr.).

The COVID-19 pandemic brought to light challenges and inequities for working mothers that have always existed. While there have been additional layers of pandemic-related complexity that I highlight in this narrative, I am also reminded that I have consistently experienced challenges as a mother in academia—taking my doctoral exams while pregnant, writing my dissertation while holding an infant, and traveling for campus visits during a national job search with a breast pump in my briefcase. My experience is hardly unique; as Ruth Osario writes, "Even in the 1970s, 80s, and 90s, [women faculty] were wandering the halls pregnant, lugging pumping equipment . . . , and setting up their children with a coloring book in the back of class when childcare fell through." As we enter new post-pandemic phases, I am gathering a clearer sense of the how the experiences of pandemic parenting have sharpened a set of tools I already had in my mothering toolbox. I also feel a growing sense of commitment to contribute to narratives of mothering in the academy. In working towards these goals, I reflect on the following lessons from mothering, teaching, and researching during a pandemic:

Embrace the Tactical

As a person who thrives on strategic approaches like making a plan, putting it on the calendar a month in advance, and confirming the details, the instability

FIGURE 6.5. *Screenshot of BrainPOP Jr. video "Temperature."*

and constant changing of things beyond my control made pandemic parenting particularly disorienting. However, when I began to embrace a more tactical approach, using what limited control I could have to "seek rhetorically timely actions," I was able to orient myself in a way that felt more manageable (Mathieu, 17). The perception of stability in my domestic space and time—even as a raging pandemic surged outside of my home—became a central tactic. Even as the pandemic reached some stages of relative stability, I continue to use these tactics—weekly family calendar planning, alarms on my phone, email reminders—to navigate the ongoing instability of parenting, whether during or post-pandemic.

Acknowledge the Tools You Already Have

In embracing the tactical, I realized that I already had many of the tools I needed, but I needed to use them in slightly different ways and to recognize their value in bringing some feeling of certainty to a wholly uncertain situation. Parents and caretakers are already problem-solvers by necessity—whether we are parenting an infant or a teenager, caretaking for a niece or an aging father. There are so many factors beyond our control, and when we encounter obstacles, we do our best to improvise. I already used planning, lists, and reminders to help me parent prior to the pandemic, and while there were added extra stressors and exhaustion, I was able to draw on a set of strategies I had already been using to make it through. When things such as a worldwide health crisis cause us to doubt our efficacy as parents, I try to remind myself to trust the tactical knowledge, competence, and practices we bring to challenging situations, rather than letting a sense of inadequacy or limitation wield too much influence over my assessments.

Tell Your Story

We can never fully understand someone else's lived experience and reality; but we can listen to their stories, and we can sympathize and empathize. Despite the excellent models I've had in the scholar-mothers who mentored me, I have always struggled to fuse these identities, opting largely to downplay my motherhood and how it impacts my work in the academy. As my relationship to parenting through the pandemic has evolved, I have a new sense of determination to speak up about the unique needs and, through storytelling, share some of the complex challenges facing scholar-parents.

For example, I recently wrote to the chair of a tenure track search committee in my department who was organizing virtual campus visits for candidates, and I shared the challenges I faced when my campus visit schedules at some schools didn't include adequate breaks for breast pumping. I also suggested that there may be times during the day that the candidate has childcare or other personal needs that make them unavailable, using the example that I am the only caretaker able to pick up our children from school most days. Telling my senior colleague these stories was not easy for me, and I had to fight the thoughts that sharing them would contribute to a perception of mothers in the academy as being distracted from our jobs, demanding of special treatments, or unprepared by not having full-time childcare coverage. However, my colleague responded with kindness and thanked me for calling attention to the possible childcare conflicts, which he had not considered since his children are now grown.

Use Your Story for Change

As a faculty member who was tenured in that department, I see how important it is for those with tenured job security to tell our stories and speak up for those who are not in secure enough appointments or privileged positionalities to do so. "Storying *is* mothering. Mothering *is* storying," writes Rosario: "Both can generate possibility. . . . Both can serve activist goals by burning a fire inside us to change the material conditions of our homes and communities, to transform the world for the next generation." As I write this chapter and begin telling one piece of my parenting journey, I hope to contribute to this work by changing the narratives we tell about working mothers and addressing inequities in the workplace.

Bibliography

BrainPOP Jr. "Temperature." YouTube, October 29, 2024. https://www.youtube.com /watch?v=bfEwyMTUHio.

Cooper, Marianne. "Mothers' Careers Are at Extraordinary Risk Right Now." *The Atlantic,* October 1, 2020. https://www.theatlantic.com/family/archive/2020/10/pandemic -amplifying-bias-against-working-mothers/616565/.

Enoch, Jessica. *Domestic Occupations: Spatial Rhetorics and Women's Work.* Southern Illinois University Press, 2019.

Mathieu, Paula. *Tactics of Hope: The Public Turn in English Composition.* Boynton/Cook Publishers, Inc., 2005.

PhonicsMan. "Spell Sight Words in FortNite." YouTube, January 4, 2019. https://www .youtube.com/watch?v=dJtjkn59CFo.

Rosario, Ruth. "Constellating with our Foremothers: Stories of Mothers Making Space in Rhetoric and Composition." *Constellations: A Cultural Rhetorics Publishing Space,* no. 4 (August 18, 2021). https://constell8cr.com/articles/mothers-making-space -rhet-comp/.

Sinker, Dan. "Parents Are Not Okay." *The Atlantic,* August 22, 2021. https://www .theatlantic.com/ideas/archive/2021/08/parents-are-not-okay/619859/.

"It's Not Like I Have Anything Better to Do!"

Rhetorics of Abundant Time During the COVID-19 Pandemic

Meaghan Brewer

In May 2020, my department held its first Zoom meeting since going remote in response to the COVID-19 pandemic. As the meeting ended, the chair asked if we should have another meeting next month during the semester break, something that would have been unheard of prior to the pandemic. "Sure!" one of my colleagues chimed in with a smile. "It's not like I have anything better to do!" As my colleagues laughed and nodded, alarms sounded in my head. As the mother of two young children, the youngest of whom was eleven months old, I *did* have other things to do, especially since I no longer had available childcare and was the default caregiver.

In this chapter, I describe how this early pandemic construction of time—depicting it as something people now had in *abundance*[1]—created additional strains on working academic mothers. Before the pandemic, our default way of thinking about time in modern Western culture was more in terms of *scarcity.* We "spend" time rather than "passing" it (Lakoff and Johnson, 8–9). And, as philosophy and linguistics scholars George Lakoff and Mark Johnson assert, our conceptual systems (which are fundamentally metaphorical) are important because *we live by them*—they "govern our everyday functioning" and define "our everyday realities" (3).

As my experience above illustrates, the metaphors we used to think about time changed, or perhaps grew more polarized, with the onset of the pandemic. As the first lockdowns went into effect in the United States, people suddenly had "free time," and news sources began publishing articles advising people of what to do with this "extra" time (see, for example, "30 Creative Ways"). Social media feeds were suddenly full of people who had adopted dogs or were trying out sourdough bread starter kits.

Of course, this sense of time abundance occurred in concert with a general kind of time distortion, what *Wired* journalist Arielle Pardes dubbed "Coronatime." Pardes argues that without events and interactions with people beyond our households, which humans use as time benchmarks, we were no longer registering time passage in the same way. In fact, my sense from interactions with colleagues was that it became a signal of virtuosity for someone to say they had abundant time because it meant they were doing what they were supposed to do—staying home and avoiding contact.

My reference to time abundance (as a norming device) also draws on discussions of non-normative conceptions of time in writing studies. Most notably Margaret Price and Tara Wood have applied the concept of "crip time" from psychology and disability studies to composition and rhetoric, noting the constraints people with disabilities have on their time and describing the various ways in which university processes create rigid structures around time. Drawing on work by disability studies scholars Carol Gill and Irving Kenneth Zola, Price defines crip time as referring to "a flexible approach to normative time frames" (62). In rhetorical terms, crip time aligns with the concept of *kairos,* which, in contrast to *chronos* (normative, linear time), is "a more subjective dimension of time" in which the savvy rhetor might identify the timing that feels right for action (Crowley, 83). Arguing that it is "the notion of *flexibility* (not just 'extra' time) that unites kairos and crip time," Price argues that accommodations for faculty with disabilities can't just involve quantitative shifts (i.e. more time) but also qualitative reassessments about how we think about tenure clocks, concepts of "productivity," and what it might mean to have a "modified work schedule" (108). Understanding that time has this metaphorical, subjective dimension and that it is, as Lakoff and Johnson argue, part of a conceptual system dictated by Western culture, helps us to recognize the differing needs of caregivers. As I will argue later, a dramatic shift in our conceptions of time might be necessary for the many of us who are academics and caregivers. Particularly for writing program administrators (WPAs), who are often called upon to manage crises[2] like the sudden pandemic switch to online education, such shifts must include creative restructurings of normative university systems and expectations.

Time abundance acted as a troubling backdrop that made it more difficult for caretakers, already strained in our time resources, to assert our needs when we were being asked to take on additional burdens. We now had fewer hours in the day for work and household tasks due to the absence of childcare associated with schools and daycares closing or going remote. Concurrently, at my university, Pace in lower Manhattan, committees that once met two or three times during a semester were now meeting five or six times, often extending meeting times into between-semester breaks. The reasoning behind the increase in meetings often wasn't transparent or fully articulated. In some cases, committees met more to address issues arising from our shift online, while in others it appeared that they were meeting more often simply because it was now, supposedly, easier to do so over Zoom. In some cases, additional meetings helped us maintain contact and kept people connected, which seemed like a good thing on the surface but negatively impacted caregivers who were juggling additional childcare responsibilities during the day.

While Pace's administration acknowledged that caregivers in particular would be less "productive" during the pandemic, the proliferation of meeting requests as well as my colleagues verbal constructions of time as abundant (as in the meeting I describe), put me and others in a double bind in which we felt compelled to attend meetings and enter workstreams that contributed to Pace's pandemic response and shift to remote learning, even as our scholarly outputs ground to a halt. Although the administration verbally acknowledged the additional stresses caretakers were under, the normative simulacrum of abundant time, along with statements that everyone needed to "pitch in" to deliver quality education to students during the pandemic, made caretakers' time scarcity invisible and created even more strains than they had pre-pandemic. (For more on this invisibility, see Nancy Myers and Heather Brook Adams, this volume.) I also felt guilty when I had to leave meetings early or push the timeline for a task off because I also *wanted* to be included, since this inclusion was a sign that my institution valued my expertise, representing yet another double bind that has always been present for working mothers but was made worse with the pandemic.

In what follows, I offer two brief vignettes of my experiences as a working academic mother during the pandemic to demonstrate how my institution constructed time as abundant, while at the same time depicting the university as understanding and family friendly. While in some cases I believe fellow faculty and administrators were simply uninformed in these constructions, in others it's possible that the "family friendly" front was a more purposeful veneer created to get us to be productive. I end with strategies for faculty with caregiving responsibilities to recognize and respond to these rhetorics of abundant time.

Before continuing, I also want to acknowledge that while I draw on my local context for examples because they're what I (a white, cisgender woman and mother) experienced, I don't believe the dynamics I describe are particular to my institution. In fact, Ashley J. Holmes (this volume) describes navigating similar double binds as she negotiated her role as a mother and faculty member. Throughout the pandemic, I interacted with colleagues (most of whom are WPAs) at other universities who described moments that echo those I narrate in what follows. Moreover, feminist scholars in rhetoric and composition have long documented the double binds and constraints experienced by women, caregivers, and other marginalized groups, particularly Black women and other people of color, as they labor in university settings (Gabor et al.; Kynard; Miller; Perryman-Clark and Craig; Schell; Wenger).

Rhetoric and writing studies scholar Kim Hensley Owens' description of the negotiations she had to make when she had two children while on the job market and in the first years of a tenure track job, including requesting time to pump at interviews and negotiating a lighter teaching load in the semester after her second child was born echo my experiences. Owens demonstrates how university administrators can often easily revoke accommodations agreements for caregivers with excuses like "the crashed economy," the pandemic, or, more recently, the decline in international student enrollment (Owens in Cucciarre et al., 53). The tenuous nature of these agreements shows the extent to which universities still operate according to normative timeframes. To put it again in terms from disability studies, such accommodations function as what writing studies scholar Jay Dolmage would call "retrofits," which are "component[s] or accessor[ies added] to something that has already been manufactured or built" (20). While retrofits are preferable to no accommodations, or what Dolmage calls the "steep steps" that make laboring within the university inaccessible, they often, by giving the appearance of fairness, render the struggles faced by those with disabilities or challenges invisible (16, 21).

In what follows, I expand on the discussions mentioned in the prior paragraph by showing how many of the conditions faced by caregivers were exacerbated during the pandemic, even as these conditions were rendered invisible by retrofits and rhetorics of abundant time. However, I also want to reiterate that the experiences I describe below may also pale in comparison to the experiences of caregivers who are part-time and contingent faculty and/or members of multiply marginalized groups.

Vignette 1. Writing Task Force Meetings

In February 2020, my colleagues in composition and rhetoric and I received an email from the office of the provost stating that the new Associate Provost was going to be forming a "Writing Task Force" and that our first meeting would be held on March 13. The Associate Provost provided no overriding purpose or agenda for the meeting, merely stating that "March 13th will be our organizational meeting and we will discuss the frequency of our meetings" (email, February 28, 2020). When I asked colleagues what the meeting was about, everyone had a different take. One colleague suggested it was about what we were doing in place of CAP, a program in place to support students who were admitted provisionally to Pace, which was in the process of being dissolved. The Writing Center director thought we were meeting about moving the Writing Center to a new space.

When Pace went remote on March 11, 2020, the meeting was rescheduled for the end of March with the following agenda:

> Introductions/How is Everyone Doing?
> Current COVID-19 Challenges? Current Good News?
> Writing Centers & the Learning Commons
> Space in New Building in NYC
> Concerns, Challenges, Recommendations
> Next Steps

As vague as this agenda was, it at least gave us a sense of what to expect (that the meeting would be about the new space being created for the Writing Center in New York City and new expectations for reporting structures for the Writing Center directors on both campuses). However, most of our meetings lacked agendas altogether or simply weren't constructive, partially because of our two-campus structure; Pace has campuses both in lower Manhattan and Pleasantville, NY, and our English departments have largely functioned independently. The Writing Task Force meetings did have the positive effect of motivating us to work more with our counterparts on the Pleasantville campus, although this arrangement, of course, led to more meetings that took away from already constrained time.

Another issue during these meetings was that the frequent (often unannounced) presence of administrators on the Zoom calls made us more performative than productive. At first, I appreciated administrators' attention to the programmatic issues that necessitated these meetings, but as the semester wore on, it seemed like their presence was more for surveillance. Resolving the issues facing us sometimes necessitated frank talk among the writing experts that we would have preferred to have off the record. I also felt pressure to keep my camera on to project professionalism, even though I was often watching my kids.

During one noon-time call, I was breastfeeding my son (camera turned off) when the Associate Provost suggested we introduce ourselves to the new Dean of Arts and Sciences. "Jon!" I yell-whispered to my husband, "you have to take Jeremy so I can introduce myself to the new dean!" I carefully transferred my now-sleeping child before turning my camera on in time to mumble out an introduction, just as my son began crying in the background.

Vignette 2. "Just Get It Done"

One of the most frustrating things about the Writing Task Force meetings is that they took away time when I could be doing research or class prep and left me with little in terms of tangible results. This situation wasn't just the case for this set of meetings. During the 2020–2021 academic year, in addition to teaching my classes and directing a program, I also served on several newly formed committees, including two subcommittees under our school's curriculum committee devoted to revising our core curriculum.

The initial meetings for these subcommittees, dubbed as "information gathering" or "brainstorming" sessions, were two hours long—an almost impossible chunk of time for me to find while sharing childcare responsibilities with my husband. In the fall, my daughter's school district announced that students would be in-person for half days every other day (staggering two "A" and "B" cohorts). Somewhat similarly to the schedule that Holmes (this volume), describes in her chapter, my husband and I had to arrange for one of us to pick up my daughter at noon every day, feed her lunch, and then be available during her afternoon Zoom.

I thus went from having some decently long stretches of time pre-pandemic to my time being divided into *much* smaller chunks when I could count on getting things done. Of course, my time has always been under some constraint; even pre-pandemic, I often had to leave campus meetings that went past 4:30 PM because my commute was almost two hours, and I had to pick my kids up from daycare.

Despite my and others' complaints about constrained time, members of the administration repeatedly told us that we needed to "find time" to complete tasks. One example of this demand involved Faculty Annual Reviews (FAR). During the summer of 2020, the administration announced that due to budget shortfalls, not only would we not be receiving raises but we would also lose our 403B match, amounting to a pay cut. The FAR had always been the tool that merit raises were based upon (promotions and performance reviews go through a separate process, so FARs were only for the purposes of determining merit raises). Without raises, faculty asked why we had to go through the time-consuming task of writing up our achievements. However, during a Faculty Council Meeting, members of the administration told us that it was still important to record what we had accomplished, ending with the command that we, "Just do it. Just get it done."

Also, during the fall, another member of the administration approached our department about having an outside evaluator service visit to help us develop a strategic plan for the future of the Writing Centers, which would be moving out of our English departments to report directly to the provost. While we were excited about having input from scholars in our field, we also knew that one of the initial steps would be generating a lengthy report for the evaluators, something we thought could be postponed until we had fewer pandemic-related strains on our time. When some of my colleagues and I (all parents) raised our objections, another administrator responded that we shouldn't feel "scared" to have these evaluators visit and that we would "always have constraints on our time." Ironically, the administrator's statement that such constraints would continue was true, but she used this fact to minimize and invalidate our concerns.

Some Takeaways and Strategies for Dealing with Rhetorics of Abundant Time

As the introduction to this collection also attests, disparities in time availability between caretakers and those who don't have these kinds of responsibilities have long existed. However, as I've suggested here, the pandemic at first hid and then exacerbated them. To put it another way, it wasn't an aberration that I had constraints on my time and had to make difficult choices in managing my workplace and childcare duties. In fact, during lunch with colleagues before the pandemic, one of my male colleagues who doesn't have children and who had similar administrative duties guilelessly asserted that he had "ten times as much work" as I did. In reality, as someone with administrative duties on a larger campus, my obligations were probably equal to, and likely exceeded, his.

The strategies I suggest here have to do with making these disparities more visible. At my institution, the upper administration often paid significant lip service to the additional burdens the pandemic had placed on caregivers, and during meetings across the university, we were instructed to allow for disruptions, for example, when kids made appearances on Zoom or colleagues had to leave a meeting early. There was a lot of cooing at babies and telling parents that it was "no problem!" when we had to hop off to get our child a snack.

This lip service worked as a retrofit that obscured the severity of the struggles caregivers were facing. Caregivers still had to "just do it" in terms of work output, and we often failed at negotiating smaller workloads. So, my first recommendation is simply to recognize when rhetorics of abundant time are at work, so we don't feel guilty when we point out that a proposed timeframe isn't feasible. As Lakoff and Johnson contend, even as our realities are structured by metaphors, they are "so much the conventional way of thinking . . . it is sometimes hard to imagine that . . . [they] might not fit reality" (11). One example of a rhetoric of abundant time is the "return to work" rhetoric that began circulating in the public sphere in 2021, as if what we had been doing for the past year and half prior was something else entirely.

Thus, a second strategy is to keep self-advocating by making the invisible visible. I remind administrators that even as the pandemic (supposedly) wanes and children (sometimes) return to school, we still have additional burdens on our time. Often these strains on our time are invisible unless we draw attention to them, or, worse, we feel shame about mentioning them (see Holmes; Myers and Adams, this volume). In spring 2021 when I met with my chair about my FAR, I told her frankly that while I had had a good year in terms of publications, sooner or later there would be a gap in my output because I hadn't been putting more things into the pipeline. This concern demonstrates that simply granting a clock stoppage for 2020, an allowance that reflects views of time constraints in linear, normative terms, doesn't address the qualitative and continuing ways our work as scholars will be affected (see Myers and Adams, this volume; Price).

Third, accept help when it's offered, something I almost never did before because I was cognizant of giving the appearance of doing my fair share. I now know that, as Dolmage argues, "fairness is an underdefined term" (21).[3] One advantage of our increased use of Zoom was that it allowed me to share labor with the co-director of our WAC program on the other campus, who not only offered his help when I was having particularly busy weeks but also checked in to see how I was doing. Women professors and WPAs often find ourselves doing extra work because we're seen as default caregivers even beyond the home, something that has been well established in the WPA literature (see, for example, Holmes, this volume; Leverenz; Schell; Wenger). But it's important that we allow ourselves to be cared for and perhaps even rotate these responsibilities differently. Especially at the beginning of the pandemic, time scarcity registered as physical pain, and on more than one occasion I found myself sobbing in frustration when my son awoke early from a nap or I had spent so long helping my daughter with schoolwork that I didn't have time left for class prep. Having colleagues acknowledge my struggles (when it appeared genuine) and occasionally take over some of my responsibilities went some way towards relieving my mental anguish. In the longer term, not seeing work sharing as individual failure helps to disrupt the individualistic ethos that characterizes much academic work but that can be damaging to caregivers (see Gabor et al.).

Unfortunately, women and caregivers continue to be at a disadvantage in the workplace because appropriate supports aren't in place and because, culturally, caretaking responsibilities aren't a priority, either in universities or more broadly. I've recently joined a new group advocating for more family-friendly policies at my university that I hope will work to expose these rhetorics of abundant time and advocate for those of us harmed by them.

The Persistence of Time Abundance and Scarcity

As I reread this chapter in December 2022, two things strike me. First, even though the events of the pandemic are relatively recent and their effects are ongoing, I am amazed at my persistence in the face of having to work in the absence of childcare. As a mother of two children, I am always at the whims of life events that take me away from my work. These days, a two (or more)-day bout of sickness feels insurmountable. And yet, somehow, then and now, I have continued to push through. Looking back also reveals that I was right to resist meetings and initiatives that required a time commitment with no discernible accompanying benefit, either for me or my institution. In fact, some of these initiatives, like the revision to our core curriculum, have come to nothing.

Second, and relatedly, there are, and continue to be, psychic costs to my persistence because the twin rhetorics of time abundance and scarcity are still at play. I am currently on sabbatical, a semester off that I had to delay by a year because my institution opted not to fund semester-long sabbaticals in the 2021–2022 academic year.[4] Sabbaticals are often portrayed as a period of time abundance. Without the burdens of teaching and service, we (supposedly) have extra time to pursue research. Perceptions of sabbatical time outside of academia are perhaps even more damaging, as many see it as just "time off." Both perceptions reflect normative, chronological constructions of time. And while I'm grateful for my sabbatical, my subjective experience of time hasn't changed. In the year prior, I took on a large-scale empirical study of undergraduate reading practices. I've had breakthroughs and wonderful moments as I analyze my data, but I'm not doing it at the unrealistic rate of efficiency that I had imagined.

All to say that time *scarcity* still feels like my default experience, leading me to wonder whether time abundance will always be a fantasy, at least while I have small children. In fact, perhaps time abundance and time scarcity are flip sides of the same coin reflecting linear, normative conceptions of time, and even as I resist such constructions, I still find them holding powerful sway over how I conceptualize and experience time.

Before meeting with my department chair to assess my performance over the past year, I had been reading Nap Ministry founder Tricia Hersey's *Rest is Resistance: A Manifesto.* Hersey reminds us of the necessity of rest, showing how we need it to resist capitalistic grind culture and imagine new realities. My chair reiterated seeing the sabbatical as a time to rest when I recounted my struggles with self-doubt at my limited productivity (productivity, again, being a term that reflects normative conceptions of time.) And don't we all need to rest and heal after these past few years? For me now, resisting rhetorics of time abundance is also about reminding myself to rest.

Notes

1. In rhetorical scholarship, the term "abundance" is associated with Desiderius Erasmus's *copia.* Erasmus refers to abundance in terms of stylistic richness (having on hand a rich variety of expressions) and subject matter richness (knowing several examples that can be referenced with ease to build a case.) What I argue here, however, is that we can extend rhetorical abundance beyond these concepts to think about ways that metaphorical constructions of time as abundant during the pandemic made time *scarcity* less visible.

2. Invoking the rhetoric of a crisis is another well-established tactic university administrators use to reinforce normative constructions of time. By creating false senses of urgency, they force faculty and particularly WPAs into a pattern of, as writing studies

scholar Lydia Wilkes describes it, "quick reaction" rather than "intentional, principled response" (21; see also Welch and Scott).

3. Citing work–family researchers Robert Drago and Carol Colbeck, Owens describes similar moments of trying to avoid "mother-bias" by overcommitting to service work and avoiding or minimizing family commitments. Of course, during the pandemic, family commitments were often quite visible during meetings on Zoom (Gabor et al., 52).

4. This was a cost-saving measure pursued by my institution in response to current and projected revenue shortfalls due to COVID-19. Faculty still had the option to take a year-long sabbatical at half pay, which I couldn't afford to do. Semester-long sabbaticals at full pay were reinstated for the 2022–23 academic year.

Bibliography

"30 Creative Ways to Spend Your Free Time During the Pandemic." Northwest Arkansas Community College, 2021. https://www.nwacc.edu/.

Crowley, Sharon. "Rhetoric and Kairos: Essays in History, Theory and Praxis by Phillip Sipiora, James S. Baumlin." *Rhetoric Review,* 22, no. 1 (2003): 82–85.

Cucciarre, Christine Peters, Deborah Morris, Lee Nickoson, Kim Hensley Owens and Mary P. Sheridan. "Mothers' Ways of Making It—or Making Do?: Making (Over) Academic Lives In Rhetoric and Composition with Children." *Composition Studies* 39, no. 1 (2011): 41–61.

Dolmage, Jay. "Mapping Composition: Inviting Disability in the Front Door." *Disability and the Teaching of Writing: A Critical Sourcebook,* edited by Cynthia Lewiecki-Wilson and Brenda Jo Brueggemann. Bedford/St. Martin's, 2008.

Erasmus, Desiderius. *On Copia of Words and Ideas.* Translated by Donald B. King and H. David Rix. Marquette University Press, 1963.

Gabor, Catherine, Stacia Dunn Neeley, and Carrie Shively Leverenz. "Mentor, May I Mother?" in *Stories of Mentoring: Theory and Praxis,* edited by Michelle F. Eble and Lyneé Lewis Gaillet. Parlor Press, 2008.

Gill, Carol J. "A Psychological View of Disability Culture." *Disability Studies Quarterly* 15, no. 4 (1995): 16–19. https://kb.osu.edu/items/67583305-241e-4a7a -aecf-c9a1998688ca.

Hersey, Tricia. *Rest is Resistance: A Manifesto.* Little, Brown Spark, 2022.

Lakoff, George, and Mark Johnson. *Metaphors We Live By.* University of Chicago Press, 2003.

Leverenz, Carrie. "Don't Worry, Be Happy." *The Things We Carry: Strategies for Recognizing and Negotiating Emotional Labor in Writing Program Administration,* edited by Courtney Adams Wooten, Jacob Babb, Kristi Murray Costello, and Kate Navickas. Utah State University Press, 2020.

Kynard, Carmen. "Teaching While Black: Witnessing and Countering Disciplinary

Whiteness, Racial Violence, and University Race-Management." *Literacy in Composition Studies* 3, no. 1 (2015): 1–20.

Miller, Susan. *Textual Carnivals: The Politics of Composition.* Southern Illinois University Press, 1991.

Pardes, Arielle. "There Are No Hours or Days in Coronatime." *Wired.* May 8, 2020. https://www.wired.com/story/coronavirus-time-warp-what-day-is-it/.

Perryman-Clark, Staci, and Collin Lamont Craig, eds. *Black Perspectives in Writing Program Administration: From the Margins to the Center.* NCTE, 2019.

Price, Margaret. *Mad at School: Rhetorics of Mental Disability and Academic Life.* University of Michigan Press, 2014.

Schell, Eileen E. *Gypsy Academics and Mother-Teachers: Gender, Contingent Labor, and Writing Instruction.* Boynton/Cook Publishers, 1998.

Welch, Nancy, and Tony Scott, eds. *Composition in the Age of Austerity.* Utah State University Press, 2016.

Wenger, Christy I. "Feminism, Mindfulness and the Small University jWPA." *WPA: Writing Program Administration* 37, no. 2 (2014): 117–40.

Wilkes, Lydia. "From Putting out Fires to Managing Fires: Lessons for WPAs from Indigenous Fire Managers." In *Toward More Sustainable Metaphors of Writing Program Administration,* edited by Lydia Wilkes, Lilian W. Mina, and Patti Poblete. Utah State University Press, 2023.

Wood, Tara. "Cripping Time in the College Composition Classroom." *College Composition and Communication* 69, no. 2 (2017): 260–86, http://www.jstor.org /stable/44783615.

Zola, Irving Kenneth. "Self, Identity and the Naming Question: Reflections on the Language of Disability." *Social Science and Medicine* 36, no. 2 (1993): 167–73.

CHAPTER 8

The Labor of Inquiry

Women's Writing and Research During COVID-19

Elizabeth Ellis Miller

Feminist inquiry does not shy away from the personal. Indeed, feminist scholars have long insisted that the personal—our experiences, our bodies, our emotions—shapes and informs knowledge-making; it is only privilege that provides a mask of disembodied objectivity. Feminist rhetoricians take this insight in many directions, considering the theoretical, pedagogical, and methodological implications of experience, the body, and emotion for the field (Glenn; Royster; Logan; Kirsch and Ritchie; Kirsch and Royster). As Jessica Enoch, Cheryl Glenn, and Jordynn Jack contend, "Feminist rhetorical methodologies center on and wrestle with the fact that *all* research contains elements of subjectivity. . . . Doing research does not mean denying our subjectivity, but rather taking responsibility for it, openly acknowledging what it is we are trying to find out—and why we are trying to find it out" (11). At the heart of feminist rhetorical studies, then, is attention to the messy relationship between the material conditions and experiences of the researcher and the questions she is asking.[1]

As integrally connected to the personal, feminist inquiry is not static: our questions shift as circumstances change, whether challenges, crisis points, or joys. In *Teaching Queer,* Stacey Waite models this type of inquiry in response to writing pedagogy, a project she asserts developed "from the difficult challenges of teaching in my own body" (49). Reflecting on her experience, Waite writes, "Our ways of knowing are intrinsically linked to our ways of being, our becoming" (49). Jessica Restaino likewise considers embodiment and inquiry, writing about the final years of friend and collaborator Susan Lundy Maute's life with terminal cancer. Restaino argues, "Surrender, risk, and love . . . have a rightful place in the study of rhetoric and in our writing, as a function of method" (90). Waite and Restaino thus model—and interrogate—how we inquire and write into difficulty, pain, and crisis. They urge researchers to mine experiences of difficulty or joy and to be reflective about method in this work.

It is well-established, then, that feminist methodology accounts for and acknowledges how experiences inform *all* our inquiries. Given the feminist imperative to reckon with the personal in our research, in what ways might we acknowledge and examine this dimension of inquiry as *labor*? As a case study in dramatic, sudden shifts in ways of being, COVID-19 provides rich ground for considering this question. In what follows, I move into this terrain through a focus on Emily Oster, one woman whose writing and research explicitly turned to COVID-19 during the 2020 pandemic from the position of a parent. Examining Oster's newsletter *ParentData,* this chapter details the shape and process of inquiry for Oster during the crisis of the pandemic. I read Oster's newsletter through Arlie Holschild's notion of emotional labor, or "the management of feeling to create a publicly observable facial and bodily display; emotional labor is sold for a wage and therefore has exchange value" (7). Feminist inquiry demands being honest about the personal; it also requires one to *manage* one's feelings and consider audience expectations for emotion and identity.[2]

I have selected Oster for this study because she did a lot of public writing and research about COVID-19 during 2020, a time when many women, and I count myself among them, wrote and researched little because we lost access to childcare, resources, and other necessary supports for work. Oster, by contrast, shifted her research and writing into one of the most controversial arenas of the pandemic—kids and the virus—and thus invites attention to the ways that women's writing during 2020 reveals the labor of inquiry. I selected Oster for the additional reason that her pandemic writing, like most of her public writing, emerges from her identity as a mother, and thus offers additional insight into the ways that asking questions intertwined with embodied experience impacts the labor of research and writing. Before turning to analysis of *Parent-Data,* I begin with a brief overview of Oster's public career and her writing during COVID-19 and my experience as a reader of her work.

From Parenting Advice to School Policy

In February 2020, Emily Oster launched a SubStack newsletter titled *Parent-Data,* a new project for her, one that she intended to cover everyday pregnancy and parenting-related issues. Oster, a professor at Brown University, writes and teaches for academic audiences about economics, particularly health economics. Her public writing focuses on explaining academic research about issues of pregnancy and parenthood, and post-2020, COVID-19. Before 2020, Oster had generated a devoted following among parents through the "data-driven" approach to questions about pregnancy and family life she outlines in books *Expecting Better* and *Cribsheet* (the third installment, *The Family Firm,* was released in 2021). *Expecting Better,* for instance, synthesizes journal articles about topics pregnant women typically get brief advice about, such as alcohol use. *Cribsheet* applies this same type of analytical lens to discussions parents face in the early childhood years. Oster's data-forward rhetoric offers more details, science, and reasoning than is often offered at prenatal or pediatrician's visits, satisfying a certain type of pregnant person or parent who wants more information but doesn't have the time or skill set to sift through the PubMed database.

ParentData was thus a way for her to connect with her audience and write in response to new developments in pregnancy and parenting research. She recalls that she planned the newsletter to center on mundane topics like whether or not juice is part of a healthy diet for children. Indeed, the first topic-oriented newsletter released on February 26, 2020, tackles the relationship between antibiotic use and allergies. According to Oster, she writes to help parents be more relaxed and to feel like they made good decisions (North; Oster, *Cribsheet*).

As this brief overview indicates, Oster's readers prior to 2020 included those who find academic reasoning and data helpful for thinking through pregnancy and parenting. While we cannot know the exact demographics of this group, most critics assume a few things—these were middle- and upper-class, educated, "coastal types" (Goldstein; North). When her newsletter turned into a discussion about parenting during a pandemic, however, Oster's reach suddenly expanded. Rather than writing for parents thinking about drinking wine during pregnancy or baby-led weaning, Oster was writing about issues facing a much wider variety of stakeholders—parents, teachers, school staff, policymakers—from across socioeconomic and geographic lines. As the news cycle turned to COVID-19, parents across the United States looked to Oster with new, pandemic-specific questions: Can I take my child to the playground? When will be we able to visit grandparents? Rather than eschew these questions, Oster pivoted and attempted to bring her data-driven approach to the pandemic. Oster, like many, recognized the federal government was not proactively addressing family issues, and in response, spearheaded her own systematic attempts to collect and analyze data about COVID-19, schools, and childcare centers. This effort resulted in mixed success, with both praise and intense public scrutiny and criticism. Oster admits she did not fully recognize the stakes of writing for this larger, more diverse audience, and she acknowledges had she reflected on it more, she would have made different choices (North). For this expanded audience, Oster led conversations about child-related issues during COVID-19—what became some of the hottest-button debates of the pandemic. She has been criticized throughout her career by various groups, but the pandemic heightened the polarity of Oster as a public figure and researcher. The *New York Times* reports, "She fought to reopen schools, becoming a hero and a villain"; a 2021 *Vox* piece similarly explores, "How Emily Oster became one of the most respected—and reviled—voices of the pandemic" (Goldstein; North). Some of the criticism was certainly warranted, which, to her credit, Oster admits. Wholesale judgements make good headlines but rarely offer insight into a figure's rhetorical career. Neither heroine nor villain, Oster represents a small group of individuals who stepped into a void and responded to the pandemic in ways that the federal government failed to do (North).

As a working mother and reader of *ParentData,* I followed Oster's pandemic-related writing because it provided me with *some* sense of a national conversation about COVID-19 and kids. My firstborn daughter was seventeen months old in March 2020, and my second daughter arrived in July 2021. I experienced the pandemic as a mother of small children and as a pregnant woman. *ParentData* was useful for contextualizing certain family-related pandemic decisions, but more than an information resource, I found that Oster facilitated a discussion few others were having at the time about parenting toddlers and infants during COVID-19. Over the summer of 2020, the school debate generated a lot of national discussion; not much of it focused on very little kids. I signed up for the newsletter expecting to track topics like the American Academy of Pediatrics' guidelines on screen time, and I kept reading as Oster moved into COVID-19 and family life. To be clear, I disagreed with some of Oster's positions. I valued *ParentData* because it documented the realities of pandemic parenting in a moment when this conversation was difficult to find.

Turning now to analysis of *ParentData,* my goal is not to evaluate the variety of pandemic-related arguments Oster made, but instead to reflect on how her newsletter suggests a complex dimension of inquiry that manifests from personal experience—emotional labor. As a public "parenting guru" and mother, her writing during COVID-19 reveals the pandemic-specific emotional labor of writing for parents during a crisis and a more generalizable type of emotional labor, one that emerges from investigating out of experience and identity. Specific to inquiry during COVID-19, Oster's writing offers insight into what it meant for a private individual—not trained or experienced in policy discussions—to research and write for the public *about* the pandemic while *experiencing* the pandemic. More generally, as a mother writing about parenting and pregnancy topics, her work brings attention to the weighty expectations of stepping into public conversations about kids.

Feeling COVID-19

While experiences of the pandemic differed vastly, it seems fair to say everyone *felt* some effects of COVID-19. In the United States, these felt effects were especially acute for parents, many of whom suddenly found themselves working at home while caring for their children for extended periods of time and faced with constant decisions about how to parent during the pandemic. Consider the headlines—"Parental burnout: how juggling kids and work in a global pandemic brought us to the brink"; "The parental burnout crisis has reached a tipping point"; "The Pandemic is a 'mental health crisis' for parents" (Mir; North, "The parental burnout"; Grose). Of course, as commentors note, these stresses fell disproportionately on mothers, and many women decided to leave their jobs or cut back their hours due to the demands of caregiving during and after 2020 (Hsu). It is also important to point out that the parental burnout rhetoric elides the fact that caregiving circumstances have *always* been untenable for many parents and disproportionately affects people of color, due to class and racial inequities in the United States (Goldfield).

This brief context brings to fore the emotional labor expected of public writers, like Oster, who published and circulated work during the pandemic. Writing for an audience of parents required navigating an emotionally fraught moment through both the expression of *feeling* and *managing* it. Extending Holschild's earlier work, Sharon H. Mastracci, Meredith A. Newman, and Mary E. Guy write that emotional labor entails the "*expression* of one's capacity to manage personal emotions, sense other's emotions, and to respond appropriately, based on one's job" (125, emphasis mine). This theory invites consideration of how feminist researchers are expected to align experiences with emotions: expressing appropriate feeling, understanding others' responses, and navigating the rhetorical implications of both. Given the context of parenting in the pandemic, this type of emotional labor is complicated by the high stakes of the conversation and a generally anxious national mood. For the public writer, on the one hand, there is an expectation that professionally you should be managing feeling appropriately, and then on the other, that you should not be unaffected. And, particularly for Oster writing for parents, there is a desire for empathy and understanding.

Examining *ParentData* issues from March 2020 through August 2021, Oster straddles these emotional lines, regularly expressing feelings of fatigue, stress, and anxiety, while assuring readers she is managing these emotions. For example, in a piece titled "A Short Reflection" published on June 25, 2020, Oster writes, "The NYT Parenting has been doing some excellent COVID-19 writing, and the awesome Jess Grose piece on parental burnout is no exception. This really resonated with me because, basically, I'm very tired" ("A Short"). This reflection reveals Oster expressing her own feelings, "very tired," and acknowledging the national mood on parenting in the pandemic. The overall purpose of the essay is to make space for negative feelings about the crisis and to situate herself in relationship to them.

Other posts make this same move but more quickly, as an acknowledgement before getting into discussion of a parenting or pregnancy topic. For example, on November 19, 2020, Oster writes, "Let's put it out there: this is a very high stress time. Most days, I feel like the only time I'm actually relaxed is the ten minutes after I finish running in the morning" ("Antibiotics"). Again, Oster acknowledges that she is writing during a period of heightened stress, and readers may be feeling anxious or sad. She observes her own emotional state through humor and lightness, noting that she is not emotionally protected from the challenges of the holidays during COVID-19. This piece then discusses toddler toothbrushing, a survey about the tooth fairy, and a recent news story focused on antibiotics and babies. This example reveals Oster's general approach to navigating the demands of emotional labor: she recognizes the national mood, acknowledges she feels it too, and then moves on to the kind of discussion she is known for, presenting summaries of academic studies that speak to the everyday concerns of parents.

Emotional labor, as Mastracci, Newman, and Guy posit, is not just about recognizing and expressing feelings; it also requires demonstrating the *management* of feeling. Applied to writing about parenting during the pandemic, then, not only does the public writer need to show the audience they are not above feeling the emotions of the crisis, but they are also expected to show that they are handling these feelings appropriately. In Oster's case, she explains she manages fatigue, uncertainty, and anxiety through writing, talking to friends, running, and focusing on small things she can control, such as an ice rink she created with a hose in her backyard. She offers her experiences to readers as encouragement and assurance, often with a dose of self-deprecating humor. In the June 25 issue, for example, Oster writes: "I suspect I'm echoing the feelings of many of you. I do not have any great solutions. But as my daughter's millennial teacher would say, 'I want to name this feeling.' So I'm naming it" ("A Short"). The "naming the emotion" strategy comes up in other issues. This example offers the typical strategy for emotion management discussion in the newsletter—it's brief, direct, and clear about what the action point is.

While these emotional references most often serve as newsletter introductions or conclusions, Oster devotes a few posts entirely to reflective writing, where the focus is on how she manages a difficult moment. In an extended entry "Control," written on February 15, 2021, Oster writes: "I hosted a conference last week (on Zoom, obviously) and in one of the breaks another organizer asked one of the presenters how she was doing. And she said, to paraphrase, 'Bad.' When she elaborated, it wasn't just one thing. Her kid's daycare was still closed. Adapting to remote teaching was challenging. It's cold" ("Control"). As this excerpt indicates, the beginning of the post explores general feelings of frustration, fatigue, and anxiety where Oster recognizes how parents are feeling and why. The remainder of the piece details Oster managing her feelings and the ways she copes. She documents her backyard ice rink, including a photo, and explains this activity provided her a positive space for frustration and worry. She writes:

> A lot of us are feeling it . . . It's easy for this to manifest in a desire to take control where we *can* get it. For me, it's my backyard ice rink. With repeated applications of water when it's under 15 degrees, I can control having an ice rink in my backyard. In a normal year, this might be a fun activity. This year, it's perhaps gone a bit beyond that. As I realized when I got the hose caught in the hose spool and spent 30 minutes in my basement screaming profanities as I tried to unspool it. This may have reflected a frustration that went beyond the ice. ("Control")

Characteristic of Oster's discussion of emotion, she does not get too serious. Even in admitting that she is struggling, the tone is light; the story is humorous and self-deprecating. The humor aligns with the message. She understands and feels the stress of the moment, but she is okay, still making jokes, and therefore capable of tracking down the latest helpful data and synthesizing it for readers.

Since *ParentData* readers expect advice, Oster takes her discussion of emotional management further. She acknowledges that ice rink creation is not for everyone, but she suggests a similar type of activity might be helpful for others: "[A]t least for me, it's productive to acknowledge that it's okay to be a little more obsessed than usual with the things we *can* control" ("Control"). She suggests that it is helpful to recognize where actions are possible and make a deliberate plan about what your family will do, and then consider what pieces of the puzzle are beyond planning or individual choice. She writes, "I will sit with it, even if just for few moments. I will recognize it for what it is (and reflect on how much I dislike it). And then I will try—really, really, try—to (at least briefly) let the feeling go" ("Control"). It is important to note that Oster is not telling people to just let all their feelings go, but she is suggesting that it can be helpful to distinguish between what her family can make choices about and what is not within their realm of influence.

Writing about the parenting in the pandemic, then, cannot mean turning away from the *feelings* about parenting in the pandemic. Even for a writer like Oster, who regularly hails data as a key insight for parenting decisions, the rhetorical situation requires recognizing and responding to heightened anxiety. Since she writes as a fellow parent, this recognition entails sharing how she is feeling and managing the anxiety herself.

The Emotional Labor of Inquiring as a Mother

As the previous section outlined, emotional labor refers to the expectations for expression of feeling as well as sensitivity to others' feelings that are intertwined with our work. However, the concept also captures the identity-based labor many professions (unfairly) require and fail to recognize. Here the definition offered by Ronnie J. Steinberg and Deborah H. Figart is helpful. They write that emotional labor is "the relational rather than task-based aspect of work" (9). Kate Navickas writes that in this case, the labor may emerge from "negotiating who one is going to be in a position in relation to what is expected to them" (62). This theory is especially apt for examining the emotive expectations surrounding the identity of *mother* in relationship to one's professional position. The rhetorical situation of being a mother at work is tricky and complex to say the least. Feminist scholar Ruth Osorio writes about mothering in academic spaces, opening with her experience of becoming a mother during graduate school. While she had the benefit of supportive mentors, Osorio observes, "[A]cademic culture continues to punish mothers and caregivers at every stage of an academic career. . . . [M]others were [and often still are] largely instructed to keep their identities as mothers apart from their identities as scholars" ("Constellating with our Foremothers"). In and out of academia, emotional labor for mothers entails negotiating how parenthood figures into one's work and how a profession views and understands this role.

In choosing to inquire from the experience of mothering, writers and researchers have to do this identity construction for themselves *and* for audiences. For anyone who enters academic and public discussions about parenting and pregnancy as a mother, the emotional labor gains different resonances. How will I construct my identity as a mother for audiences? What "kind" of mother does my audience expect me to be? Since the beginning of her career as a public writer, Oster has negotiated this terrain through selective and strategic revelations. For a writer whose arguments hinge on particular kinds of evidence and nuanced economic analysis, she is very open about her experiences. Writing about parenting issues as a mother requires navigating audience's expectations and desire to know about your kids.

In general, Oster constructs herself as a funny, nerdy, somewhat anxious, present and deliberate mother, often through pithy examples laced with sarcasm. For instance, in the first installment of *ParentData* she explains, "In 2010 I turned 30 and got pregnant (as one does). And like a lot of women I found myself frustrated with the lack of data and evidence behind the pregnancy recommendations I was getting" ("Introducing"). This opening to the newsletter sets the tone for how Oster's constructs herself: a not-too-serious economist who blends her job with her role as a mother. She goes on in this piece to convey that the purpose of *ParentData* is to continue the kind of analysis and writing she has been doing, just on a more regular basis. The "About" page elaborates on who Oster is and the purpose of the newsletter. To describe herself, she writes:

> Here's one version: I'm a Professor of Economics at Brown University. I'm also an author of three books—*Expecting Better, Cribsheet* and *The Family Firm* . . .
>
> And here's the second version: I'm a mom of two kids who doesn't sleep enough. I'm married to a great guy who puts up with all our business being turned into books and newsletters. I like to run. I think I'm funny but the kids do not. ("About")

Through the "two version" approach, Oster plays with the idea that these roles are separate, with one identity represented as serious, professional, and industrious, and the other as silly, family-and-fun-oriented, though, of course, they overlap considerably. The construction is strategic, to identify with parents and to present herself as relatable expert and dedicated mother.

Given that *ParentData* emerged from Oster's identity as a mom, when the newsletter turned to pandemic-related issues, the emotional labor of writing from this identity continued. Oster developed a reputation for distilling academic articles, but as a mother writing about this data, people also really want to know about her experience *using* available evidence. Data alone does not tell one how to parent. Oster acknowledges this to be true; her perspective is that it is helpful to know what the scientific evidence says, to be able to discern what data is helpful, what can be set aside, and then to come to the data with your own set of personal circumstances and values (Green). She lays this framework out in her 2021 book, *The Family Firm,* but before the book was published, she offered this material in snippets in the newsletter, applied to pandemic issues. For example, in the top post of the entire newsletter, "Grandparents and Daycare," published May 18, 2020, Oster writes about a framework for making pandemic-decisions. The essay is long compared to other posts. The main point is that she cannot tell everyone what choice to make about the variety of issues they are facing, but she can offer some help thinking through the best way to frame questions. The close of the post is telling, however, as Oster discusses her own family's decisions:

> No, Seriously, What Do You Do?
> Yeah, yeah, okay. Even though I know I will be crucified, I will tell you.
>
> - Our nanny has continued to come; she works a half day. She lives alone and we have asked her to socially distance. I trust her, but do not police her behavior.
> - If camps open, I will send my kids.
> - We saw my parents, who are older, for a socially distant hike last weekend. We did not touch them and the adults wore masks.
> ("Grandparents and Daycare,")

Oster's audience looks to her for data, but they also expect her to explain what choices she is making. This expectation is a double-edged sword. On one side, it is an innocuous curiosity and desire to know what Oster is doing—What does motherhood look like for you right now? On the other, it is an expectation that cannot please or satisfy everyone in the audience, and that will certainly result in anger among some—How could you mother that way right now? For mothers writing about parenting, the personal is not a choice; it is an unavoidable labor that one has to negotiate. Understood through Waite's theory of inquiry, the individual's experience is inseparable from the "body of knowledge." As Waite writes, "It is no accident, then, that the idiom of body of knowledge takes the metaphor of the body . . . in the echoes of the idiom's erasure of the body, we can still hear that somehow what we know, or what we have come to know, is part of bodily composition. What happens when we ourselves become bodies of knowledge?" (18). For mothers stepping into public conversations about child and family life, audiences expect to learn about the material, personal dimensions of what they know. For Oster writing during the pandemic, this expectation meant including her own experiences navigating childcare, grandparents, and more.

Arguably, given the lack of pandemic-related data about children, there was more pressure on Oster than ever to reveal her own positions and experiences with issues. For example, on April 13, 2020, Oster wrote an essay titled, "Will the Kids Be All Right?" She writes, "A lot of you have written with concerns about how this will affect your kids, so I thought it would be good to do a rundown of what we know, or what the data *might* say. . ." ("Will the Kids"). Oster emphasizes "might," she says, because really, the data does not say very much that is useful. Recognizing this void and the anxiety it may create, Oster writes about how things are going in her own home. For instance, she opens saying, "I feel bad for my kids. I am trying to make the home school isolation fun (more TV time! Recess in the backyard! Take-out lunch on Mondays!) but the bottom line is that they miss school. It's a little heartbreaking watching my son Google Hangout with his teachers and sing the 'Hello' song" ("Will the Kids"). Oster tries to be honest with readers about how little can really be known, data-wise, about parenting in a pandemic. In the absence of abundant evidence, she writes out of her own experience, sharing small details about how her own kids her doing. As this post indicates, audiences continued to look to Oster to answer their questions about parenting in the pandemic, and part of this writing included discussing her own experience of what was happening, how her family was handling it, and who she was as a mother in the moment. Oster stuck to the persona she had created pre-pandemic—as witty and smart, encouraged by data, and deeply invested in being present to her kids and family.

This chapter reflects on the idea that feminist inquiry requires emotional labor. Broadly speaking, women disproportionately face emotional labor, as the management and performance of feeling for audiences. Journalist Rose Hackman observes, "[W]omen across the world are taught from a very young age to regulate, modulate, and manipulate their feelings in order to have a positive effect on the feelings of others. Women, endlessly told to smile but also tasked with making other people smile, are held accountable not only for the expression of their own feelings but also for the feelings of others" (4). While Hackman's writing here, like Arlie Hothschild's initial work on the topic, speaks about the inequity of emotional labor across the work spectrum, my chapter centers on the specific arena of academic women developing research and writing from personal experience.

Emily Oster's public writing in the context of the pandemic provides a window into this dynamic. As a woman writing about pandemic parenting issues from the position of a mother, Oster faced expectations to speak from experience and to express emotion appropriately—to manage her feelings about the pandemic and to articulate her understanding of other's feelings. Given her reputation as an analyst valued for her training in economics and skill parsing data, it is at first somewhat surprising how often she speaks about the personal and how she and everyone else is feeling. Yet, her routine and persistent turn to writing from and about her experiences reveal the demands of emotional labor on women (and perhaps especially mothers) writing about topics that emerge from our identities.

This analysis of Oster's public pandemic writing provides a heightened context for reckoning with a reality that women working in academia have faced and will continue face—researching, teaching, and leading from experience requires more and different kinds of work, much of it related to navigating feeling, our own and others. To most fully support women in these spaces, we have to first fully understand the kinds of work we do, and feeling work needs more attention, particularly as universities do not value or recognize this kind of labor. The upshot of this essay focused on Oster's pandemic writing in her newsletter, *ParentData,* and generally speaking, this body of public writing has won Oster a wide readership and success. However, in researching from her experience—truly, asking questions from her pregnant body—she has certainly encountered other felt effects of being a "vagina economist" in a field infamous for being inhospitable to women (Levitt). As a junior faculty member at the University of Chicago, she was denied tenure. When asked about the rationale, she speculates that her work in her first book, *Expecting Better,* played a role in the decision. *Expecting Better,* by Oster's own description," is "part memoir, part metanalysis" focused on her experience of becoming pregnant and using her economic training to navigate her journey (Lammer, Druckerman). While it is impossible to parse a tenure decision from the outside, what the decision makes obvious is just how inhospitable some disciplines are to researching from experience. To fully grapple with the emotional labor of Oster's inquiry from the body, then, means also situating this work in a university context that ultimately rejected her and her research.

Most concretely, this chapter and the work of this collection might help us better understand the challenges women and mothers encounter in academia so that we might create better supports. One of those challenges is certainly the felt effects of researching from our bodies. As academics, when we research and write—and teach and lead—from our experiences as women, we take on and navigate additional emotional labor. Naming this dimension of feminist inquiry as labor is not to diminish the practice or argue we should not intertwine our questions and our identities as women and mothers. As the opening to this chapter establishes, this relationship is inseverable. My goal instead is to bring attention to the emotional labor, to name it as a challenge, so that we might do more to acknowledge it and carry it together. For women researching from their bodies, then, the recommendation is to make visible and value the emotional labor of this work.

For mothers in the university, however, the recommendation is to create cultural shifts that diminish the emotional labor around being a parent at work. By many metrics, becoming a mother makes it difficult to succeed in academia (Torres). Conversations about supports for academic parents typically focus on the concrete realities in play, like so-called "work-life conflict," loss of opportunities, and limited access to childcare and maternity leave (Misra). However, as this chapter argues, there are other mundane and diffuse ways that being a mother negatively affects our work, and one of them is certainly the labor of managing our own and everyone else's feelings about our position as mothers. In most universities, we work in spaces designed to suppress indicators of parenthood, and therefore encourage our silence about being a mother—leave your children and all signs of them at home or in the childcare center. Yet, well-meaning (and sometimes not so well-meaning) colleagues ask questions about our family lives that require quick and careful thinking about what type of anecdote appropriately matches the emotional needs of the audience. The moment one becomes a parent there is an expectation that you understand and can manage this odd dynamic, recognizing the appropriate spaces and moments to speak from the position of parent, having pleasing stories at the ready, and remaining silent about it otherwise. In sum, we need the material supports, and, at the same time, we *also* need cultural shifts that offer women guidance and freedom to configure the identity of mother in academia in ways that work for them without also being expected to manage others' feeling about this role.

Notes

1. See also writers such as Sarah Ahmed, Gloria Anzaldua, and Pauli Murray.

2. For other women writing publicly about parenting during the pandemic, consult Jesse Grose's *New York Times* column. In the podcast vein, see "Best of Both Worlds" and

"Psychologists Off the Clock." This collection will also add to our archive of women's public writing about COVID-19. See, e.g., Cooper, Martini, and Miley, and Matravers. Likewise, Grose's 2022 book *Screaming on the Inside: The Unsustainability of American Motherhood* reflects on pandemic parenting from a slightly more distant vantage point.

Bibliography

Ahmed, Sarah. *Living a Feminist Life.* Duke University Press, 2017.

Anzaldua, Gloria. *Borderlands / La Frontera: The New Mestiza.* Aunt Lute Books, 2022.

Druckerman, Pamela. "Can a Little Bit of Data Make Parenting Easier?" *Literary Hub,* April 26, 2019. https://lithub.com/.

Enoch, Jessica, Cheryl Glenn, and Jordynn Jack. "Introduction: The Endless Possibilities for Feminist Research." *Retellings: Opportunities for Feminist Research in Rhetoric and Composition Studies,* edited by Jessica Enoch and Jordynn Jack, 3–16. Parlor Press, 2019.

Goldfield, Hannah. "Deb Perelman Is Thankful for Tacos." *The New Yorker,* November 25, 2020. https://www.newyorker.com/.

Goldstein, Dana. "She Fought to Reopen Schools, Becoming a Hero and a Villain." *New York Times,* June 22, 2021. https://www.nytimes.com/.

Green, Emma. "How to Avoid the Worst Parenting Mistake." *The Atlantic,* August 2, 2021. https://www.theatlantic.com/.

Grose, Jessica. "The Pandemic is a 'Mental Health Crisis' for Parents." *The New York Times,* September 9, 2020. https://www.nytimes.com/.

Grose, Jessica. *Screaming on the Inside: The Unsustainability of American Motherhood.* Mariner, 2022.

Hackman, Rose. *Emotional Labor: The Invisible Work Shaping Our Lives and How to Claim Our Power.* Flatiron Books, 2023.

Holschild, Arlie. *The Managed Heart: Commercialization of Human Feeling.* University of California Press, 2012.

Hsu, Andrea. "Millions of Women Haven't Rejoined the Workforce—And May Not Anytime Soon." *NPR,* June 3, 2021. https://www.npr.org/.

Kirsch, Gesa, and Jacqueline Jones Royster. *Feminist Rhetorical Practices: New Horizons for Rhetoric, Composition, and Literacy Studies.* Southern Illinois University Press, 2012.

Kirsch, Gesa, and Joy Ritchie. "Beyond the Personal: Theorizing a Politics of Location in Composition Research." *College Composition and Communication* 46, no. 1, (1995): 7–29.

Lammer, Aaron, Max Linsky, and Evin Ratliff. "468: Emily Oster." *Longform.* December 8, 2021. Podcast, MP3 audio, 51:01.

Levitt, Steven D. "17: Emily Oster: I Am a Woman Who Is Prominently Discussing Vaginas." Podcast produced by Morgan Levey. *People I Mostly Admire.* February 26, 2021.

Logan, Shirley. "'When and Where I Enter': Race, Gender, and Composition Studies." In *Feminism and Composition Studies: In Other Words,* edited by Susan C. Jarratt and Lynn Worsham, 45–57. Modern Language Association, 1998.

Mastracci, Sharon H., Meredith A. Newman, and Mary E. Guy. "Emotional Labor: Why and How to Teach It." *Journal of Public Affairs Education* 16, no. 2 (2010):123–41.

Mir, Saima. "Parental Burnout: How Juggling Kids and Work in a Global Pandemic Brought Us to the Brink." *The Guardian* Sept. 8, 2021. https://www.theguardian.com/lifeandstyle/2021/sep/08/parental-burnout-how-juggling-kids-and-work-in-a-global-pandemic-brought-us-to-the-brink.

Misra Joyra, Jennifer Hickes Lundquist, and Abby Templer. "Gender, Work Time, and Care Responsibilities Among Faculty." *Sociological Forum* 27 (2012): 300–23.

Murray, Pauli. *Song in a Weary Throat.* Liveright, 1987.

Navickas, Kate. "The Emotional Labor of Becoming: Lessons from the Exiting Writing Center Director." In *The Things We Carry: Strategies for Recognizing and Negotiating Emotional Labor in Writing Program Administration,* edited by Courtney Adams Wooten, Jacob Babb, Kristi Murray Costello, and Kate Navickas, 56–74. Utah State University Press, 2020.

North, Anna. "The Parental Burnout Crisis Has Reached a Tipping Point." *Vox.* December 8, 2020. https://www.vox.com/.

North, Anna. "How Emily Oster Became One of the Most Respected—and Reviled—Voices of the Pandemic." *Vox.* July 26, 2021. https://www.vox.com/.

Osorio, Ruth. "Constellating with Our Foremothers: Stories of Mothers Making Space in Rhetoric and Composition." *Constellations: A Cultural Rhetorics Publishing Space* Vol. August 4, 2021.

Oster, Emily. *Expecting Better: Why the Conventional Pregnancy Wisdom is Wrong—and What You Really Need to Know.* Penguin, 2014.

Oster, Emily. *Cribsheet: A Data-Driven Guide to More Relaxed Parenting, from Birth to Preschool.* Penguin, 2019.

Oster, Emily. "Introducing . . . ." *ParentData.* Substack, February 24, 2020.

Oster, Emily. "Will the Kids Be All Right?" *ParentData.* Substack, April 13, 2020.

Oster, Emily. "Grandparents and Daycare." *ParentData.* Substack, May 18, 2020.

Oster, Emily. "A Short Reflection." *ParentData.* Substack, June 25, 2020.

Oster, Emily. "Antibiotics and the Tooth Fairy." *ParentData.* Substack, November 19, 2020.

Oster, Emily. "About." *ParentData.* Substack, 2021.

Oster, Emily. *The Family Firm: A Data-Driven Guide to Better Decision Making in the Early School Years.* Penguin, 2021.

Oster, Emily. "Control." *ParentData.* Substack, February 15, 2021.

Restaino, Jessica. *Surrender: Feminist Rhetoric and Ethics in Love and Illness.* Southern Illinois University Press, 2019.

Restaino, Jessica, with Susan Lundy Maute (in memoriam). "Surrender as Method: Research, Writing, Rhetoric, Love." *Peitho* 18, no. 1 (2015): 72–95.

Royster, Jacqueline Jones. *Traces of a Stream: Literacy and Social Change Among African American Women.* University Pittsburgh Press, 2000.

Steinberg, Ronnie J., and Deborah H. Figart. "Emotional Labor Since the Managed Heart." *Annals of the American Academy of Political and Social Science* 561, no. 1 (1999): 8–26.

Torres, Ana Júlia Calegari, Letícia Barbosa-Silva, Ligia Carolina Olivera-Silva, et al. "The Impact of Motherhood on Women's Career Progression: A Scoping Review of Evidence-Based Interventions." *Behavioral sciences (Basel, Switzerland)* 14, no 4 (March 2024): 1–17.

Waite, Stacey. *Teaching Queer: Radical Possibilities for Writing and Knowing.* University of Pittsburgh Press, 2017.

CHAPTER 9

Reimagined Productivity

Narratives of Academic Mothers
Who Choose to Homeschool

Heidi M. Williams, Laura Seroka, Abby Arnold-Patti,
Nandini Deo, and Ceceilia Parnther

For years, even prior to the pandemic, academic mothers have chosen the "traditional" route of homeschool, acting as the primary educator for their children, not a virtual facilitator. While the specific number of academic homeschooling parents is unknown, many parents took the opportunity to reevaluate, reprioritize, and reconceptualize work and home during the pandemic. This led to the number of homeschooling households in the United States doubling by the Fall of 2020 (Eggleston and Fields for the US Census Bureau). According to reports from the National Home Education Research Institute (NHERI) (2021) and the National Center for Education Statistics (NCES) (2019), the number of homeschooled children with a parent with a graduate degree climbed from 15 percent in 2016 to 21 percent after COVID closures in 2020 (Cui & Hanson; Ray). Studies also revealed the labor of homeschooling holds a gender disparity with mothers overwhelmingly (78 percent) taking the role of instructor and the labor of designing a home education curriculum (NCES). Whether new or existing homeschooling academic mothers, the pandemic required a reimagining of productivity and balance in both professional and home realms in attempts to meet the needs of their families amid a global health scare as well as survive the career progression requirements of academia.

Indeed, chapters throughout this volume have outlined the labor issues facing women in academia. In addition, business and communication scholar Rachel Pettigrew identified that women, in particular, were faced with working a "split shift" during the pandemic whereby they completed paid labor early in the morning, domestic and care labor while children were awake, then returned to paid labor before sleep (8). This split created enhanced emotional labor and tensions as mothers juggled two identities, that of an "ideal worker," who is committed to their job, and that of a "good mother," who puts her children's emotional, educational, and physical needs above all else (Cooper; Hermann and Neale-McFall). Prior to the pandemic, organizational communication scholars Patrice Buzzanell and Meina Liu found that when women become mothers, their professional identity was reconstructed, and the mother worker identity was often negatively judged against that of the ideal worker. Therefore, working mothers often seek to solve problems alone rather than speaking with their colleagues or employers about changing needs. In academia specifically, research showed the pandemic further reduced the already minimal blocks of time available for conducting research, especially for mothers (Ross). Academic women are losing moments of productivity as the increase in time spent on care and home responsibilities decreases time available for professional research and service to communities (Moodley and Gouws). *Washington Post* reporter Caroline Kitchener showcased this disparity noting that men's journal submission rates rose during COVID, while those of women's decreased. These trends place women fighting to show their "good worker" status amid decreasing availability to be professionally productive, potentially harming their ability to maintain a viable research trajectory (a common academic expectation). Adding homeschooling labor to the responsibilities magnifies those challenges in terms of time constraints and emotional labor. Yet, the narratives of homeschooling academic mothers are often missing from conversations about professional, mother, and educator identities and productivity. If two identities (mother and professional) create unfair barriers to productivity, it is essential to understand how a third criterion, homeschooling, impacts those productivity expectations.

This chapter highlights and celebrates the narratives of academic mothers through their understandings of home education and their versions of productivity. The authors of this chapter live in widespread localities, academic disciplines and colleges, ages of children, and length in homeschooling, yet are all connected through the shared decision to adopt the identity of homeschooling academic mother, and navigate the professional and personal challenges which come from this decision. The authors connected in a social media group entitled "Support Group for Professors Who Homeschool" during 2020 as a means of creating community and knowledge sharing. Through their experiences, they share threads of divergence from social expectations as they reimagine productivity including understanding homeschooling as productive even if it falls outside their professional identities and ways homeschooling pedagogical practices informs their professional work. There are also similarities among experiences including a lack of institutional support for holding multiple roles and identities of labor, the emotional labor of being an academic homeschooling mother and engaging in 'split-shift' work, and the need to view productivity across colliding identities rather than within each role. Points of divergence arise as they made decisions on how to homeschool, how to balance the identities of being a professional and mother, and ways to be productive while also striving for work–life balance.

As Jessica Edens McCrary acknowledged in the introduction of this book, to suggest a singular experience would falsely flatten the myriad individual circumstances of women during the pandemic and the years in its wake. Our chapter outlines five varying narratives of professorial mothers who homeschooled during 2020 and its residual years.

Heidi M. Williams

I am an Associate Professor at Tennessee State University, a Historically Black University in Nashville, TN. I have two daughters—a four-year-old who loves ballet and singing, and a seven-year-old who is a tiny environmental activist. I am in my second year of schooling my children at home.

A month after my oldest daughter turned five, she entered kindergarten in public school. Since she was so young, I was concerned about her emotional readiness, the maturity level required to take ownership of her learning, and her overall physical ability to wake up every day at 6:00 AM and rush out the door to endure an 8-hour school day. Maybe she was ready, but I can say with certainty that I was not ready for kindergarten. My concerns regarding school-readiness only expounded when our hometown experienced an EF3 tornado in the middle of the night, which hit several of our area schools. Effective immediately, just six months into kindergarten, our district was closed, only to have that announcement overlap with the announcement closing our schools until further notice due to the pandemic.

As a result, my child's elementary school moved to optional virtual sessions for the kindergarteners once a week, and my youngest was home from preschool. However, in no fashion was I prepared, equipped, or educated in early childhood education enough to begin teaching a kindergarten and preschool curriculum. Since my institution moved online as well, my children and

I essentially started our spring break early and it moved us directly into summer break; we spent our days playing and visiting the lake, as Alice Cooper's "School's out for summer, School's out forever" played on rotation in my mind.

The following school year, I watched parents in complete panic and disarray as they held their breaths to see if schools would open in the fall. I cowered silently while parents fought between mask mandates and various school reforms. Ultimately, when my institution made the decision to continue with online instruction the upcoming school year, I decided to homeschool. My daughter was stripped from a "normal" kindergarten experience, and I felt like it was my obligation to move her forward academically. We converted our guest bedroom into our classroom, found a curriculum we could loosely follow (with plenty of nature-based learning suggestions), and set forth on our homeschool journey.

I plummeted myself into homeschool literature (specifically, Julie Bogart's work) and found that I have been educating my children through various forms of "play-based"/"discovery-based" learning all along. Whether by choice, or by demands of balancing a career while homeschooling, we are "relaxed homeschoolers," in that we are not led by a schedule. We work throughout the day in chunks, often in 15-minute increments, and we spend a great deal of time outside of our home learning and exploring. My decision to continue to homeschool rests on these points:

- There is a strong and growing community of academic mothers, and fathers, who school their children at home. As a mother in academia, my emotional well-being rests on the fact that many women in academia choose to homeschool as a form of empowerment, and now I am one of them. Furthermore, the academic motherhood community has largely been silent and not widely accepted within higher education; now, more than ever, women are identifying with and advocating for their dual roles, and we must continue to do so.
- My position as a homeschool parent has informed my college-level pedagogy on profound levels. I will continue to immerse myself in homeschool literature, as well as best practices within my field of rhetoric and composition while enjoying the beautiful intersections of those two fields.
- The work I'm doing at home and at work are equally important. I am raising tiny scholars and critical thinkers, while also teaching argumentation, research writing, expository writing, and technical writing at the college level. The work I am doing at the elementary level and the college level will impact the generations.

The challenges of balancing homeschooling while maintaining my role as professor, committee member, researcher, and community volunteer come with an infinite number of shortcomings. Nothing is ever complete, but we finish each day and are done with it. Tomorrow is a new day, and we pick back up where we left off . . . and mostly, I work in the evenings after daddy arrives home from work, and I binge-work on the weekends. I also rely on the homeschool community around us and send my daughters to tutorials. My children are curious, have remarkable imaginations, and are their own little people with individual interests and personalities. I am still drowning in the demands of academia, but I can at least say I'm doing so between witnessing the exact moment a butterfly emerge out of its cocoon, learning about blown glass and visiting large-scale sculptures made by Dale Chihuly, and of course, making paper-mâché volcanos.

Abby Arnold Patti

I am a tenured communication professor at a community college, teaching a 5/5 load. In addition to teaching my courses, I am responsible for advising students, serving on college and state committees, and remaining an active scholar through research, publication, and engagement with professional associations. I am also a mother of three—an eighth grader, a sixth grader, and a first grader.

My children had always attended a traditional school until the pandemic sent students home during the Spring of 2020. After a few months of tears, frustration, and setbacks doing virtual school, I made the difficult and scary decision to withdraw them completely and enroll in independent homeschool. This meant, much to their relief, that they would no longer be held captive to a computer screen, YouTube tutorials, and standardized, auto-graded tests. It also meant that I would be solely responsible for designing their curriculum, instructing them, assessing them, and documenting their attendance and progress. The term "overwhelmed" fails to capture the feeling and experience. One colleague, another mother, made very clear her disapproval of my choice and her doubts at my capacity to fulfill my professional duties and meet the educational needs of my children. I carried that criticism and doubt with me throughout the next year.

The days are endless. My alarm wakes me at 5:00 AM, and I begin my day by responding to emails. By 6:00 AM, I have moved to grading assignments or preparing for the courses I'm teaching that day. I have one more hour before the children wake up, so I rush to get to a stopping point. At 9:00 AM, I shift gears and serve as middle school teacher, elementary school teacher, and cafeteria manager until noon when I must get back online to meet my students via

Zoom. The older children work independently for a few hours in the afternoon while I teach. My first grader spends this time coloring, playing computer games, and playing in the backyard. I feel guilty that his afternoons seem to lack the structure that I imagine a homeschool day should have. I reconvene with them around 5:00 PM to review their work and plan for tomorrow. Then, it's to the kitchen to prepare dinner. While others report culinary creativity during the pandemic, at my house we are defaulting to frozen pizza too often as I am exhausted by this point in the day. After they eat, I go back to work. There is more grading, emails, and course prep waiting for me.

Typically, I work until midnight or later, since so much of my typical workday is now spent homeschooling my children. This cycle repeats itself as if one day bleeds into the next and my exhaustion continues to build. Imagine the film *Groundhog Day,* on endless repeat.

However, there are beautiful moments as well. The children have blossomed in many ways. They are more creative and independent. They have learned to love reading for its own sake, not only for an assignment. They are journaling, and their writing skills are improving markedly. We do school outside, on the ski slopes, on a hiking trail, and in our pajamas. My son expresses gratitude for a break from the social pressures of middle school. I struggle with the idea of ever sending them back to traditional school, although my career practically demands that I do.

Borrowing from the work of Keith Berry,[1] I offer some key takeaways of my homeschooling experience using the idea of "Things I must think about" and "Things I no longer must think about."

Things I must consider as an academic homeschooling parent:

- State education standards and homeschooling laws. These were completely foreign and nearly unintelligible to me when I began this journey. I cannot imagine how difficult it must be to navigate these landmines without the privilege of my years of experience as an educator. This information should be more readily accessible to parents.
- Managing how my department chair, deans, and colleagues perceived my work. Like many academics, I found myself doing much more work during the pandemic. However, for me, taking on more work became a type of cover stemming from fear any professional boundaries I set would be misattributed to my decision to homeschool. Of the many lessons we can take from our collective experience in the pandemic, one primary one is a

fundamental reimagining of workspace and work boundaries. Professors have always enjoyed a greater degree of freedom than many, however the blurring of boundaries created during the pandemic led to working mothers like me feeling the need to constantly prove themselves via increased productivity during a time when we were simply trying to survive.

- Creating and maintaining boundaries. All boundaries seem to dissolve as home and work collapse into one space and time when I am lecturing from my kitchen table. My role as educator and mother role collapse into one another as I'm attempting to teach middle school algebra to my reluctant daughter. The professional and domestic collide as I quickly unload the dishwasher between virtual committee meetings. Holding mental space for these competing goals is exhausting.

Things I do not need to consider as an academic homeschooling parent:

- Bedtimes, alarm clocks, and school calendars. Being free from the chains of the tardy bell and the carpool line granted me much-needed relief. I found that my children are naturally night owls and allowing our school day to begin late morning and end after dinner granted me time to work uninterrupted for several hours before they woke up each morning. Frequently we would skip an entire day of school and make it up on a Saturday when I did not have work obligations. We chose to extend the school year rather than rush through material. It was a gift to work with a schedule that met my children's individual needs and that could be adapted to the ebb and flow of my academic calendar.
- Homework, tests, and school projects (educational norms in general). It felt as if a heavy weight had been lifted from the shoulders of my dyslexic son (and me) when the pressure of weekly spelling tests was removed from our lives. It was transformational to see my children learning without the pressure of a unit test looming. Our family's overall quality of life improved when we were no longer at the mercy of school project deadlines. As a professor, I certainly understand the importance of these capacities, however our time homeschooling made clear the limitations of these educational paradigms, and the burden these taken-for-granted norms place on families who are often under-equipped to fulfill them.
- Interpreting assessments. Homeschooling provided precious time with my children that I otherwise never would have experienced, including unique

opportunities to witness their academic and personal growth firsthand, in the moment. Those were the magic moments that we educators live for, and to experience them with my own children was lifechanging. I had felt the pride of seeing a good grade come home from school but witnessing the light-bulb moment a concept "clicked" for my child was priceless. Being able to watch their growth, learn their strengths, and discover their interests firsthand alongside them granted me incredible insight into their personalities and their academic progress.

Nandini Deo

At the time of this writing, I was a tenured associate professor of political science at Lehigh University. I began working at the department in 2008 and achieved tenure in 2015. My children were born in 2012, 2016, and 2019. My oldest spent one year in a play-based preschool but otherwise has been homeschooled. My middle child started in the same preschool but dropped out halfway through because pandemic preschool lacked joy and connection.

We opted to homeschool so we could spend more time with our children, nurturing their natural curiosity and to maintain their sense of a half-Indian identity as a source of pride. I am inspired by child-led learning but find my own "schoolishness" requires that we also integrate some formal academic work into their days as they get older (Richards 2022).

My greatest challenge is feeling like I don't have enough time to do everything as well as I wish—to conduct my research, teach my students, serve my university community, my discipline of political science, my neighborhood; and custom tailor our days to meet the needs of each child. The COVID-19 pandemic robbed me of the part-time childcare I usually rely on, which let me get some of my academic work done and it took away our access to community learning and socializing resources for the children.

One of the things I have learned to do is creatively combine research and teaching. Now I want to figure out how to integrate our homeschooling into my academic life. I love my work, and I love my children—keeping them separated feels artificial and limiting.

I would feel supported if it were easier to bring my children to campus so they could work on their projects while I am in the office, if I was better paid and could buy more time to think and write by hiring more babysitting, and if there were more opportunities to network with other homeschooling faculty. When I think about the advice that I wish I had received when I started on this path, these are the three things I could have benefited from:

First, building community at work and in the homeschool work takes time and effort—choices about time and emotional resources must be made and you should make those choices consciously.

Second, you are swimming upstream by choosing to homeschool and work—the reality is that no one is going to reward you or recognize you for this, so make sure you really want to blend both tasks.

And finally, allow what you learn as a homeschooling parent to soften and shape how you are as a classroom instructor. Bringing that same love and care to your students that you have for your children will make you a much better teacher and human being.

Ceceilia Parnther

I am on the tenure track as an Assistant Professor at a private urban research university in New York. I have three daughters, ages four, nine, and eleven. I kept my four-year-old at home, supplementing care with a part-time caregiver who would give me space to work and play with my daughter. Homeschooling is something I have considered for a long time. As the years passed, I became increasingly more comfortable with the schools I chose for my children. I chaperoned field trips, joined the PTA and school leadership teams, and sold pickles, popcorn, and cookies. These activities were close to the action but included the security of teachers and school administration. Finally, I made peace with my reticence to homeschool.

I have heard of parents who homeschool while navigating a career and never believed I had what it took to manage both while adequately providing the fundamentals that my daughters need to succeed. I worked every weekend and most nights well into the morning but felt I had managed a delicate balance.

The pandemic upended so much of what I thought I knew. As school doors shut indefinitely, all of my thoughts and research went out of the window. I could not consider a path where I felt adequate. I immediately put my research skills to use, tirelessly identifying educational tools and resources aligned with their current studies. Supplementing the offerings of my daughters' schools, I used a designed curriculum and my desired learning outcomes for my children to round out the spring 2020 school year. I put together a calendar of academic and cocurricular activities. To do this, I used advice from online homeschool groups and the Teachers Pay Teachers (TPT) online resource.

Early on, I overcompensated, overscheduling to gain a sense of control and order. I now realize this response was a coping mechanism. Lack of time was my greatest challenge and exacerbated feelings of inadequacy. As a partner, a parent, a teacher, and a professor, nothing ever felt done.

By Fall 2020, I found my footing and chose to continue to homeschool. We remained completely remote, and I began to listen to my children more. I found solace in mother-scholars who were experiencing similar things. This situation is not perfect, but neither are parenthood or academia. My advice for anyone considering homeschooling is:

> Know that every choice is hard. Make the decisions you can find peace with and do so unapologetically.
>
> Make dedicated, uninterrupted time for scheduling meetings where grace is not easily extended.
>
> Recognize that whether homeschooling by choice or by chance, you bring an understanding of your child that no one else has.
>
> Embrace that it is not possible to do everything at once. However, schedules, honesty, and grace go a long way in homeschooling.
>
> Acknowledge disturbances, but don't dwell on them.

We are all dealing with unfathomable challenges, and grace and care are necessary. I am fortunate to have learned the beauty in the vulnerability of homeschooling as a mother in academia.

Laura Seroka

I am an Assistant Professor at Berea College with a focus on environmental communication. I started homeschooling with one child in pre-K in 2018 while working on my PhD. Now, I have a second grader (age 7) and a kindergartener (age 5). When we began homeschooling, in the Midwest state I lived in, childcare and school fees for one toddler and one preschooler were more than $1600 a month or almost $20,000 a year (Child Care Aware of America). Minimal teaching assistant wages, matched with flexible schedules thanks to my wife's pediatric nursing job, made homeschooling in the early years the smart and easy choice.

My daughters thrived doing hands-on projects at home, guided by a STEAM-based curriculum. They loved being home with their moms, and we loved spending extra time together. When kindergarten came, we kept homeschooling—why enroll when we would leave as soon as I finished my doctorate program? Homeschooling offered stability and the flexibility to move anytime. I accepted a teaching-focused, tenure-track job in the American South serving at-risk youth of Appalachia. Due to the move, new jobs, and no time to vet schools, we decided to homeschool "just one more year." Living in the American South, we worried: Will our kids be bullied and excluded at school for having two moms? But I also worried—Are we teaching them enough? Are we stretching ourselves too thinly?

The pandemic shifted us to survival mode. I taught online, balancing my family's needs alongside my students. In my faculty/advisor role, "high-touch teaching" took on new meaning. I had daily meetings with my virtual students because the pandemic returned some to unsafe home environments, caused some of them to experience depression as they also dealt with economic struggles. Weekends were for "catching up," and days off became a thing of the past. There was not enough of me to go around, not enough of me to carry the mental load, not enough of me for me. There were no field trips, clubs, or sports; I was in "mom mode" 24/7. My college recognized parents' loads and offered amendments such as letting us limit our teaching loads to two sections of one class to minimize prep or optional delayed tenure reviews, but as the pandemic dragged on, those amendments disappeared. Now we are required to be back on campus, but I am still homeschooling my children. Due to low county vaccination rates, poor public-school ratings, and seeing my children thrive in a homeschool setting, we will continue homeschooling as long as they want to do so. The flexibility of academia is one reason I can offer this arrangement to my kids; yet it took a pandemic for administrators to acknowledge and address issues faced by homeschooling faculty and staff.

The biggest question I get asked when other academic parents find out I homeschool is "How do you fit it all in?" Homeschool requires the reimagining of work and education, and there is a learning curve. I tell them if you want to homeschool:

> Let homeschool fit your schedule. Homeschool can happen anytime of the day and at any location, whether you start at 7 AM or 5 PM.
> Seek a support group. Seeing others in similar situations and hearing their solutions makes you feel understood, heard, and valued.
> Don't become invisible. Keep talking about homeschooling with college administrators and voice your needs.

As our narratives thread together, we find that our productivity as academic mothers who homeschool relies on three important factors. First and foremost, we acknowledge that having a *choice* to homeschool is at the forefront of our decisions to continue to school at home. We recognize that homeschooling increases our overall responsibilities, but we are thankful our careers afford us some freedom of choice. Secondly, we each find ourselves in a position of needing support and validation from our supervisors and administrators. By and large, academic motherhood is an anomaly. The increased need to support professorial parents is at an all-time high, as we continue to navigate the pandemic. And finally, the urgency expressed in each of our narratives is the ability to allow ourselves to set work/home boundaries. A well-balanced career is essential to our productivity and success as scholars, educators, and mothers.

As higher education institutions move away from emergency virtual learning to previous mentalities of in-person learning, pressures from administrators could potentially impact our ability and flexibility to homeschool. In fact, only three of the contributors of this chapter are still homeschooling, except for Lackey and Parnther. Indeed, Parnther admits that as a junior faculty member, it is currently untenable for her to continue homeschooling. Yet, she has "become more mindful of work–life balance" with respect to having "much more appreciation for what it means to be fully present and to create strong and clear boundaries." Moreover, Lackey says that her children are happily back in the traditional classroom, but she "misses the freedom and intimacy of homeschooling." Although Lackey's homeschool journey only lasted during the pandemic, she shares the sentiments that those of us who are still homeschooling feel—"One of the lasting gifts our season of homeschooling gave our family was a deep understanding of and appreciation for each child's unique learning style, a more nuanced understanding of each child's unique strengths and challenges, and a holistic integration of learning into our everyday lives." Collectively, we have learned as teachers and mothers that investing in our children's learning and understanding the inequalities of women's labor are the two components of homeschool consideration that we will take with us as we move forward.

Women take on a disproportionate amount of career and household labor, constantly moving between professional and mothering identities and reimagining productivity to both meet, and at times challenge, the expectations of both the "good worker" and "good mother" narratives. Deo, Seroka, and Williams acknowledge that homeschooling and being in a community with other parents who homeschool illustrate that point and provide space to collectively understand and reimagine the productivity expected of academics. We need a more visible representation of children and families in ways that do not disrupt professional obligations. Normalizing the existence and needs of families goes a long way in supporting employees and boosting morale. In addition, enhancing advocacy for practices that are mindful of children and families would go a long way toward better job satisfaction and greater chance for success. It will become essential for parents who homeschool to advocate for not just work–life balance, but work-life-homeschool balance. Prior to COVID-19, there were already long-standing gender, class, and racial inequities related to care of others and of the home with many women working paid labor during the day, then engaging in unpaid labor at home. Research shows this "second shift" inequity became more transparent during COVID as many women took over one more element of care—homeschooling (Adams-Prassl et al.). Organizations must continue seeing points and intersections of "second-shift," "split-shift" and unpaid labor, such as homeschooling, as important and worthy endeavors in the community. The contributors acknowledge that homeschooling reminds and reinforces the value of the domestic labor that we do. Too often, we believe, such labor is undervalued. It is an affirming reminder that the work we do at home with our families is just as important, perhaps more important, than the work we do at the college.

Bibliography

Adams-Prassl, Abi, Teodora Boneva, Marta Golin, and Christopher Rauh. "Inequality in the Impact of the Coronavirus Shock: Evidence from Real Time Surveys." *Journal of Public Economics* 189 (2020): 104245. https://doi.org/10.1016/j.jpubeco.2020.104245.

Bogart, Julie. *The Brave Learner: Finding Everyday Magin in Homeschool, Learning, and Life.* Penguin Random House, 2019.

Buzzanell, Patrice M., and Meina Liu. "Struggling with Maternity Leave Policies and Practices: A Poststructuralist Feminist Analysis of Gendered Organizing." *Journal of Applied Communication Research* 33, no. 1 (2005): 1–25. https://doi.org/10.1080/00909 88042000318495.

Child Care Aware of America. "Parents and the High Cost of Child Care." (2017). https://info.childcareaware.org/hubfs/2017_State_Fact_Sheets.pdf.

Cooper, Marianne. "Mothers' Careers Are at Extraordinary Risk Right Now." *The Atlantic* (2020). https://www.theatlantic.com/.

Cui, Jiashan, and Rachel Hanson. "Homeschooling in the United States: Results from the 2012 and 2016 Parent and Family Involvement Survey (PFI-NHES: 2012 and 2016). Web Tables. NCES 2020–001." National Center for Education Statistics (2019). https://nces.ed.gov/pubs2020/2020001.pdf.

Eggleston, Casey, and Jason Fields. "Census Bureau's Household Pulse Survey Shows Significant Increase in Homeschooling Rates in Fall 2020." US Census Bureau (2021). https://www.census.gov/.

Hermann, Mary A., and Cheryl Neale-McFall. "COVID-19, Academic Mothers, and Opportunities for the Academy: The Pandemic's Toll on Women Faculty Caregivers."

American Association of University Professors Academe 106, no. 4 (2020). https://www.aaup.org/.

Kitchener, Caroline. "Women Academics Seem to be Submitting Fewer Papers During Coronavirus. 'Never Seen Anything Like it,' Says One Editor." *The Lily* 24 (2020). https://www.washingtonpost.com/.

Moodley, Keymanthri, and Amanda Gouws. "How Women in Academia are Feeling the Brunt of COVID-19." *The Conversation* (2020). https://theconversation.com/.

Pettigrew, Rachael N. "An Untenable Workload: COVID-19 and the Disproportionate Impact on Women's Work-Family Demands." *Journal of Family & Consumer Sciences* 113, no. 4 (2021): 8–15. https://doi.org/10.14307/JFCS113.4.8.

Ray, Brian D. "How Many Homeschool Students are There in the United States? Pre-COVID-19 and Post-COVID-19: New Data." *National Home Education Research Institute* (2021). https://www.nheri.org/.

Richards, Akilah. Raising free people: Unschooling as liberation and healing work. PM Press, 2022.

PART III

Time, Tension, and Transition

Bringing into Focus
What's Been Blurred

Rewarding Relation-Based Work

Lee Nickoson and Mary P. Sheridan

In response to the pandemic and social justice crises of 2020, proclamations across higher education's national landscape offered students, faculty, and staff commitments of care. For example, Davidson College's "Amid Coronavirus Fear and Confusion, Compassion and Community" (DeAngelis) and MIT's "Forging Ahead with Care and Compassion: MIT Professors Adapt Advising to Pandemic Context" (Immerman) offer situated attention to the ways in which faculty were heeding the call to lead with care. For many universities, these calls to care and compassion are already part of their commitments, ones they leaned into during this time of crises. For example, Sterling University's "Ideas for Building Community Through Service and Compassion" (Foshee) states, "Compassion and service, values Mother Catherine Spalding and the Sisters of Charity of Nazareth promoted fiercely, are alive on Spalding's campus today. I am confident that our students, faculty, and staff can harness these ideals in the midst of this difficult and often unpredictable pandemic." This common caring discourse prioritized our individual and collective well-being; "compassionate" became central to developing campus cultures and reimagining faculty/staff responsibilities that, in the moment, seemed nothing short of transformative.

Enacting these transformative calls could lead to institutional resets that make higher education more equitable; however, those calls invoke institutional responsibilities as well. For example, in "Campus Life and Care Giving," Rollins College colleagues Amy Armenia, Sharon Carnahan, and Alice Davidson suggest the need to alter policies and practices that would recognize the cost of caring work. Such an imperative, we argue, could lead to transformational change if it addresses both *who* does the work of compassion and *how* this labor is institutionally shared, recognized, and rewarded.

Reflecting on this extended moment of transformative possibilities from the vantage point of 2025, we investigate the unacknowledged, often gendered and racialized, labor needed to foster a community of care. We find the promise of such work enticing, but not without unpacking what community-engaged scholars Karen Rowan and Alexadra Cavallaro call "work before the work," or the slow, preparatory labor that is often skirted in a rush for public outcomes, in their case, calls for community engaged research. For Rowan and Cavallaro, building community means investing in sustained relational labor, such as listening, reflecting, and exposing majoritarian but inequitable understandings and practices so that all voices shape collective action. Like Rowan and Cavallaro, we found that our universities had not engaged in the work before the work. In their rush for public outcomes, universities had called for communities of care but they had done so without sustained institutional attention to the labor needed to backfill our universities' public pronouncements. Where were the acknowledgement, evaluation, and reward structures?

Not surprisingly, the mismatch for solicited but unremunerated work had deleterious consequences. This chapter explores those consequences. Mary Sheridan focuses on faculty and staff perspectives of being called to enact a community of care within institutional structures not fully fit for purpose, and Lee Nickoson explores the perspectives of department chairs and mid-level administrators who are working in slightly different institutional positions. Both start with the lived experiences of people who sought to use the disruptive moment of 2020 to build infrastructures capable of cultivating and sustaining communities of care. While our hopes for deep structural transformation differ, taken together these sections detail the lacunae that hinder institutional change as well as offer concrete actions that can help institutions enact their relation-based educational missions.

Not Thinking and Its Consequences (Mary P.)

Service from minoritized groups is often expected yet unrecognized in institutionally meaningful ways. For example, COVID-19's "great resignation" exposed the untenable situation many female workers faced when required to meet the intensified ongoing structural imbalances in both workplace and family caregiving responsibilities (Donegan; Górska et al.). The racial reckonings of the 2020s highlighted how patently false is the "illusion of inclusion"—a belief by those in power that there are equitable social structures, but a belief challenged by the lived reality of those who engage in additional unrecognized labor to meet universities' anti-racist missions (Heilig et al.; Matthews et al.). This mismatch harms faculty and staff who perform such labor, and in 2021 prompted me to ask—when widespread disruptions expose long standing unrecognized labor of marginalized folks, is there an opportunity to make a change?

I explore that question in an institutional ethnography that investigates if faculty and staff can hold one university accountable to its own stated values, particularly, being a "community of care" (University of Louisville, "Mission"). Because this "Cardinal principle" is central to university branding (University of Louisville, "Core Brand"), framing the university as a community of care is the lead in many outward-facing university press releases and news stories (cf. Cappiello) as well as inward-facing emails and administrative exhortations, perhaps especially during the 2020–2021 COVID pandemic responses and antiracist agendas. In a typical example, the opening paragraph of a 2021 news story about our school's COVID response describes the "all hands-on-deck approach . . . [that] illustrated our 'community of care' Cardinal principle" (Kelso). Similarly, then President Bendapudi of the University of Louisville outlines actions the institution is taking in response to racial unrest, especially the murder of Breonna Taylor in our hometown; she framed the actions as ways the university "fully live[s] out our commitment to being a Community of Care" (University of Louisville News). Despite the omnipresent invocations of care, the labor to enact this value was and continues to be largely un(der) recognized in university structures.

This institutional ethnography explores the consequences of this mismatch, with the hopes of both documenting and ameliorating the effects. Methodologically, my research relies on two rounds of interviews (20 people in the first round; 5 in the second round) and textual analysis of institutional documents focusing on both internal documents (e.g., university, college, and departmental policies) as well as external documents (e.g., press releases and mission statements). Theoretically, this research follows academic and activist Caroline Criado Perez's research on the gender data gap, particularly a frame she calls structural "*not* thinking." Not thinking leads to a bias against marginalized people who are not valued in institutional decision making, which in turn leads to damaging consequences for those not thought about (Criado Perez, xii). For Perez, not thinking is particularly problematic when "an unintended male bias that attempts (often in good faith) to pass itself off as 'gender neutral'" becomes embedded in inequitable institutional structures (Criado Perez, xii–xiii).

Perez's argument aligns with a spate of sociological and higher educational research that examines how institutional policies anchor privilege and disadvantage (Ray et al.; Bird; Guarino and Borden; O'Meara et al.; Pyke; Wood et al.). For Perez, a key step in redressing inequitable institutional practices is to make the problem visible, which in my research might mean that the university president's acknowledgement of/call for relational effort would translate into rewarding that care-based labor. While my research participants were not as optimistic as Perez about how such visibility would redress damaging structural bias, participants shared Perez's finding about two overlapping trends of institutional not thinking—devaluing the labor of minoritized groups and institutional policies–structures that allow this situation to continue.

For those seeking to recognize relational labor, the literature and my research participants offer important lessons about the structural roadblocks erected by higher education's not thinking. These lessons call us to attend to the lived consequences of institutional not thinking for individuals doing the university's caring labor; to how policy and policy implementation become the handmaidens of institutional not thinking structure (cf. Ray); and, to the piecemeal magical thinking that this can lead to; as if good intentions can overcome institutional not thinking. For many, such lessons may seem patently obvious. For others, they may come as a surprise. In either case, documenting and spotlighting problematic practices and their consequences are crucial initial steps in making relational labor both legible and rewarded.

"Not Thinking" Devalues Gendered and Racialized Labor

Universities often manifest ignorance of academic labor by devaluing the labor of certain groups, usually minorities. This type of not thinking happens so often that research participants have a name for one version of it—the "Black tax." This gloss refers to the unpaid work people of color do in caring for those facing constant microaggressions, especially in the wake of intense racial unrest. This includes state-sanctioned violence in the streets as well as far-right White nationalist Proud Boys defacing the campus and targeting racial and gender minority groups on our campus. The effects of the Black tax are felt long beyond the workday. For example, for a female scholar of color who, as full professor, considered it a "joy" and "a privilege" to support international students of color during COVID, this caring included being "on my computer [with students] every morning to night. And that was emotional work that was neither [institutionally] acknowledged nor appreciated" (Muriel). The toll of this labor—how it siphons time and energy away from institutionally and academically rewarded activity; how it physically and emotionally taxes them—was simultaneously called for and not later validated in high-stakes academic reviews.

Similar experiences about women doing a disproportionate amount of "institutional housekeeping" or what Higher Education researchers Cassandra Guarino and Victor Borden describe as "taking care of the academic family" are well documented (690) (Bird, Litt, and Wang; Morley and Walsh; O'Meara et al.; Wood et al.). This labor of caring builds up the environment and morale that keep people connected to a university. Yet, because women, especially those of color, are in the minority in most academic departments—as is typical, female faculty of color make up only 5% of full professors in 2020 at the University of Louisville—they are saddled with disproportionate work as they are routinely tapped for these mentoring and service roles (University of Louisville, "COSW Cohort Report"; Turner). This unvalued labor functions as a drag on women's careers. The takeaway is that the university's publicly stated goal for higher education to be more caring, welcoming, and equitable is undermined by ongoing institutional not thinking about who does the labor to make this happen.

Not Thinking Is Embedded in Policies

Even when universities ostensibly mean to redress inequity, they often reinforce inequity by requiring minoritized groups to do additional, unrewarded labor, such as when institutions choose not to attend (enough) to policy consequences, especially so-called neutral policies.[1] Riece, a queer staff member of color, provides an example of this not thinking when she describes when the university had recently renegotiated contracts for promotional materials, the new companies had no people of color depicted in them. "No one else looked at that order or looked at those [vendor] sites and said, 'Well, why do they have White breasts and not have Brown breasts?' And I get tired of it always being me. Like you all should be paying attention to this too. It's burdening. It always falls on the shoulders of the people who are being oppressed to confront the oppressor." When asked about how to hold people responsible for creating inclusive learning environments, Riece laments the impotency of the existing policies when saying, "Where does that report to compliance go? . . . We kind of have a lot of words but there's nobody holding us accountable." Later in the interview, Riece returned to how people and, ultimately, institutions are not accountable for enforcing their own policies, saying, "Reporting things is like throwing them into a black hole. It's really for yourself . . . It's not that I think it will go anywhere. It's just that it's on record so I can pull it back up and say, 'It's not the first time I've brought this issue up.'"

Despite the stated intention of giving recourse to aggrieved parties, policies are often nonperformatives, public statements that an institution might do something, but they create processes that allow this something *not* to happen (cf. Ahmed, *On Being Included*). In these situations, the power of policies to enforce university values proves impotent because there is not a culture—the thick layers of education, expectation, support, and consequences that might lead to changed actions—to make these policies meaningful. That mismatch calls for examining how workplace policies function instead of how they are imagined to function (Griffin et al.; cf. Patel).

Riece's experiences are similar to that of other research participants in my study who argue that this university does not attend to how policies and policy implementation discriminate against minoritized people. For example, Muriel is a female senior faculty of color and former chair of a university grievance committee who notes, "There's a lot of unfairness in the way that policies are administered. And until we can address that, I don't know that faculty will ever be satisfied about how they are treated . . . [But] I don't hear White men complaining. So clearly there's some [other channels] that they can go through to get what they want." The paucity of workplace complaints by White men, particularly in a predominantly White institution, made Muriel wonder both about who the policies were designed for and about the invisible networks dominant groups have that allow them to circumvent non-performative policies. These invisible networks afford dominant groups access to resources that can undercut equity, since the privileged can address their concerns this way rather than going through laborious institutional practices that can exhaust and silence those attempting to hold universities accountable (Ahmed, *Complaint!*). Those without access to these privileged networks must engage with facially neutral institutional policies, a move that sociologists note often harms minoritized groups (Ray et al.).

Such patterns echo longstanding feminist critiques about how higher education seeks superficial changes toward creating equitable places to work and learn without making the deep, structural changes needed to meet their goals (Harding). This sentiment rang true for Jennifer, a White, senior, cis professor who noted that while her field says that women are welcome to join, that same field was not made for women and was not going to change. Given that it's been over fifty years since Harding's observation and given that many folks have sought to make universities more equitable, the question becomes, why do university personnel not have more to show for their time, money, and effort?

Beyond Good Intentions

Perez echoes philosopher Sandra Harding's answer when she details how people offer piecemeal, good intentions without examining the ways in which entrenched, institutional not thinking anchors what is materially encouraged in that institution. Higher education researchers Griffin, Bennett and York posit several overlapping reasons similar to those of Perez, including mis-implementations that generally begin "with promising practices" but lack a thorough understanding of underlying issues (3); and "piecemeal" implementations that are not consistently infused with accountability that "permeates all layers of an institution" (3). Traces of those underlying reasons can be found in the ways my research participants describe how even good-intentioned institutional policies are enacted in their context.[2]

While participants in my study noted both the university administrators' good intentions and how these are limited by material conditions facing public higher education, participants also decried administrators' choice to solicit ad hoc, unpaid labor instead of acknowledging that the university lacked the material and political capital to enact its values. This problematic issue is overtly explored by Rebecca, a White, queer, female junior faculty member who lists a litany of frustrations emerging from her attempts to implement the university's stated values—from establishing lactation rooms and gender-neutral bathrooms to challenging racial profiling in virtual testing software and in who has to show IDs on campus. Rebecca contextualizes these frustrations by acknowledging that "the problem [is] with how higher education has gone from the greater good to a business . . . [the University] stated these [caring] values but I do feel like the bottom line is still money and dollars." For Rebecca, this mismatch plays out when her unit talks about enacting community engaged or DEI projects—"We have no support for it. We're all so understaffed and it's like, okay, you want me to do this but how can I do this when I have this other job?" While Rebecca is angry at and exhausted by the university's lack of action, she also recognizes that university administrators are deeply limited by how funding works at this state institution (Sheridan). Similarly, Riece points out that even the university's then-president, the first female and first person of color, could not overcome the legislature's opposition to funding anti-racist caring initiatives and the fact they hold the purse strings. This obstacle, another participant states, makes clear the emptiness of university's attempts to implement its caring proclamations.

For my participants, the institutional requests for unpaid labor reflect a lack of reckoning with the underlying costs that this work has on employees. Without material support, administrators offer what are likely meant to be well-intentioned, upbeat, morale-lifting sentiments. These messages often are received as tone-deaf to the lived realities of faculty and staff. For my participants, the dilemma is real, but to frame the solution as institutionally unremunerated "caring" labor that often falls on marginalized groups is disingenuous and damaging.

The consequences of institutional not thinking place study participants in a bind as demonstrated in Riece's case, who found my question of *how* to hold universities accountable to be a question only a person with (White) privilege would ask. They note that those without such privilege have long ago learned that they can't hold the university accountable—"How are we supposed to do that? We don't have any power. You can't hold people accountable with no power . . . It's their Cardinal Principles. It's their Anti- Racist Agenda [but] we don't have any way to hold them accountable." "Frustrated," "exhausted," and "burned out" by what they considered institutional double-speak, Riece disengaged from their attempts to change the institution, and instead cared for their own mental health and supported individual people on their individual projects, an understandable move, but one that limits potential institutional change (Báez and Ore). During our second interview months later, Riece had decided to re-engage. Choosing not to be pushed out as part of the "bl-exit," the recent mass exodus of faculty of color,[3] they were once again pulled to tactically build alliances of recognition and support within and against what they consider problematic institutional care structures. As they note, history has taught that windows for change close quickly. Sherri, a senior Black female faculty member, similarly found the push and pull of caring work to be a central part of "the history of race work" that teaches the importance of using the resources at hand, in this case, the existing statements and policies that *might* provide materials to craft something structurally better. Amid this push and pull, participants who challenge institutional not thinking evince what Ahmed might call "weary hope," one that is present, but is also exhausted and worn out (*Complaint!* 289).

My participants' weary hope includes bearing witness so that these stories can circulate in productive, if unexpected, ways (Ahmed, *Complaint!*, *On*

Being). For example, raising these experiences in spaces where participants do not feel protected or heard (e.g., university commissions, college leadership meetings) can inform willing university members about what faculty and staff face and how they perceive upper administrators' attempts to address these conditions. Such moves can be part of larger efforts toward structural change. The participants who shared their experiences with me labored to expose both the continuation and consequences of institutional not thinking, with the hope that something better might result.

Even with this weary hope, I'm not optimistic about what institutional lessons have been learned from the 2020 crises about rewarding relational, caring labor. In respond to the crises of the 2020s, the drumbeat of denigrating political rhetoric has given rise to a raft of legislative and judicial actions impacting higher education, including the ongoing iterations of the 2022 Stop WOKE Act (Lu and Baumann); the dismantling of DEI programs in higher education and business; and more than 150 educational gag orders by largely Republican-leaning state legislatures (PEN America). Universities' anemic responses provide little, if any systemic, guidance on how to make higher education more hospitable for all people; and the extreme retribution that has become a hallmark of the current political climate makes this trend unlikely to change. In that void, once again some faculty and staff are tasked more than others to build "a community of care" without structural acknowledgement of that labor. Like my participants, I believe both that higher education is in a difficult spot and that upper administrators with good intentions do not have good options available to them (LeoGrande and Bass). I also believe that those with the power to call for relational labor need to align these calls with material acknowledgements of that labor, an idea Lee explores in the next section.

Recognizing and Rewarding Critical
Compassionate Faculty Labor (Lee)

Mary explored in the preceding section the importance of holding institutions accountable to the values they espouse if higher education is to be responsive to the complexities of the world(s) in which students, faculty, and administrators are asked to affect positive change. The participants in Mary's study shed light on the fallout that is a consequence of labor being unacknowledged or ignored by institutional reward structures—we lose invaluable resources and contributions from faculty feeling overwhelmed, exhausted, and excluded from decisions concerning performance expectations and evaluation. In this section, I share how an institution's commitment to care manifested itself in the early days of the pandemic before turning attention to the implications compassion-based faculty efforts have for institutional representations of faculty productivity.

Calling for Care

On March 24, 2020, my campus colleagues and I received an email from our university president announcing what would become the institutional COVID-19 messaging. Colleagues across the country—in fact, across the globe—received similar messages that referenced us being in "unprecedented times" and outlined what would become the triaging efforts involved with supporting the continuance of the university's life as fully and responsively as possible. That same email announced the move to online course delivery after what had been an emergency cancellation of classes for two weeks. Buildings were closed. Faculty would now work from home—teaching, conferencing with students, and meeting colleagues online. That March 24, 2020, email had as its primary focus an announcement of the creation of a new student emergency fund. Faculty were invited to contribute to the fund and support students who were now struggling with basic needs surrounding access in areas such as technology, housing, health care, and food. The university's commitment to supporting students' well-being was clear and reassuring. As the chair of the English Department at the time, I recall reading the email and the many that followed with grave concern for the faculty and staff who were to provide triage support including assistance for adapting to learning online and help figuring out how to navigate unexpected financial, interpersonal, social, and medical/mental health crises. Faculty shared the president's deep concern for students as well as a recognition of the unfamiliar waters in which we were swimming.

Like the sudden email and video statements shared by university administrators around the globe, local messaging from our university administration identified all of us as bound through our institutional commitment to engage one another as a community of care—that care would become the compass for us while navigating a pandemic. Again, similar to many other colleges and universities, the administration had established a formal Community of Care Coalition just a few years prior (2017) with the goal of bringing together various identifiable support resources (e.g., accessibility services, student counseling, Title IX office, and others)—"A Community of Care requires campus-wide responsibility for acting on situations that can have significant impact on individuals and the campus community. As a public university for the public good, Bowling Green State University (BGSU) prioritizes community well-being and belonging to ensure that Falcons do not struggle alone" (BGSU). To be sure, these and other support resources are crucial to any college or university as is a focus on community and community member well-being. With the spread and shutdown, however, we each needed to develop a sense of care in action. COVID presented an unimaginable situation that was already significantly impacting all of us. The question quickly became, then, how do we—faculty and administrators alike—act responsibly, and, I would argue, responsively, while triaging? How do we put into practice an institutional commitment to care for one another and for ourselves? How long would this moment of crisis operations last? And, finally, what would this emergency response—working in and through a moment of crisis for an indeterminate period—mean for faculty work expectation? Evaluation? These questions, although important, seemed less pressing at the moment than navigating the numerous immediate practical concerns revealed through the sudden abandonment of the physical campus and the move to remote work. The imperative of the moment was unique. Each faculty and administrator searched for methods of performing feelings of concern for something that we recognized as important, in other words—*care*.

Much feminist research, teaching, and administration remains grounded in Nell Noddings' ethics of care–caring for actions and practices and about dispositional commitment. Noddings argues that caring-for is most impactful when both or all parties involved engage in a shared investment in caring for the other. COVID challenged existing methods for participating in research, teaching, and service as reciprocal care through the disruption of how we studied, learned, and worked together. How to practice care during periods of uncertainty, detachment, and disconnection? We learned by doing—through the doing. The commitment to care as a shared campus disposition was imbued with a sense of urgency—each faculty member, unit chair, dean, and so on found ourselves members of this care coalition, aware of the need for us to learn together how to practice care as policy and practice, as commitment and, we soon realized, as ad hoc decision makers working within a remote community. In the next paragraphs, and in ways similar to Mary, I offer a few examples of how faculty performed acts of care. I then take up the anecdotes of these examples of compassionate practice to explore the possibilities they offer us in terms of revisiting and rediscovering faculty workload and evaluation structures. By compassionate practice, I mean the work expected of faculty performed intentionally in recognition of suffering and, because of that aware-ness, attempts to alleviate suffering through interpersonal connections with another. The same compassion-based faculty teaching, mentoring, and engage-ment efforts we learned and lived because of the sudden shift to performing our roles and responsibilities remotely and in times of crisis provide evidence that relationship-building and maintenance matter significantly in how we choose to engage our work. As a result of what may be read against existing faculty re-view and reward policies as triage efforts, we have an opportunity to redesign faculty performance evaluation policies as recognitions that include explicit at-tention to care-based labor. As Mary notes, we risk continuing to perform care-based labor as piecemeal efforts—work that is vulnerable to going unnoticed in moments of performance review because the reporting mechanism does not include the categories or measures needed (e.g., mentorship of new faculty, co-curricular professional development initiatives supporting undergraduate and graduate students).

Practicing Care

Compassion-based work, traditionally associated with caregiving (i.e., wom-en's work), was suddenly signaled as the priority for all administrators as we performed our roles across the spring, summer, and fall of 2020, including ways to approach faculty performance expectations. Caregiving work has a storied history as less recognized or ignored in faculty workload assignments and performance reviews. In a 2011 study, for example, Misra, Lunquist, and Templer report that, on average, women spent 4.5 hours more than men per week working on university service activities and 6% more time on mentoring activities than men. Underrepresented faculty, namely women and persons of color, spent more time performing service roles representative of their minority statuses. Relation-based efforts, often identified as "women's work," regularly require the faculty member's investment in emotional labor, social support, and collaboration communication (Misra et al., 310). Unpacking the time and efforts involved with relational teaching, mentoring, and engaging with the profes-sion, perhaps not surprisingly, revealed that women and faculty of color take on much of the heavy lifting in these areas.

I served as department chair during the early days of the pandemic. The work of all administrators quickly came to demand a skill set that none of us possessed—securing the physical spaces of the building; accounting for all stu-dents, staff, and faculty; working with various campus offices to triage student, staff, and faculty technology and access needs; arriving at alternative methods and processes for in-process faculty promotion and review evaluations; reimagining the tenure clock for pre-tenured faculty; assisting graduate students and their mentors as they worked to either reshape field research or, in some cases, imagine a new capstone project feasible as conducted remotely; establishing new, at-first daily, Zoom department meetings for the dissemination and discussion of emerging university response policies and practices. Department chairs collaborated with other administrators to address universal issues, as well as difficulties particular to a given department, group, or individual. We asked, for example, how much can we reasonably ask of a faculty member who now finds themselves homeschooling young children while balancing the turn to online teaching and research? Internally, I worked closely with and relied heavily upon the tremendous talent and efforts of a collection of colleagues—associate chairs, program directors, and faculty across programs and ranks—to identify strategies for supporting emerging and pervasive mental health crises shared across student, staff, and faculty.

"Pivot" soon became a tired term. The emphasis across conversations became increasingly bound to issues of labor. Recognizing the need for relationship-building as central to learning and teaching, Wright-Mair calls on university faculty and administrators to redefine expectations for productivity —"different does not mean less than" for us to lead with "compassion and critical action towards creating equitable educational environments" (n.p.). Upon reflection, I now understand that those early conversations with my faculty colleagues about reimagining labor were connected to developing a heuristic of care. We needed space, time, support, and opportunities to work with each other, to mentor and be mentored, to engage with others to realize new paths forward in our teaching, scholarship and professional commitments. We were triaging care for students, staff, and faculty, extending Zoom conversations, and discontinuing important but non-essential departmental policy and committee work. We were trying. Staff were trying. College and university administrators were trying, and yet. . . .

Fast forward to today, it's now late 2025. Students, staff, faculty, and administrators alike have developed expertise pivoting, adapting, and leading with responsivity. And although the heightened state of the pandemic has passed, new urgencies arise. Social justice crises, political unrest, and a global recession also demand attention, compassion and responsivity. We have an opportunity to apply what we continue to learn from the pandemic, namely, that relationship-based, responsive teaching, mentoring, and professional engagement is foundational for people feeling the care given to them.

Recognizing Care as Labor

Jolie Sheffer and her collaborators attend to the central role robust communication among faculty and administrators has for colleagues' experiences with shared governance. They argue for additional transparency and commitment to developing deep and wide partnerships across faculty groups as paramount to the well-being of a university community (Sheffer et al.). But how do we move beyond complaints around perceptions of buy-in, engagement, and the ways of understanding faculty and administration commonly associate with each other? How to, as they assert, "mak[e] sure more voices are heard?" The authors offer multiple suggestions in support of university administrators and faculty working together to strengthen shared governance and, in so doing, construct a roadmap for how institutional leadership might further translate a commitment to care for faculty, into policy and practice. Among their suggestions—identify whose voices are being heard and those that remain silent, build multiple communication and feedback pathways, distribute power among and across university, college, and unit leadership and membership, and offer suggestions for strengthening shared governance beyond immediate institutional rank and role. "It is only through strong relationships with diverse and multidimensional constituencies that our work has meaning, purpose, and an audience," Sheffer writes. It is certainly true that COVID's fast and vast spread in early 2020 marked an exceptional moment in our collective history. Even exceptional experiences, however, can come to feel mundane, and once-exceptional expectations can become the norm.

Over the last two years, I became increasingly eager to learn how faculty annual performance review processes and expectations would follow the many significant changes to faculty performance. How would evaluation metrics be reimagined given the need for faculty to pivot, particularly as colleagues shared narratives of individual and collective weariness associated with feeling unseen and unheard? Like so many of my colleagues, I came to realize the of-the-moment work that grew from triaged efforts to strategize and facilitate strong relationships across constituencies was labor that existing university policy largely ignored. Hanasono et al. posit the need for us to reimagine institutional policy and systemic understandings of leadership as both public-facing/task-oriented but, just as important, as private-facing, rationally based labor. They call for faculty self-representation of productivity (i.e., "authentic self-assessment"), multiple pathways for meeting expectations as contracted (i.e., "flexibility"), and adaptive frames that would provide attention to relation-based service efforts. Expanding on their call, I would argue that broadening the possible pathways for advancement to include service-based leadership would introduce a mechanism for rewarding commitments to care (i.e., relation-based academic labor traditionally marginalized, assumed and ignored as "women's work").

My experiences as a department administrator leave me understanding the disparities between the lived experiences of faculty labor and how those efforts do (or do not) get identified in annual performance reviews. Our collective experiences with finding alternative pathways for effective, responsive teaching, research, and professional engagement resulting from the pandemic provide a unique opportunity to build structural space for the recognition of relational labor into our annual faculty evaluation and promotion and tenure policies. Authenticity in the context of university policy best serves all stakeholders when it reflects a belief, a trust, in one another as operating under the shared university commitment to care. The crises of 2020 taught us the importance of strong interpersonal relationships as essential to our well-being. Connection matters. We need to feel connected; we need to feel seen, and have our voices heard. Evaluation rubrics need to align with our stated value commitments around care and compassion.

What if our performance assessment policy documents identified leadership through intentional service as a third avenue for professional contribution and advancement? Similar policy reimaginings are likely to be available at the department level. For example, what if we redefined the parameters of professional development funding to include the care costs of faculty with children or those responsible for elder care? An example of this change at my home institution is that departments are charged with arriving at a new faculty workload policy last fall. In part a response to state mandates, the dictate includes recognition of "teaching-related activity" as a marker of faculty labor, with faculty encouraged to develop policy language for how teaching-related activities gets practiced in the unit. I am hopeful that, moving forward, efforts to revise existing policy include conversations around the need for structural mechanisms for rewarding the time and labor involved with performing active membership in a community of care—responsive, reflective compassion as an ongoing institutional priority. This moment, now over four years since we learned of the pandemic, lives as an opportune time for us to build policy that recognizes and gives structural weight to performing care. The time to rebuild faculty workload and reward structures is now or we risk forgetting the powerful lessons each of us has learned about the work required to maintain our membership as practitioners in a community of care.

With a bit of distance from the initial pandemic fright and social justice activism, we bring into focus the lessons learned from universities' enactments of their stated commitments. During the traumatic time of 2020, we read repeated institutional messaging about the value of relational work. As time began to pass, we heard from those on the ground about their experiences of living universities' calls to enact this caring labor. Now, as the intensity of these crises recedes from the university's daily operations, we fear that the opportunity to call institutions to value relational labor has a "best by" date, and that expiration date may be passing. As institutions settle back into the deep grooves of not thinking, we must act if we are to operationalize the lessons learned over these past few years, to align institutional values grounded in care and compassion with policies and practices that materially account for the relational labor so recently heralded.

How we recognize ongoing relational-based labor as central to the profession may differ based on context. Nonetheless, there is a consistent need to develop institutional mechanisms that acknowledge, evaluate, and reward relational labor as teaching, mentoring, service, and at times, institutional leadership, all practices crucial for fostering equitable learning environments and retaining students, faculty, and staff. Holding extended office hours for students in need of support is labor. Reviewing university contracts to ensure equitable learning environments is labor. Challenging and working around racist testing software is labor. Exposing gendered patterns of unrewarded service is labor. Meeting regularly for conversation with a new faculty colleague to build their sense of belonging is labor. Completing classroom observations and workshopping job market materials for graduate students who are soon to be on the market is labor. Convening or participating in ad hoc committees created because of an emergent student, faculty, or campus community need is labor. Maintaining equitable grievance processes and developing alternative evaluation metrics are labor. Unfortunately, these examples of care-based labor too often go unnoticed and/or unrewarded in moments of review and promotion; in fact, people can be penalized because this labor takes time away from what is rewarded in current institutional structures.

Coming out of the crises that lauded the importance of relation-based labor, we are divided on the (potential) progress universities are making towards materially valuing that importance. One of us feels disheartened, as ongoing budget cuts and political meddling have ushered in retrenchments that forward disembodied product-based metrics as evidence of an academic's value. Such moves once again obfuscate the relational labor needed to keep students, faculty, and staff connected to the university's mission. Another of us is cautiously optimistic, seeing the university try out new leadership and pilot programs that *may* leave space for acknowledging the labor of caring. We agree, however, that we must seize the moment still resonant with the exigencies of recent crises if the expected relational labor is to be made transparent in institutional representations of faculty "success." In other words, we urge this recognition to happen now, before the lessons exposed in the recent crises become blurred, not thought about, once again.

Notes

1. As Ibram X. Kendi notes, there are no neutral policies.

2. This is a particular problem at the research site due to administrative turnover. At the time of many interviews, there were interim presidents, provosts, deans along with a host of other high-profile positions.

3. Two years later, Riece left the university.

Bibliography

Ahmed, Sara. *On Being Included: Racism and Diversity in Institutional Life*. Duke University Press, 2012.

Ahmed, Sara. *Complaint!* Duke University Press, 2021.

Armenia, Amy, Sharon Carnahan, and Alice Davidson. "Campus Life and Care Giving." *Inside Higher Education*. September 13, 2020. https://www.insidehighered.com /advice/2020/09/14/some-best-practices-college-employees-care-responsibilities -during-pandemic/.

Báez, Kristina. L., and Ersula Ore. "The Moral Imperative of Race for Rhetorical Studies: On Civility and Walking-in-White in Academe." *Communication and Critical/ Cultural Studies* 15, no. 4 (2018): 331–36.

Bird, Sharon R. "Unsettling Universities' Incongruous, Gendered Bureaucratic Structures: A Case-Study Approach." *Gender, Work and Organization* 18, no. 2 (2011): 202–30. doi: 10.1111/j.1468–0432.2009.00510.x.

Bird, Sharon R., Jacqueline Litt, and Yong Wang. "Creating a Status of Women Report: Institutional Housekeeping as Women's Work." *National Women's Studies Association Journal* 16 (2004): 194–206.

Bowling Green State University. *BGSU Community of Care*. September 2022. www .bgsu.edu/bgsucares.html.

Cappiello, Janet. "RaiseRED Planting Seeds to Grow UofL's Community of Care." *U of L News*, February 11, 2022. https://www.uoflnews.com/.

DeAngelis, Mary Elizabeth. "Amid Coronavirus Fear and Confusion, Compassion and Community," *Davidson College*, March 17, 2020. https://www.davidson.edu/news/.

Donegan, Moira. "Part of the 'Great Resignation' Is Actually Just Mothers Forced to Leave Their Jobs." *The Guardian*, November 19, 2021. www.theguardian.com/.

Foshee, Anna. "Guest Blog: Ideas for Building Community Through Service and Compassion During the COVID-19 Crisis." *Spalding University*, March 25, 2020. https://spalding.edu/.

Górska, Anna Maria, Karolina Kulicka, Zuzanna Staniszewska, Dorota Dobija. "Deepening Inequalities: What Did COVID-19 Reveal About the Gendered Nature of Academic Work?" *Gender, Work, and Organization* 28, no. 4 (July 2021): 1546–61. https://doi.org/10.1111/gwao.12696.

Griffin, Kimberly, Jessica Bennett, and Travis York. 2020. "Leveraging Promising Practices: Improving the Recruitment, Hiring, and Retention of Diverse & Inclusive Faculty." OSF Preprints. June 24. https://doi.org/10.31219/osf.io/dq4rw.

Guarino, Casandra M., and Victor M. H. Borden. "Faculty Service Loads and Gender: Are Women Taking Care of the Academic Family?" *Research in Higher Education* 58 (2017): 672–94. https://doi.org/10.1007/s11162-017-9454-2.

Hanasono, Lisa K., Ellen M. Broido, Margaret M. Yacobucci, Karen V. Root, Susana Peña, Deborah A. O'Neil. "Secret Service: Revealing Gender Biases in the Visibility and Value of Faculty Service." *Journal of Diversity in Higher Education* 12, no. 1 (2019): 85–98.

Harding, Sandra. *Whose Science? Whose Knowledge? Thinking from Women's Lives.* Cornell University Press, 1991.

Heilig, Julian Vasquez, Keffrelyn D. Brown, and Anthony L. Brown. "The Illusion of Inclusion: A Critical Race Theory Textual Analysis of Race and Standards." *Harvard Educational Review* 82, no. 3 (2012): 403–24. https://doi.org/10.17763/haer.82.3.84p8228670j24650.

Immerman, Ellie. "Forging Ahead with Care and Compassion: MIT Professors Adapt Advising to Pandemic Context. *MIT News*, October 20, 2020. https://news.mit.edu/2020/committed-to-caring-1020/.

Jennifer, interview with Mary P. Sheridan, March 18, 2022.

Kelso, Alicia. "UofL Recognizes its COVID-19 Heroes." *U of L News*, July 21, 2021. https://www.uoflnews.com/.

Kendi, Ibram X. *How to Be an Antiracist*. One World, 2019.

LeoGrande, William M., and Scott A Bass. "A MAGA Assault: Higher Ed's Leaders Need to Push Back on Attacks from MAGA Republicans, Not Try to Placate Them." *Inside Higher Education*, April 25, 2024. https://www.insidehighered.com/.

Lu, Adrienne, and Dan Bauman. "2 States Restricted DEI. Here's How Colleges Revised Their Websites." *Chronicle of Higher Education*, August 18, 2023. https://www.chronicle.com/.

Matthews, Kiernan, Todd Benson, Sara Polsky, and Lauren Scungio. "When Perceptions of Diversity Don't Match Progress: New Analysis from the Faculty Job Satisfaction Survey." *Collaborative on Academic Careers in Higher Education.* Harvard University, November 16, 2020. https://coache.gse.harvard.edu/.

Misra, Joyra, Jennifer Hickes Lundquist, and Abby Templer. "Gender, Work Time, and Care Responsibilities Among Faculty. *Sociological Forum* 27 (2012): 300–23. https://doi.org/10.1111/j.1573-7861.2012.01319.

Morley, Louise, and Val Walsh, eds. *Feminist Academics: Creative Agents for Change.* Taylor and Francis, 1995.

Muriel, Interview with Mary P. Sheridan. May 17, 2022.

Noddings, Nell. *Caring: A Relational Approach to Ethics and Moral Education,* 2nd ed. University of California Press, 2013.

O'Meara, KerryAnn, Alexandra Kuvaeva, and Gudrun Nyunt. "Constrained Choices: A View of Campus Service Inequality from Annual Faculty Reports." *Journal of Higher Education* 88, no. 5 (2017): 672–700. https://doi.org/10.1080/00221546.2016.1257312.

Patel, Leigh. "Desiring Diversity and Backlash: White Property Rights in Higher Education" *Urban Review* 47 (2015): 657–75.

PEN America, "Index of Educational Gag Orders." n.d. https://airtable.com/appg59iDuPhlLPPFp/shrtwubfBUo2tuHyO/tblZ4ow5HLBuTK9vs/viw5lFPxKHGkamFok?blocks=hide.

Perez, Caroline Criado. *Invisible Women: Data Bias in a World Designed for Men.* Abrams Press, 2020.

Pyke, Karen. "Service and Gender Inequity Among Faculty." *Political Science & Politics* 44 (2011): 85–87. https://doi.org/10.1017/S1049096510001927.

Ray, Victor, Pamela Herd, and Donald Moynihan. "Racialized Burdens: Applying Racialized Organization Theory to the Administrative State." *Journal of Public Administration Research and Theory* 33, no. 1 (January 2023): 139–52. https://doi.org/10.1093/jopart/muac001.

Rebecca, Interview with Mary P. Sheridan. July 23, 2021.

Riece, Interview with Mary P. Sheridan. June 7, 2022.

Riece, Interview with Mary P. Sheridan. January 18, 2023.

Rowan, Karen, and Alexandra J. Cavallaro. "Toward a Model for Preparatory Community Listening." *Community Literacy Journal* 33 (2018): 23–36.

Sheffer, Jolie A., Lisa K. Hanasono, Charles Kanwischer, et al. "Pieces of the Puzzle: The Importance of Shared Governance." *Liberal Education.* (Winter 2022). www.aacu.org/liberaleducation/articles/pieces-of-the-puzzle.

Sheridan, Mary P. "Out of Time: Using Emergencies to Imagine Alternatives to Higher Education's Chrononormative Possibilities." In *Writing Emergencies*, edited by Kate Pantelides and Holly Hassel, forthcoming.

Sherri, Interview with Mary P. Sheridan. March 14, 2022.

Turner, Caroline Sotello Viernes. "Women of Color in Academe: Living with Multiple Marginality." *Journal of Higher Education* 73 (2002): 74–93. https://doi.org/10.1080/00221546.2002.11777131.

University of Louisville News. "A Statement from President Bendapudi: Diversity and Inclusion, our Cardinal Principle." Accessed June 1, 2020. https://www.uoflnews.com/.

University of Louisville. *COSW Cohort Report.* Accessed October 28, 2022.

University of Louisville. "Core Brand Communication and Messaging Strategy." Accessed September 12, 2024. https://louisville.edu/brand/downloads/communication-guide/.

University of Louisville. "Missions, Vision, Principles." Accessed September 12, 2024. https://louisville.edu/about/mission.

Wood, J. Luke, Adriel A. Hilton, and Carlos Nevarez. "Faculty of Color and White Faculty: An Analysis of Service in Colleges of Education in the Arizona Public University System." *Journal of the Professoriate* 8 (2015): 85–109.

Wright-Mair, Raquel. "A Work of Heart: Practicing Critical Compassionate Pedagogy in the Face of Adversity." *Diverse Issues in Higher Education.* July 17, 2020. https://www.diverseeducation.com/covid-19/article/15107342.

CHAPTER 11

"But He Isn't *Your* Kid"

Stepparenting and Work–Life Balance, COVID-19 Edition

Molly E. MacLachlan

Since accepting my first tenure-track job in 2016, I've worked toward the submission of my tenure and promotion portfolio, due the second Monday of September 2020. New Faculty Orientation in August 2016 focused on the three tenets of tenure and promotion—Teaching, Service, and Research. There was no forgetting what was expected and when, so I accepted role after role to be sure I was doing the work necessary to satisfy each area: committees upon committees, university wide initiatives, system wide initiatives, mentoring, publications, conferences—the works. These tenets drove pre-tenure review processes in 2018, and every professional development workshop offered by the university between and thereafter.

Then, COVID-19 happened.

In March 2020, life as we knew it turned upside down for everyone. Suddenly in my capacity as Co-Director of Composition, I found myself sharing teaching materials to help faculty transition all at once to an online environment for students who hadn't chosen to learn remotely. The chaos and uncertainty required supporting faculty in new ways and calming students' worries about school and fears about the pandemic. But these tasks comprised only one part of my life; chaos and worry were everywhere else too. My partner is a nurse, and his (then) 4-year-old son moved between our house and his mother's while the hospital protocols constantly changed because there was no national standard available. I navigated synchronous/asynchronous learning, received many emails about delays in reviews of articles, taught yoga virtually, and cleaned constantly. We also taught virtual school to his son on our custody days. Work and life were as unbalanced as one could imagine. My looming tenure and promotion portfolio was not on my mind, due in September 2020.

As the chaotic spring 2020 semester closed, the provost sent out an email about pausing tenure clocks because of the pandemic on April 30, 2020, with a deadline of May 20, 2020, to apply. This is not an offer available regularly; it only came about because of the global pandemic. I talked to my department chair about taking that opportunity, and I talked to many other colleagues too. I didn't *want* to delay moving forward because, aside from my pride, there are also financial considerations because "any extra time required to reach tenure lengthens the lower paid period of an academic parent's working years and so threatens her financial welfare" (Allison, 28). Although everyone understood the effects of having a child at home and trying to get a preschooler to do virtual school, most people suggested I not center that as a reason—I was awaiting some acceptances or rejections for a few peer-reviewed articles after all—because, well he isn't *mine.* If I included parenting in my discussions, people encouraged me to leave it at parenting, omitting my role as stepparent. As Jennifer Marson-Reed et al. suggest, "While *some* progress has been achieved at *some* institutions (e.g., paid maternity leave and options for 'pausing the tenure clock'), the traditional and unofficial rules and subsequent academic culture remain far more powerful and potently present," and this is only really applicable to traditional motherhood (19). My institution, arguably, is not a part of the *some* alluded to here. On the surface, I did not fit into the version of mother that might get options like these due to motherhood. Ultimately on May 19, 2020, I did apply to pause my tenure clock because it was what I *needed* to do not what I *wanted* to do—my well-being needed it; I cited delayed acceptances/rejections, mental health, and managing virtual school for a child (no, I did not call him my stepchild in that application). There was no guarantee that an application would be honored; we had to justify the need. My application was narrowly accepted after a conversation with the dean—he had initially denied my request—because I appeared ready for tenure and promotion, but the delay in publication notification emails won him over; the need to support my (step) child did not.

Faculty Life, Family, Failure

Outside of the impacts of COVID-19, "managing the demands of the tenure process along with the practicalities of raising children and managing a home presents a formidable challenge for academic parents. This generalization is especially true for women, who, even in dual career families, still often shoulder most of the day-to-day household work and childcare" (Allison, 26). Many of us just see this situation as our regular day-to-day life. Jennifer Marson-Reed et al. acknowledge that "parenting is a full-time, hands-on job and living out motherhood alongside an academic appointment presents a unique challenge all its own" (16). We are needed fully in both spaces, and often suddenly. Kelly Ward and Lisa Wolf-Wendel remind us that "the general narrative suggests that both faculty life and parenthood are all consuming and irreconcilable, and that only a fool would attempt to balance a tenure-track academic career with the desire for children and a family" (1). In other words, we are already set up to fail because we are needed too much in both of our spaces to be successful at both—the likelihood of failure looms. These challenges also impact those of us who are stepparents because, when our child is with us, we cannot be absent. Even though we were in a global crisis, applying to pause my tenure clock felt like a failure. I've felt this sense of failure before—when I committed to the 5-year-plan of completion for my PhD instead of the 4-year-plan.

None of these delays *actually* represent failure; I am not a failure. Needing time and a pause button isn't a sign of failure. Delaying career advancement isn't a sign of failure. But, in many ways, the culture of academia tells us that getting off the prescribed track is failing. Intersections of professional advancement (and delayed advancement), gendered work-life expectations and the shades of grey of motherhood aren't new junctures for junior faculty women; however, the pandemic has intensified the need to explore and understand these intersections through a feminist lens so that we can push back against the problematic, patriarchal structures to arrive at a more equitable "new normal." Our careers don't have to take precedence over lives. As Loren Marquez reminded us a decade ago, "when we tell and write our stories, we are creating an alternate rhetorical history of women professionals in our field, and by extension, we complicate and deconstruct the often-patriarchal construction of professionalization" (84). Therefore, my experience can contribute to how we frame motherhood as visible labor that works in tandem with our academic careers instead of in conflict with them. My entry point into conversations of motherhood is through the role of stepmother, which is a relatively unexplored position in our field, so interrogating stereotypes of motherhood matters here too. For example, I stepped into a role that is viewed as evil in so many instances (I am no Lady Tremaine from *Cinderella*) or, even worse, not "actually a mom" (Sanner and Coleman, 1470). Motherhood is complex, particularly when put into conversation with careers. However, the global pandemic has thrown work/life balance into chaos, so the exigence of our moment gives us the opportunity to redefine and improve gendered work/life expectations, so they are (more) sustainable and equitable in a post-pandemic economy.

Most of us didn't plan upon becoming a stepparent "when we grew up." It is, however, a very conscious choice that is made early in a relationship with a person who has a child; I was ready(?) to be a stepmom. Becoming a stepmom doesn't wait for official marriages or preparation: it started a random Wednesday afternoon with pizza and goldfish crackers when I met his red-headed 2.5-year-old, two months into our relationship. One of the major complexities of being a stepmom is navigating how much voice is too much voice, when my voice matters in decisions, and what is worth a battle between households. The dynamics of being a stepmom means there is *technically* a co-parenting unit of four (in my case) that makes decisions, negotiates differences, and respects the way two entirely separate households share one very important member. I had to decide what I wanted to be called (Molly and Mommy sure sound alike). I had to navigate how to honor his mother without dismissing myself. I had to remember that building my relationship with him was as important as supporting his relationship with his dad. Every parenting decision I make does not just affect my household because it reverberates through him to his other home. Luckily one of my closest friends is also a stepmom, so I wasn't alone in figuring it out, much like a first-time mother relying upon her own maternal figures. Early on, I was told "you wouldn't understand since you're not actually a mom," from my own family. That has improved over time, thankfully, as my family learned with me about stepparenting; everything is underscored by custody schedules.

Faculty and Gendered Expectations

Unsurprisingly, "the fallout from the patriarchal structure of the tenure track and the notion that one must first achieve success along the timeline most beneficial to men—often at the expense of women's ideal reproductive years—is manifested in a very real fear and anxiety" (Marquez, 79). Many decisions I have made regarding my life outside of the academy have been in response to this fear and anxiety: I have not had a child, although I am a stepmother, and if we do decide to have another child, it will be after tenure. This structure does not support motherhood of any kind. Revisiting this structure and integrating *flexibility,* perhaps varied timelines that make room for pause, is one way we could work toward more equitable gendered work/life expectations that include mothers instead of excluding them.

As many of us experienced while moving through the ranks of academia, junior faculty, particularly women, take on labor (visible and invisible) at a much higher rate than male counterparts because we are told it will help us get tenure and saying no rarely feels like an option. We should say "no" more often. Elizabeth Kleinfeld argues for saying no in her blog "Privilege and Saying No," but acknowledges the role of privilege, recalling her own choices prior to tenure. She remembers that those "inviting" her to service would have a say in her tenure and promotion so she feared they would vote against her, and she believed these people had her best interest at heart for success. As Kleinfeld points out, saying no just didn't seem like a viable option. Taking on extra committee work, administrative positions, mentoring, and even agreeing to teach overloads do two things: 1) they get in the way of our path to tenure because they take attention away from researching, writing, and publishing, and 2) they pull us away from life outside of our offices and classrooms. These roles aren't inherently problematic; in fact, they are valuable, but they make work/life balance impossible, especially when we are not just responsible for ourselves. Personally, I have had many female students come to me for mentorship because they feel like they have no agency over their education due to family expectations of women, being mothers themselves, or being unsure of how to navigate academia. Perhaps these students seek me out because "having a [child] makes gender saliant and often causes a woman to be viewed as not just a professor, but a female professor with a child" (Ward & Wolf-Wendel, 8). I'm doing it, and so can they. Lidia Martinez and Luisa Ortiz establish that "female academics are the ones who have a greater workload of teaching and mentoring, as male researchers consider these activities to be unproductive or time consuming" (163). They are time consuming, but they aren't unproductive; however, they don't always result in scholarship. Similarly, Eileen Schell states, "the work of the university, like the work of most institutions, is made possible by women's 'support work'" (406). In other words, the university relies upon my support work as a junior tenure-track female academic but doesn't value it in tenure and promotion decisions.

The pandemic challenged me to reassess how I work toward work/life balance, especially when work and life were sequestered into the same space. Spatially compartmentalizing work and life was no longer an option, so I had to find balance within my tandem experiences. Suddenly, I was "available" to students 24/7, and in many ways, it was expected so that students felt supported through this chaotic time. Often, I'd ask, but what about faculty? How is the university supporting us? I've yet to hear these answers. This work of availability and support of students is often invisible, but it is mental and emotional work that takes a toll on us, the whole person—mind and body. We are expected to sacrifice our own mental and physical well-being in the name of care of students and the university. This scenario is not sustainable or equitable.

The pandemic highlighted just how much sacrificing we are doing in the name of support; although support is expected of all faculty, it often falls more heavily upon women. Gendered expectations also suggest that moms are responsible for the uptake of figuring out virtual school with children who are suddenly at home all the time while we are also trying to teach, research, write, and do service. In chapter six of this book, Ashley Holmes unpacks this experience; she outlines the lived experience of working from home with virtual learning, speaking to how it was "nearly impossible to separate home and work, mother and professor" (see p. 97, this collection). Often working hours were after bedtime, but synchronous class time was coupled with virtual school, explaining directions to a child who is in the process of learning how to read, and reminding him to pay attention—all while simultaneously teaching via zoom. This experience isn't unique, and my partner and I were able to approach much of this as a team, so it didn't fall completely on me. But, as you may know, a four-year-old is loud, so distractions were at an all-time high. Holmes was right, contrary to schools' perceptions—he did need a lot of help. One might say, but he isn't your responsibility; he isn't your kid; you're *just* a stepmom. While it is true that I didn't birth him, it is false that he isn't mine; stepparenting begins upon entering a relationship with someone with children, a conscious choice I made: he *is* mine. Mothering and motherhood are often reduced to free labor and justified by the patriarchal structures "as a selfless expression of love" (Martinez and Ortiz 163). An expression of love makes the work of motherhood invisible, or at least easy to devalue in professional settings. This situation is only more complicated by the position of stepmother because many "descriptions serve to reproduce dominant ideological systems and serve to reinforce the secondary status of stepmothers" (Renegar and Cole 516). With this line of thinking, being a stepmother is inferior and highlights why I was advised not to mention it in my tenure clock pause application or why someone might say you're just his stepmom—as if that precludes me from the work and love of motherhood.

Success on Both Fronts

I compiled, drafted, polished and submitted my Tenure and Promotion portfolio in September 2021 in the midst of the largest spike of COVID-19 post vaccination (not the calmer atmosphere I had hoped for when I chose to pause), and in February 2022, I was awarded tenure and promotion. *Success!* Actually, it was pretty anticlimactic like many milestones in academia. Arguably, we are still learning what it means to be post-pandemic; my university resumed "business as usual" well before we were post anything. Unfortunately, I am not sure we have learned as much from the pandemic as we had hoped. Flexibility in professional advancement and teaching modalities seems to have waned instead of increased, and we are all struggling—students and faculty alike. We are witnessing (what feels like) colleagues leaving in mass, huge enrollment drops, massive budget cuts, and entire programs disappearing throughout our university systems; we are newly overburdened with additional committee work and increased course caps as we lose colleagues, experiencing hiring freezes, and supporting students who need so much more than we can give. *Pauses are no longer offered for Tenure and Promotion.* There is no clear room for life and academia to coexist.

As a stepparent, I am also doing more: volunteering regularly in his classroom (they call me Dr. M), making sure we have the outfits for dress up days (there are *many*), supporting him while he does homework and reads—even when he doesn't want to do it, helping at school events, and reminding everyone that I am his stepmom, not his mom, out of respect for his mother. First grade is a lot. While I love my career and my students, the pandemic reinforced that work does not surpass life in value. I may not always make time for a meeting scheduled after working hours, but I will always find the time to make sure he has a dalmatian outfit for the one hundred first day of school. I say *no* to extras at work, but I also have the security of tenure, as little as it provides. If we cannot see systemic change that implements needed flexibility, I hope that we, at least, can choose ourselves instead of overburdening our schedules. The reality is our institutions will never choose us, so we have to make that decision with all the precarity it brings.

Even in the best of times (and we can all agree a global pandemic is not that), motherhood is complicated and messy, which is often why we are just supposed to act like that doesn't exist while working. But what happens when it all plays out on screen together? We can no longer ignore the ways our professional lives intersect with our personal lives nor is the goal to draw hard boundaries between them. We cannot continue making the labor of motherhood invisible within the academy nor can we privilege one kind of motherhood over another. COVID-19 has only intensified how traditionally viewed female tasks impact productivity for mothers because "female faculty members are still expected to maintain the same levels of productivity required by their job, thereby putting them in a precarious situation" while also caregiving, maintaining households, homeschooling, and countless other tasks (Martinez and Ortiz, 154).

Normalizing and not penalizing the pause button would support mothers in academia. Stories like mine speak to the truth that "academic women with children can do more than simply survive the rigors of the tenure track—they can find satisfaction and success in all of their many roles" (Ward and Wolf-Wendel, 1). Paths toward professional advancement, in my case tenure and promotion, currently only support patriarchal notions of linear progression, one version of success. These paths situate motherhood as an obstacle whereas fatherhood is not—how many of us have heard: babies after tenure? Schell reminds us that "this observation is hardly original; socialist feminists have long pointed out how women's domestic labor enables men's productive labor" (406). The only reason I was permitted to pause my tenure clock "without penalty" is the global pandemic. I am not advocating this option solely for mothers; instead, it would support all faculty. I became a mother in a non-traditional way, but the system doesn't have allowances for that. So, yes. I paused my tenure clock and delayed my career advancement so I could embody all my roles—stepmom, teacher, scholar, mentor, and administrator. But hitting pause should be an option outside of a global pandemic—it creates the possibility for sustainability and equity, thus shifting motherhood away from the position of obstacle to professional advancement. Pausing is just one way to support all forms of mothers, fathers, scholars, and teachers. As we continue to establish our "post-pandemic" work-world, it is important *not* to return to outdated structures; instead, centering flexibility in professional advancement and teaching modalities provides a more sustainable and equitable professional landscape in academia.

Bibliography

Allison, Juliann. "Composing a Life in Twenty-First Century Academe: Reflections on a Mother's Challenge." *NWSA Journal* 19, no. 3 (2007): 23–46.

Kleinfeld, Elizabeth. Review of *Privilege and Saying No.* June 1, 2020. https://elizabeth kleinfeld.com/2020/06/01/privilege-and-saying-no/.

Marquez, Loren. "Narrating our Lives: Retelling Mothering and Professional Work in Composition Studies." *Composition Studies* 39, no. 1 (2011): 73–85.

Marson-Reed, Jennifer J., Olivia M. McLaughlin, Jacquelynn Doyon-Martin, Angela M. Moe, Jaclyn M. Cwick, and Adrian Copeland. "It's as Hard as It Looks: Motherhood and Academia." *Sociological Imagination* 58, no 1 (2022): 16–34.

Martinez, Lidia, and Lucia Ortiz. Review of *Motherhood and Academia in Mexican Universities: Juggling Our Way through COVID-19.* In *Mothers, Mothering, and COVID-19,* edited by Andrea O'Reilly and Fiona Green, 153–67. Demeter Press, 2021.

Renegar, Valerie R., and Kirsti K. Cole. "'Evil Is Part of the Territory': Inventing the Stepmother in Self-Help Books." *Women's Studies in Communication* 42, no. 4 (2019): 511–33. https://doi.org/10.1080/07491409.2019.1660745.

Sanner, Caroline, and Marilyn Coleman. "(Re)Constructing Family Images: Stepmotherhood before Biological Motherhood." *Journal of Marriage and Family* 79, no. 5 (2017): 1462–77. https://doi.org/10.1111/jomf.12428.

Schell, Eileen. 2002. "(Un)motherhood: Reigning Rhetorics of Mothering Inside and Outside of Academe." *JAC* 22, no. 2 (2002): 404–13.

Ward, Kelly, and Lisa Wolf-Wendel. "Motherhood and an Academic Career: A Negotiable Road." *Academic Motherhood: How Faculty Manage Work and Family.* Rutgers University Press, 2012, 1–12.

Pandemic Writing in Crip Time

Tense Dispatches from Mid-Rank

Shannon Walters

In late 2019, I found in my campus mailbox a ten-year service gift from my university, a timepiece. I had to smile—I'd missed the deadline to choose my own gift so received the default one, a small but heavy silver-toned clock that looked like it belonged on an office desk rather than a mantel at home. The clock's face, a circle of roman numerals inside a rectangular box, was hard to see from more than a few feet away, but brought it home I did, and put it on my mantel, because the clock was stopped anyway, and I was going to be home for the next academic year, during my long-awaited first post-tenure sabbatical.

At first, I tried to fix the clock myself. Then, partly on a lark, I emailed human resources, asking if any instructions came with the clock. The irony of a broken clock wasn't lost on me. I had spent most of the last ten years thinking about time—measuring it, treasuring it, stretching it, losing it. Like many cisgender academic women privileged enough to secure a tenure-track job, my experience being on the "tenure clock" aligned with my "biological clock." I got pregnant right after finishing my first book, already at an "advanced maternal age" and just prior to going up for tenure. Nine months later, my eleven-day old daughter in one arm, I bent down carefully to retrieve a package from the mail carrier—my book in print. Eight months later, my daughter swatted at my tenure letter while I opened it with one hand, the other arm holding her.

When I had my second daughter two and a half years later, I was just finishing a stint as a writing program director, during which I had little time for research. Less than a year later, I was serving as interim graduate director. During the years of administration and early days of parenting, I had eagerly looked forward to the sabbatical as dedicated time to delve into my second book. Indeed, I had banked on this time, feeling secure that I could regain some of the intense time spent both parenting and administrating immediately post-tenure. I had expected administrative obligations, graduate student mentoring and increased service work to meet me at the middle of my career, challenging me to create new ways to become more efficient with my research time, especially as I parented. I did not expect a pandemic to ask this of me as well.

Although I was in the extremely privileged position to take a sabbatical, it was a balancing act. To take the full year, I would receive only a portion of my salary. To make the time productive, I enrolled both of my young children in full time daycare. So, in the middle of March 2020, when daycare abruptly shut down to halt the spread of COVID-19, I found myself ill-prepared for what lay ahead. I was paying for childcare I wasn't receiving, earning only a percentage of my salary, and losing sabbatical time that I had waited six years to acquire and would not acquire for another six years. I had been making good progress on my manuscript, in a rhythm of research and writing that felt productive and even luxurious. I finally had the mental space to imagine a large project again. Then, in the span of twenty-four hours, I went from a working mother with full-time childcare engrossed in research to learning how to parent in a pandemic and watching my sabbatical time dwindle.

At first, I thought I could recapture the lost time. I got up before my kids, I worked after they went to bed, and all weekend. Quickly the pressures of the pandemic made this pace unsustainable. Some days I spent hours just hunting down available online grocery delivery slots while trying to parent—cajole for naps, potty train, prepare snacks, clean messes, and entertain for hours on end with nowhere to go. The deep and "slow" time that a sabbatical was supposed to provide—open for tackling large questions and swaths of research—was completely obliterated in these early pandemic months, and I quickly learned that a new perspective was necessary (Berg and Seeber).

To try to reorient my attitude toward time in the pandemic, I turned to the concept of crip time, which also featured prominently in my research project. Crip time, an alternative to quantitative time, is rooted in the experiential knowledge of disabled bodies and minds moving through time and space differently and the strategies developed to resist normative time. My project, occurring at the intersection of disability studies and rhetorical studies, sought to use the concept of the paranormal to shift ways of approaching the binary categories of normal and abnormal. Using etymological and definitional underpinnings of the prefix "para-" as "beyond," I sought to reframe critiques of the norm by going *beyond* normal through the paranormal rather than "away" from normal, as implied by "abnormal." Crip time facilitates this movement, warping time and space. Alison Kafer writes that "rather than bend disabled bodies and minds to meet the clock, crip time bends the clock to meet disabled bodies and minds" (27). Ellen Samuels, describing various approaches to crip time, states: "Disability and illness have the power to extract us from linear, progressive time with its normative life stages and cast us into a wormhole of backward and forward acceleration, jerky stops and starts, tedious intervals and abrupt endings" ("Six Ways").

In ways such as these, crip time can be understood to resemble what many people—disabled and nondisabled—came to experience in pandemic time. Undoubtedly, disabled people experience crip time more intensely, creatively, and precariously than nondisabled people (Piepzna-Samarasinha). For almost everyone, however, the passage of time during the early stages of the COVID-19 pandemic was frequently described as warped, repetitive, flowing differently or just plain stopped. Pandemic time also made the categories of disabled and nondisabled more porous, as people became ill (acutely or long-term) or more aware of their vulnerability and interdependence. As the rhythms of daily and working life changed, people lost track of time, felt it was never ending or simply didn't matter anymore. Bodies and minds accustomed to a fairly linear passage of time suddenly attempted to accommodate themselves to radically different experiences of time and space.

While the concept of crip time helped me reorient my approach to time, there were hard limits and fraught tensions. I could not simply apply crip time to pandemic time. Here is where my research project and real life collided—in the paradoxes of pandemic time there was no way to be also *beyond* time. No amount of conceptual apparatus could create time or recover the lost time of my sabbatical. Similarly, when I returned to teaching, readily importing concepts of universal design for learning (UDL) into my classes, no amount of accessible teaching was enough for some students struggling with pandemic stress, who simply disappeared. However, the tensions that crip time threw into relief during the pandemic are helpful to understand from the unique context of the mid-rank academic, in the areas of research, teaching, administration and service. These tensions identify specific problems as well as potential opportunities.

By definition, the concept of tension or the state of being "stretched tight" relates to crip time and pandemic time. As Samuels explains, crip time is a complex concept, with tension built in, as it involves contradictions, including fits and starts, jerky transitions and abruptness. This is the physicality of tension, or when a force is applied to something to stretch it. Tension, in colloquial terms, can also connote mental and emotional strain. As pandemic time wore on, its elements of crip time acquired more emotional and physical tension. Nowhere did this resonate for me as an academic parent more than in my belated learning of the *New York Times'* "Primal Scream Line," a phone line set up "where the floor is yours to yell, laugh, cry or vent, for a solid minute," part of a series leading the paper to make visible the obvious fact that America's working mothers were "in crisis" (Grose). A "solid minute"—finally, a discrete sense of time in which to do anything. Had I known of this option while it was in operation, I could have made great use of it. It may have spared me and my family my own particularly terrifying primal scream, which happened on a weekend in April as I finally sat down in my home office, door locked, on a deadline, to complete a grant application for which I would certainly be rejected, only to hear "Mommmmmmmmm?" for the millionth time that day. "What?!" I roared back so loudly that I strained my vocal cords.

The form of tension most identifiable to me as an academic mother working during the pandemic is the feeling of being stuck or squeezed, feeling the pressure from two opposing forces. I was intrigued by affect theorist Ann Cvetkovich's descriptions of being "stuck" and her identification of depression as a "public feeling," which resonated broadly with the cultural experience of pandemic burnout and specifically with the academic experience of feeling unable to write in pandemic times, for a variety of reasons (21). Similar to the effects felt by the "sandwich generation," the group of people in their forties and over caught between caring for their own children and their ageing parents, I felt a form of academic squeezing both personally and professionally at mid-rank (Parker and Patten). For example, I could not ask my parents, who had preexisting conditions that necessitated trips to medical facilities, to help with childcare during my working hours because I wanted to protect both my kids and my parents. Also, like many parents fumbling through the pandemic, I felt continually pulled between my kids and my job. Whether I was on sabbatical and juggling my research with childcare in the early days of the pandemic or teaching online or in-person during the mid-to-late days of the pandemic, with my kids home during intermittent school closures, the feeling of being stretched too thin was ever-present.

I felt this tension most acutely while on sabbatical because of my position at mid-rank. The pandemic intensified obstacles commonly experienced at the mid-rank level, particularly in the area of research. Having been in the classroom for almost twenty years and consistently practicing concepts such as UDL, I moved my teaching online fairly easily. Losing time to my sabbatical was significantly more detrimental for me at the mid-rank stage because it coincided with and intensified all the other time-intensive transitions that characterize that time period. For example, burnout after tenure is a common experience among tenure-track faculty that affects performance at mid-rank. Many faculty use their first post-tenure sabbatical not only to recover from burnout but also to rediscover the joy of learning and researching that may have originally led them to their profession. I had been treasuring my sabbatical in part because it was my first time feeling "off the clock," open to pursue whatever academic inquiry I wanted, not simply the ones that would help me earn tenure. Being subject to "the clock" again so quickly after my shortened sabbatical, while also attempting to navigate a pandemic, was draining. The workload review at my university, for example, during the pandemic asked us to report our number of works published, students taught, dissertations chaired and committees served, just as in any other year.

Crip time, including the tensions it reveals, also throws into relief the challenging experiences of teaching in pandemic time. I felt pulled between students and administration, particularly with graduate students, who often needed more time in their various stages, and with a range of undergraduates. Stressed by a pandemic and a summer of social unrest, students at every level experienced crip time and teaching necessarily took on more intensity. And so, I felt even more tension between my teaching and my research, with teaching and mentoring, however still enjoyable for me, taking more time than usual. The first outside childcare I benefitted from, four months into the pandemic, was spent completing a comprehensive online teaching certification, required if one wished to teach online. In general, faculty at a range of institutions invested considerable time into negotiating, often in piecemeal ways, to secure online teaching or flexible scheduling not only to protect themselves before vaccination but also to protect their young children not yet eligible. To undertake this in a context of a national childcare shortage was daunting. Scholars and activists in disability studies were often called on to share their strategies for navigating the challenges that the pandemic posed and noted that accommodations they had sought and been denied for years, such as teaching online, were suddenly common (Accessible Campus Action Alliance). Disabled people felt disappointed that it took a pandemic to make access a key conversation in academia and for accommodations to be understood as benefitting broader populations, such as academic parents.

Also, I watched as my colleagues who were senior to me retire, sometimes early, in record numbers, leaving those of us at mid-rank with more graduate students to mentor and administrative loads to bear, while my junior colleagues rightfully received an extra year on the tenure clock. While I certainly did not begrudge either of these sets of colleagues, it struck me as posing unique problems for faculty cohorts in the middle, who would arguably spend even more time feeling pressure from both sides, mentoring junior colleagues and filling the gaps in teaching, advising and mentoring from retiring colleagues. With similar trends happening more broadly across universities—with junior faculty taking longer and senior faculty retiring earlier—shifts such as these may have wide-ranging effects on faculty at mid-rank across disciplines, producing vacuums of leadership or, more optimistically, opportunities for different leadership.

Approximately 4,637,000 payroll jobs have been lost by women in the United States since the pandemic began, many of these because of issues with childcare. At my most difficult moments, I thought to myself, "I'll just quit my job," a fantasy of the highest degree because this wasn't possible—my income and benefits were a key part of my family's livelihood. Part of my fantasy of quitting, however, is rooted in privilege; I could dream of quitting because it was unlikely that I would lose my job. This fantasy underscores just how difficult navigating the pandemic is for the majority of people with less secure jobs, inside and outside of academia. I did not actually want to quit my job, but the illusion that I might was liberating, if only for a moment, because at least it released the tense feeling of being stuck.

The next time I ventured onto my eerily empty campus, during the summer of 2020 when infection rates were briefly low, I found another timepiece like the one from the year before in my mailbox. Someone had read my email and apparently sent another. This new clock didn't work either, but almost an entire year had gone by at this point, and so I wondered, how would I know if it ever had? By this time, I was a few months pregnant with my third child, and time began to acquire more familiar contours: the exhausting first trimester, the exhilarating first kicks, my growing impatience toward the end of term. This rhythm was familiar to me and comforting, a way to mark pandemic time differently. Still, I was concerned, and spent free moments searching far and wide for a vaccine, adding my name to dozens of waitlists and contact forms.

Then, eleven days before I went into spontaneous labor, I was fortunate to secure a time slot for the COVID-19 vaccine, even before clinical trials began on pregnant people, and long before most of the general public was vaccinated. A photojournalist interviewed me and the other women in line, and we discussed the mix of emotions surrounding the occasion. My words didn't make it into the story, but my photographs did, and the images began to take on a life of their own. My mom saw me while watching cable news over breakfast, I discovered myself in a newspaper from India, and I tracked myself and other women I spoke with in articles dispensing basic information about COVID-19 and pregnancy (Smalls-Mantey; Awasthi; Hopkins). In one photo, I am pictured receiving the shot, eyes closed, double masked, belly round with what will be a nine-plus pound baby taking up the middle and largest part of the frame. My left arm is exposed, sleeve up, elbow sharp, and there is a watch prominently displayed on my wrist. In the moment, I am bracing myself, but I am also relieved, although not quite sure how this will play out. I have been in a race against time to secure a vaccine slot, knowing that once I deliver, I will not be eligible. My biggest fear is giving COVID to my newborn or getting it myself and not being able to take care of her; I worry less about the effects on the pregnancy. I sign up for two research studies that will follow me and the baby, hopeful to contribute to the data that will make this decision easier for the next person.

Looking back, after clinical trials show safety and efficacy, after the kids are back in school, after masks become an afterthought, I marvel at how post-pandemic time is a lot like post-partum time. There is an emphasis on "getting back" in both cases: getting back to work, getting back on track, getting back your body, getting back to normal. Everyone knows that things change, but we collectively wish to get it back, whatever "it" is. If we don't, there is the feeling that the world is moving on without you. Society leaves new mothers behind similarly to how it leaves people living with long-term COVID, disabled people and chronically ill people behind; there is the implication that one cannot keep up.

The clock from my ten-year service anniversary still sits on my mantel at home. It still doesn't work. The other clock, its double, sits in my office somewhere, still in its box. I am tempted to think optimistically of the old adage that a broken clock is still right twice a day. But it's not quite right in this case; the clock was never right to begin with. I've tried to fix the clock, a few different ways, but it arrived broken. What remains to be seen is how it's worth fixing.

Bibliography

Accessible Campus Action Alliance. "Beyond 'High-Risk': Update for 2021," August 25, 2021, https://bit.ly/accesscampusalliance.

Awasthi, Prashasti. "COVID-19 Risk Could Be 70% Higher in Pregnant Women: Study." *Hindu Businessline,* February 17, 2021, https://www.thehindubusinessline.com/.

Berg, Maggie, and Barbara K. Seeber. *The Slow Professor.* University of Toronto Press, 2016.

Cvetkovich, Ann. *Depression: A Public Feeling.* Duke University Press, 2012.

Grose, Jessica. "This is a Primal Scream." *New York Times,* February 4, 2021, https://www.nytimes.com/.

Hopkins, Jared, S. "Pfizer Study of COVID-19 Vaccine in Pregnant Women Delayed by Slow Enrollment." *Wall Street Journal,* September 22, 2021, https://www.wsj.com/.

Kafer, Alison. *Feminist, Queer, Crip.* University of Indiana Press, 2013.

Parker, Kim, and Eileen Patten. "The Sandwich Generation." *Pew Research Center,* January 30, 2013, https://www.pewresearch.org/.

Piepzna-Samarasinha, Leah Lakshmi. "How Disabled Mutual Aid Is Different Than Abled Mutual Aid." *Disability Visibility Project,* February 28, 2022, https://disabilityvisibilityproject.com/.

Samuels, Ellen. "Six Ways of Looking at Crip Time." *Disabiliooty Studies Quarterly* 37, no. 3 (2017). https://dsq-sds.org/article/view/5824/4684.'

Smalls-Mantey, Adjoa. "Here's What Pregnant Women Should Know About the J&J COVID-19 Vaccine." *ABCNews,* March 12, 2021, https://abcnews.go.com/Health/story?id=76327748.

CHAPTER 13

Challenging Ageism Through Intergenerational Initiatives

Michael Harker

Bringing old age to the forefront of the discussion causes difficulties
for a general theory of how we should live, or how we should
think about our values, interests, selfhood.
—Helen Small, *The Long Life*

Helen Small's sentiment in *The Long Life* resonates deeply with the experiences I've navigated in both personal and professional spaces. As a teacher-researcher in literacy studies, my work in aging studies has led me to explore how entrenched attitudes about aging emerge in scholarly and everyday settings, sometimes with profound implications for how we conceptualize how we work, who we are, what we value, and what we see as our purpose. In this chapter, I'm hoping to connect the personal with the scholarly. As I reflect on the difficult labor and isolating moments of managing a community during a global health crisis, I also consider how universities might labor more meaningfully to address ageism. It is by complicating and questioning commonsensical beliefs that shape our perceptions of aging that we foster the complexity and importance of aging in our current moment.

All condominium association presidents quickly learn that the job is a thankless one and that, at some point, you will undoubtedly experience the worst of some neighbors. The position comes with many obstacles and, at times, even unkindness from those the association is meant to represent. For me, one such incident involved a resident who, in response to my polite request to pick up after his pet, felt it best to leave a bag of dog feces tied to my doorknob. Another example led to my tires being deflated under curious circumstances after I reminded a guest about the reserved parking spot for those with disabilities. Neighbors even threatened me with a lawsuit for calling the police to report an active domestic violence case. Despite all of these frustrating moments, my background as an eager-to-serve preacher's son taught me to find fulfillment in serving my community under the most difficult circumstances and to celebrate those moments when I could see first-hand goals becoming reality.

Early in 2020, I was at the end of a three-year term as association president. By then, we had overcome budgetary constraints and completed a significant capital project. I could see the light at the end of the tunnel and was looking forward to rotating off the board to fulfill the far less demanding roles of resident and neighbor. At this time, I felt good about the impact the board had made in our community, but none of our accomplishments or lessons could have prepared us for the arrival of the COVID-19 pandemic and the challenges it would bring.

Pool Closed Until Further Notice

The first wave of the pandemic brought concerns and complaints from some residents about how the association handled the situation. In emails to me, my neighbors wondered if we were doing enough to sterilize our common areas. On our neighborhood messaging board, folks speculated about the communicability of the virus and the impact it might have on city services. Perhaps an indication of how well-intentioned these discussions were, we explored how our community should respond to acts of vandalism targeting Asian Americans. Many of these issues raised by my neighbors reflected those playing out in the media. Looking back, what happened in our 59-unit complex was symptomatic of the contentiousness, anxiousness, and speculation that generally characterized the United State's overall response. But the concern that became the most contentious and divisive issue in our community was one I could have never anticipated: "Why can't we open our pool?"

We had decided to keep the pool closed on the advisement of our association's attorneys. In the absence of decisive decision making, clarity of thought, or effective leadership from city management and public health organizations, we made a decision that we thought was in the interest of the safety and well-being of our community. After all, other city public pools in our area were closed, and condominium and apartment communities of similar size were doing the same. At the time, the city's public health office was not inspecting pools, which was evidence enough for me that the situation warranted erring on the side of caution.

Most folks in the community took our decision in stride. It was far from an ideal scenario, but they understood, especially in the early months of the pandemic, with no vaccines or antivirals available, we were not sure about the virus's transmissions nor its short or long-term effects (some of us were even sanitizing our groceries). However, one resident, someone I knew well and admired for their progressive activism in the city, could not accept the decision. This neighbor asserted many personal reasons for wanting the pool open—all of them valid—but the one argument that sticks with me even today was, "COVID-19 only affects old people. If old people don't want to come to the pool, they don't have to." With the support of kind and smart mentors, managing conflict is a skill I have honed over time; I pride myself in being able to do this task well. But when I heard these words, I knew my days as association president were numbered. Everyone has their limits.

Part of the reason these words affected me so much was that I could sense how the COVID-19 pandemic was impacting my role as association president. As a white male living in a diverse city and community, I was deliberate about transparency in communicating our board's decisions. At our monthly and annual meetings, I led by consensus, working to promote inclusive representation and participation on our board and to maintain standards that would allow our community to qualify for Federal Housing Administration funding. But as the world began to deal with the challenges of an unprecedented public health crisis, and in the absence of the usual support networks, such as in-person meetings and informal interactions with community members, the weight of the responsibility of this role shifted primarily to me. As demonstrated by other contributions in this collection, this created a not-so-uniquely isolating experience in terms of leadership and labor that pushed me into a position of having to act with limited information, elevated scrutiny, and limited resources. Physical distancing guidelines, supply chain disruptions, and social unrest on a scale unlike anything I had known added to this sensation of seclusion. The emotional toll of this isolation was only increased by the burden of shouldering the well-being of the most vulnerable members of my community, older adults and infants, as well as those of other community association board members.

Another reason these words impacted me was that my work as a teacher-researcher in literacy studies was evolving, leading me to the understudied but increasingly relevant field of aging studies. My review of aging studies scholars' works, such as those of Mary Catherine Bateson, Simone de Beauvoir, Lauren Marshall Bowen, Sarah Lamb, and Lynne Segal prompted me to ask new research questions about our current moment and the future: How might English studies develop more progressive understandings of the aging process as not only biological but as culturally and socially situated? In what ways do youth-centric views of identity, especially at the intersections of LGBTQ+ and BIPOC conversations, elide the experience of older adults? How might university strategic plans be revised to reflect the reality of their aging workforce and students? But aging studies also drew me to reconsider history, a path that led me to particularly dark events that played out during the summer of 2003—The Paris heat wave.

"Discovering Its Elderly"

The Paris heat wave of 2003 was a natural disaster that resulted in nearly 15,000 excess deaths (some experts put the toll at 19,000 over the entire summer). Reports indicate that 82 percent of victims were 75 or older; 92 percent of those victims lived alone. Stories emerging from this catastrophe are alarming, horrifying, and gruesome. Documented reports indicate that many families continued vacationing (so as not to disrupt holiday weekends) even after being informed of deceased relatives who had stayed home and succumbed to the heat. Some victims were discovered only when decomposition accelerated by the heat had caused bodily fluids to leak through the ceilings of neighbors below. In Paris, where the excess mortality rate was 141 percent compared to an average summer, the city exceeded its capacity for storing bodies, running out of refrigerated spaces to store victims of the heat wave.

This tragedy resulted from a conflation of pressures/causes. Daily maximum temperatures exceeded 35 degrees Celsius (C) [95 degrees Fahrenheit (F)] for weeks, with many days in and around the region of Paris exceeding 100 degrees F. The physical infrastructure of Paris itself contributed to what urban planners call the Heat Island Effect, a consequence of reduced green spaces in the city. Others have concluded that poor urban planning and climate change contributed to the severe conditions that brought about the event (Goodell). Regardless of the initial cause of this unprecedented event, additional factors impacted the course of the crisis. Pascal Champvert, the president of the French umbrella organization for homes for the aged, noted, "One has the impression that only now France is discovering its elderly" (Tagliabue).

Twenty years have passed since the heat wave, and with this anniversary comes reflection, challenging questions, and reformed policies. "How can the nation that claims to be the originator of the notion of human rights and dignity," Richard Keller writes, "be in such a place that people could die in such misery, and completely alone, completely isolated?" (Phelan). Similar questions have led to the type of recommendations found in France's recently published "Heat Wave Management Plan" (Garric), which includes, among many things, the importance of monitoring working conditions, improving green spaces in cities, and enlisting "volunteers and postal workers" to enroll older adults and those people identified as vulnerable in a registry. Also under consideration is the use of emergency text message services to be sent out to all citizens, regardless of age, in the event of another heat wave (Phelan).

Such recommendations are undoubtedly rhetorically powerful, with the twentieth anniversary of the heat wave as a backdrop. But these proposals do little in the way of addressing the underlying attitudes about age that led so many older adults to be left alone, vulnerable to exposure, and ultimately to die. Indeed, the Paris heat wave is an extreme example of how ageism, when intertwined with crisis and inequity, can be deadly (Vandentorren et al.). But this example also reveals how subtly ageism might impact the trajectory of a crisis, shifting priorities and values of communities away from public health and the obligations we share to protect people regardless of age.

Coming of Age in Higher Education

As scholars, teachers, and administrations in academia, we need not look far to find a context in which the lessons of aging studies are relevant, and the stakes involve the livelihood of both young and old. Phyllis Moen and Kate Schafers contend, "Universities are among the most age-segregated of institutions, catering almost exclusively to young people in their late teens and early 20s, even as new demographic realities render this educational model obsolete," (n.p.). Additionally, the US "65-plus population is projected to climb from about 17 percent today to 21 percent in 2030" (Kim). A 2019 CUPA-HR Report, "The Challenges of an Aging Higher Ed Workforce," notes that "higher ed staff that is already older than the US workforce. Over half of all staff at colleges and universities are today 45 and older, compared to a quarter under age 35" (Kim). With a workforce skewing older than the broader US labor force, we must confront the implications of these changes in ethical, constructive, and pedagogically sound ways that emphasize genuinely inclusive and equitable academic spaces.

Foundational scholarship by researchers like Lauren Marshall Bowen, Debra Journet, Heidi McKee, Kristine Blair, and others has established connections between aging studies and rhetoric and composition scholarship. Still, these connections remain on the periphery of our field's list of sound practices and priorities. Those who aspire to contribute to understanding the fundamental nature of the gap between emerging research on identity/subjectivity and aging studies might consider Lauren Marshall Bowen's and Suzanne Kesler Rumsey's engaging work. Their special issue in *Literacy in Composition Studies,* appropriately entitled "Composing a Further Life," delineates topics, methodologies, and themes that invite timely reflection. Given the profound demographic shifts in higher education and the need for further research on aging studies, they write: "How can we compose narratives of late careers or post-retirement lives within the framework of composition studies? What does it mean to navigate the aging process as both a writer and a writing teacher? How might community literacy pedagogies foster opportunities for cross-generational composition?" (Bowen and Rumsey). As noted in a contribution to "Composing a Further Life," pedagogical approaches to aging must acknowledge that "ageist ideologies are not inherent but are learned and reinforced" (Hall and Harker, 162). As a result, any cross-generational approach to prioritizing aging studies must, at the very least, explicitly resist prevailing characterizations of aging that "reduce old age to a process of decline" (Bowen, "Beyond Repair," 437). Below I profile a series of cross-generational communities that speak to these questions and priorities in varying degrees.

Events leading up to and after 2020 brought profound economic dislocation, social unrest, and significant shifts in how workers' needs are valued and understood. According to *Harvard Business Review* authors Fuller and Kerr, over 47 million Americans voluntarily left jobs, an exodus from employment that has been termed The Great Resignation (Fuller and Kerr). While many have speculated that Gen Z and younger folks accelerated this event, it is clear now that older adults of varying ages are responsible for permanently leaving positions rather than simply shifting sectors or changing jobs (SHRM). Bradley Schurman's *The Super Age: Decoding Our Demographic Destiny* makes a convincing case for refiguring higher education in a way that makes it an attractive place for older adults who wish to rejoin the workforce. Other resources, like those by Phyllis Moen and Kate Schaefers of the University of Minnesota Advanced Careers Initiative agree, noting that most folks "in their 50s, 60s, and 70s are healthy, energetic, and often surprised to be pushed into retirement or laid off with few job prospects" (n.p.); however, "few roadmaps and few options for long-life learning" are available through universities (n.p.). Moen and Shaefers identify several institutes and programs that might function as models:

- *Emory University's Osher Lifelong Learning Institute:* A lifelong learning program for older adults seeking connections with like-minded individuals who relish learning for enjoyment, this program offers diverse classes and social programs aimed toward fostering "mind, body, and soul" enrichment (OLLI).
- *Harvard's Advanced Leadership Initiative:* Focuses on unlocking the potential of experienced leaders with a focus on societal challenges. Fellows of this program engage in a year-long interdisciplinary immersion, developing a social impact strategy (HALI).
- *Notre Dame's Inspired Leadership Initiative:* Intended for accomplished individuals across various fields who have concluded their careers and seek to explore, discern, and design their next stage in life; this program is guided by Notre Dame faculty with goal of positioning older adults as university community leaders (ILI).
- *Stanford's Distinguished Careers Institute:* What happens when your professional identity goes away? Participants in this program "share their experiences and insights of creating new purpose, vision and joy in their post-career years" (SDCI).
- *University of Minnesota Advanced Careers Initiative:* Tailored for "encore adults" managing work and life transitions, this nine-month program offers a transformative curriculum, multigenerational learning, and a hand-on internship in nonprofit, social enterprise, or public service (UMAC).
- *The University of Texas's Tower Fellows Program:* "Adventure Awaits" Offering a two-semester program led by "word class thinkers and doers," this initiative offers participants access to "the best courses and professors on campus and a backstage pass to the best events and programs the University has to offer" (TFP).

Moen and Shaefers caution that such initiatives often encounter unstable funding and emphasize the importance of determining funding requirements and streams in advance of initiating programs; in my own experience with university initiatives, I find that they sometimes "over promise and under deliver" in the wake of one university Quality Enhancement Plan (QEP) replacing another. These university-wide reforms shift priorities for faculty, staff, and students alike, raising the possibility that any meaningful change must go beyond institutes and initiatives to hold a more prominent place among strategic commitments at the highest levels of universities. We must do the double work of acknowledging the importance of understanding aging and longevity from a biological perspective *and* do the difficult work of prioritizing aging as a socially constructed pressure, one that deserves the same enthusiasm, attention, and funding that we give research grounded in contemporary identity studies.

Ageism

Aging studies provides language, insights, and lessons to integrate intergenerational university initiatives with the research and instructional goals for students. In the wake of the COVID-19 pandemic, an event that impacted the physical, mental, and emotional well-being of millions of older adults, and as we move into a "world with more people over age 65 than under age 18" (Moen and Schaefers), university leaders and program directors must consider the lessons that go beyond subject areas typically associated with considering age in fields like gerontology, public health, physiology, and health care. Our priorities and commitments must transcend these traditional approaches to considering aging. Furthermore, in our efforts to complicate singular and cliché understandings of aging, we must recognize the importance of interdisciplinary projects like intergenerational learning communities. As noted above, although many of these projects are in nascent stages with unpredictable funding, they hold significant potential for (re)establishing networks of support through intergenerational community. Indeed, one purpose of asking younger students to engage with older adults in a university setting is to promote deeper understanding between generations, especially when it comes to considering the role of education and literacy among generations. However, realizing the more significant outcomes, as, for example, cultivating empathy, understanding, and promoting collective responsibilities, particularly considering events like the Paris heat wave, requires tangible, real, and inclusive interactions among younger and older generations.

Bibliography

Bateson, Mary Catherine. *Composing a Life.* Plume, 1990.

Beauvoir, Simone de. *The Coming of Age.* Translated by Patrick O'Brian. G. P. Putnam's Sons, 1972.

Bowen, Lauren Marshall. "Resisting Age Bias in Digital Literacy Research." *College Composition and Communication* 62, no. 4 (2011): 586–607.

Bowen, Lauren Marshall. "Beyond Repair: Literacy, Technology, and a Curriculum of Aging." *College English* 74, no. 5 (2012): 437–57

Bowen, Lauren M., and Suzanne K. Rumsey. "Composing a Further Life: Introduction to the Special Issue." *Literacy in Composition Studies* 6, no. 2 (2018).

Brandt, Deborah. *Literacy as Involvement: The Acts of Writers, Readers, and Texts.* Southern Illinois University Press, 1990.

Brandt, Deborah. *Literacy in American Lives.* Cambridge University Press, 2001.

Brandt, Deborah. "Accumulating Literacy: Living and Learning in a Sea of Change." In *Literacy and Learning: Reflections on Writing, Reading, and Society.* Jossey-Bass, 2009.

Fuller, Joseph, and William Kerr. "The Great Resignation Didn't Start with the Pandemic." *Harvard Business Review,* March 23, 2022. https://hbr.org/.

Garric, Audrey. "France Adopts Its First Heat Wave Management Plan." *Le Monde,* June 8, 2023. https://www.lemonde.fr/.

Goodell, Jeff. "Paris When It Sizzles: The City of Light Aims to Get Smart on Heat." *Yale Environment 360,* July 18, 2023, https://e360.yale.edu/.

HALI. "Harvard Advanced Leadership Initiative." Harvard University, October 3, 2023, https://www.advancedleadership.harvard.edu/.

Hall, Douglas, and Michael Harker. "Coming of Age in the Era of Acceleration: Rethinking Literacy Narratives as Pedagogies of Lifelong Learning." *Literacy in Composition Studies* 6, no. 2. (2018). https://doi.org/10.21623/1.6.2.10.

ILI. "Office of the Provost Inspired Leadership Initiative." Notre Dame University, October 3, 2023. https://ili.nd.edu/.

Keller, Richard C. *Fatal Isolation: The Devastating Paris Heat Wave of 2003.* University of Chicago Press, 2015.

Kim, Joshua. "'The Super Age' and Our Aging Higher Ed Workforce." *Inside Higher Ed,* January 1, 2022. https://www.insidehighered.com/.

Lamb, Sarah. "Preface." In *Successful Aging as a Contemporary Obsession,* edited by Sarah Lamb, xi-xiv. Rutgers University Press, 2017.

McKee, Heidi, and Kristine Blair. "Older Adults and Community-Based Technological Literacy Programs: Benefits and Barriers to Learning." *Community Literacy Journal* 1, no. 2 (2007): 13–39.

Moen, Phyllis, and Kate Schaefers. "Long-Life Learning and the Age-Integration of Higher Education." *Stanford Social Innovation Review,* April 21, 2021. https://ssir .org/.

OLLI. "Osher Lifelong Learning Institute at Emory." *Emory University,* October 3, 2023, https://olli.emory.edu/.

Phelan, Jessica. "Twenty Years after the Deadly 2003 Heatwave, What Lessons Has France Learned?" *RFI,* 8 Aug. 2023. https://www.rfi.fr/.

Schurman, Bradley. *The Super Age: Decoding Our Demographic Destiny.* Harper Business, 2022.

SDCI. "Distinguished Careers Institute." *Stanford University,* October 3, 2023, https:// dci.stanford.edu/.

Segal, Lynne. "The Coming of Age Studies." *Age, Culture, Humanities: An Interdisciplinary Journal* 1 (2014): 31–34.

SHRM. Society for Human Resource Management Executive Network. "The Big Question: Great Resignation." *Society for Human Resource Management Executive Network.* Accessed October 3, 2023. https://www.shrm.org/.

Small, Helen. *The Long Life.* Oxford University Press, 2007.

Tagliabue, John. "Heat Death Toll Forces a Shocked France to Question Itself." *New York Times,* August 20, 2003. https://www.nytimes.com/.

TFP. "Next Begins Here." Towers Fellows Program. University of Texas at Austin, October 3, 2023, https://towerfellows.utexas.edu/.

"Twenty Years After Deadly 2023 Heatwave What Has France Learned?" Radio France Internationale, August 8, 2023, https://www.rfi.fr/.

UMAC. "U of M Advanced Careers Initiative." UMAC Fellows Program. University of Minnesota, October 3, 2023, https://umac.umn.edu/.

Vandentorren, S., P. Bretin, A. Zeghnoun, et al. "August 2003 Heat Wave in France: Risk Factors for Death of Elderly People Living at Home." *European Journal of Public Health* 16, no. 6 (December 2006): 583–91. https://doi.org/10.1093/eurpub/ckl063.

Woodward, Kathleen. "Performing Age, Performing Gender." *National Women's Study Association Journal* 18, no. 1 (2006): 162–89.

Woodward, Kathleen. "Rereading Simone de Beauvoir's *The Coming of Age.*" *Age, Culture, Humanities: An Interdisciplinary Journal* 3 (2016): n.p.

PART IV

Emotional Labor and Equity in Higher Education

CHAPTER 14

Are We Done Yet?

Disruption, Inevitable Fatigue, and Reimagining Our PhD Exam Timetables

Kelli R. Gill and Angela D. Mack

> Living in a body that contests the status quo is an unrelenting
> process; it is indeed exhausting. Normative standards and classifications
> must move over and make room for the rest of us.
> —Christina V. Cedillo

Guilt. Apathy. Fear. Shame. Grief. Gratefulness. Disruption. These are a few of the words that describe our experiences completing (or not completing) our comprehensive exams. The pandemic has brought many trials for graduate students, one of which has been significant delay of degree completion. For ourselves, both PhD students completing our coursework at the end of spring 2020, we faced all the stress, delay, and inconveniences of the pandemic at the very time we would be starting our comprehensive exams. Facing crises, mental health decline, a racial reckoning, and additional labor due to added academic tasks and family life, our deadline for exams of fall 2020 creeped its way into winter . . . spring . . . summer . . . and then fall of 2021. While extensions were granted and the writing process continued, exams weighed over us in a way we had not anticipated. As cohort members and friends, we found ourselves reaching out to each other for emotional support. Why were we the only ones not yet finished? Why was the exams process—a requirement for most Rhetoric and Composition doctoral programs across the country—so difficult for us? Why was it such an emotional process? As we shared our experiences and connected over this dilemma, we found comfort in being able to name the emotions associated with our delayed exams. Sharing our stories helped us to create a connection and also to identify the norms perpetuated in the exams process, which labeled our situation as "unique" even in a time in which nothing is "normal."

Within this chapter, we demonstrate how our personal stories reveal cracks within the myth of academic productivity and how the constraint of rigidity fails to provide space for predictable disruption and fatigue (Delgado; Lawrence; Martinez, "A Plea"). Throughout our journeys as women in the academy, we have had to accommodate and reshape ourselves to move through universities while managing our own crises and barriers (Pinault and Rouzer; Gutiérrez y Muhs et al.). Each family death, health crisis, financial problem, or local/national tragedy stretches us thinner, until we cannot stretch anymore. We call this collapse "inevitable fatigue." We see the pandemic not as an isolated, extraordinary event, but rather as one of many catalysts for this occurrence of inevitable fatigue. Within this essay we offer our doctoral comprehensive exams as one example of an institutional structure that induces inevitable fatigue by perpetuating productivity myths in rigid programmatic timetables.

We use emotions as a thematic device to shape our narratives. We believe that careful attention to our emotions is an important feminist practice that helps us to identify inequitable social structures in the academy and cultivate relationality (Ahmed; Royster and Kirsch). In this chapter, we draw inspiration from feminist studies, disability scholars (Dolmage; Hubrig et al.; Kerschbaum; Titchkosky; Yergeau et al.), and Critical Race Theory Counterstorytelling (Delgado, Stefancic, and Harris; Lawrence; Martinez, *Counterstory*) to reimagine the doctoral journey which normalizes, rather than penalizes, disruption.

Story as Methodology in a Journey from *Guilt* to *Anger*

This essay is born out of stories. Our friendship is born of stories. As the pandemic beat us down, we were able to survive because we could tell each other our stories and found connection in them—not stories of triumph or optimism, but stories of guilt. In our Zoom rants we did not share study tips, we didn't tell each other to *look on the bright side* or *it could be worse*. We revealed that we felt guilty and ashamed of our lack of progress. Together we let ourselves be angry. We let ourselves sit in the terrible feelings and revel in the ability to voice them to another person who felt the same way. We imagined aloud what we wished the process had looked like. We storied together and, in this chapter, we do the same.

Our co-authorship in this piece rests upon the work of scholars who have modeled vulnerability in the field—rhetoric and composition scholars who have not only demanded that stories be recognized as a scholarly meaning-making practice, but who have made anger visible so that we do not have to be alone. We rely on the work of Critical Race Scholars who argue that storytelling has the power to expose myths by "assert[ing] our stories within, and in many instances counter to, hegemonic narratives of the institution" (Martinez, *Counterstory*, 51; Delgado, Stefancic and Harris). We also remember the disability scholars who have been doing the work of advocacy, vulnerability, and storying against normativity long before us. We honor this remembrance by articulating our own proximity and familiarity with disability. By sharing our stories, we put into practice what Ellen Samuels conveys in "The Six Ways of Looking at Crip Time." We express our stories as examples of time travel, grief, brokenness, sickness, and writing time. Because as Samuels explains: "Crip time means listening to the broken languages of our bodies, translating them, honoring their words." Likewise, we offer these stories up in succession, because as modeled by Jacqueline Jones Royster, "individual stories placed one against another build credibility and offer . . . a litany of evidence from which a call for transformation in theory and practice might rightfully begin" (When the First Voice, 30). We offer these stories to you not just because we think many in the field feel the same, but because we believe that transformation must begin now.

Pride, Shame, Fear (Kelli)

I was in the first grade when I received the student of the month award. In addition to a small stuffed animal, I posed with our principal for a newspaper photo. I remember everyone noting what a great student I was, particularly during such a tough time for my family. This was the same year my older sister had suffered a brain injury as a result of a car accident and had not yet woken from her coma. Something about this moment always stuck with me—it was important, dare I say admirable, to continue doing well in school even as my family was experiencing medical trauma.

I was in my first semester of my senior year in undergraduate school when I received a call that my mother had died. After a week of phone calls, funeral planning, and grieving, I quickly returned to my classes. We weren't even a month into the semester, and not only was I worried about falling behind, but I was worried about my grades. Unlike in the first grade, there were no awards to commend me for continuing through adversity. In fact, many of my professors seemed to have forgotten completely when I had to remind them about excused absences or late papers. Even without an award or praise, there was this sense of what had to be done. Taking a semester off would affect my student aid and scholarships. A part-time job was the only way to pay for my graduate school applications, my bills, and some of my family's bills that I needed to pick up after we lost my mom's income. Like many women, I felt a need to step into my mother's role after her death. Someone needed to make sure things were getting taken care of. What's more, I felt a sense of pride at being able to maintain my 4.0 GPA. Grieving was something I did in the moments in-between. Over the next few years, I would face four more family deaths, medical issues, and mental health problems but I just kept going.

I am reminded of a story my colleague Elise Dixon posted to Twitter. She recalls hurrying to her class right after finding that her house had been broken into: "I went to class because I was conditioned to feel like my education was more important than anything else, even my well-being, both physical and emotional. Part of that was because no one had EVER told me otherwise" (@dr_dix). When my family faced tragedy, I was conditioned to continue doing well in school regardless of how difficult things were at home. When my mother died, no one urged me to take a break or properly grieve. Looking back, I realize how much my status as a first-generation, working-class student impacted my decision to "keep going along" even during a crisis. I didn't know what an Incomplete was. There was no one in my family who could help me navigate the process of taking a semester off, much less pay my bills while I was away. With my mother gone, I often had to step in as a financial and emotional support system for my family. Likewise, I'd grown up in a household without health insurance—finding a psychologist wasn't something I knew how to do and my university's waitlist for counseling was miles long. It took a pandemic for me to step back and realize that my coping strategies weren't going to work anymore.

In the summer of 2020, I couldn't do my exams. I wasn't just facing anxiety around world health, but I was facing personal difficulties in my own family and a general mental decline. I took my first Incomplete. I asked for exam extensions. I started counseling. While many people were supportive, I still couldn't shake a feeling of shame. *I managed a 15-credit course load when my mom passed away, why couldn't I manage just to read?* Each email I received celebrating a cohort member's passed orals was just another reminder that I couldn't cope. *Others have more to deal with—kids, multiple jobs, heavier course loads—they can do it, why can't I?* While my department was accommodating to extensions, there was no clear path or support for extending my exams. In my semester advising appointment, I was questioned about why I hadn't yet finished. When I pointed out how much it would help to have more guidance on the exams process or to have a set path and guidelines for extensions, I was told that it was preferred to handle these things on a "case by case" basis. These types of conversations made me feel incredibly alone at a time when quarantine was already isolating me. However, it also demonstrated how the university and graduate departments consider situations like mine to be special cases.

One of the most debilitating parts of this process has been my sense of fear that I was losing myself. As I once explained to my therapist, so much of my identity is wrapped around being a hard worker. If I can't work, who am I? As Taylor M. Jackson, a sociologist and graduate student at the time of writing, explains, "I felt I was failing because I was not living up to these expectations, and it shattered my sense of self. I began to feel I was inadequate, not smart enough, and not cut out for academia. Was I lazy? Did I not really want it bad enough?" (223). So much of graduate school ties our self-worth to productivity, and rewards those who power through adversity.

There was not a single "thing" that led to my inability to work during the pandemic. Rather, the pandemic was simply the final straw. For when a student goes from K to 12, from freshman to senior, from master's to PhD (as many students are widely encouraged or required to do because of individual circumstances) it makes sense that eventually you will reach a breaking point that no amount of "self-care" will fix. A bubble bath will not fix a global crisis. A week off is not enough time to grieve. A summer is not enough time to learn the discipline of the field, yet this is how long we are expected to take, and any diversions are considered "exceptions" rather than the rule.

Necessity, Safety, Anxiety (Angela)

Kelli and I are not strangers to pursuing education even while enduring personal hardships. At the time of this writing, my father is battling a second bout with cancer, a more aggressive one than the Stage 3 pancreatic cancer he fought and overcame in 2018–2019. My Dad battled Stage 4 cancer that has metastasized and was permanently placed on a chemotherapy regimen at the time of this writing. Sharing my story is an ongoing reminder of how precarious it is for me, for both of us, to do this work. While my father fought for his life once again, I wrestled with a diagnosis that has come about since the onslaught of the pandemic. Because of it, it severely compromised my mobility, a condition wholly different than where I was when all of this began. Having to forge ahead through overlapping crises has turned into an ongoing part of the lived and embodied experience I have become uncomfortably adapted to. But my story begins elsewhere, with my mom, and with how my personal history has been a balancing act I have had to negotiate until I seemingly could not.

My mother has been disabled my entire life, and as her only child I have been chiefly responsible for her welfare. She has epilepsy, and I grew up in my grandfather's house with her as a single parent. Unlike the commonly seen tonic-clonic seizures (formerly known as grand mal seizures) where someone may convulse and fall, my mom has focal impaired awareness seizures (once known as partial seizures) where a convulsion could be anything from staring, screaming, rapidly repeating the mantras she has spoken since being first diagnosed, complaining about smells or seeing things, losing consciousness, losing awareness of surroundings, losing memory, losing recognition of herself or of people she knows, and at times becoming combative, be it to a stranger or close relative. I grew up learning how to be ready at any moment's notice because even with her regular adherence to medication, my mom could have a seizure at church, at the grocery store, in the movies, at a school function, or at any time, in any situation. Once she was in an episode, it could be anywhere from a day to even close to a week where she could barely get out of bed. I had to learn early on to maneuver my life to accommodate her illness, to take care of her and myself, and it was one of the primary factors of me choosing to stay close to home for my undergraduate education. With my own issues of being acutely asthmatic and my mom being uniquely epileptic, school was the one place that gave me continuity and substance beyond the constant state of hypervigilance I had grown accustomed to. I always had to learn to "do" despite her illness, my illness, any death in my family, and any other crisis near or far. There was nothing new, nothing unfamiliar with my capacity to keep going despite what I had to deal with. I have always had to deal with something.

The dealing with the stuff of my life did not change after undergrad. It shape-shifted into a greater expanse of stressful circumstances. When I got married, went to grad school, had a son, worked, then decided to go into a PhD program, I had already dealt with the deaths of numerous loved ones, the death of my sister-in-law, two heart attacks from my dad, the illness and death of my mother-in-law, and a melee of crisis after crisis. If I could get through my dad's cancer struggle; two home burglaries where I was the intended target; an emergency displacement and move; a car accident; and support my spouse while he emotionally recovered from being in a store robbed at gunpoint; and *still* be named Graduate Student of the Year, how is it possible that anything else could slow me down when I have already tackled the worst?

Kelli shared that facing tragedy caused excelling in school to be a conditioned response, I on the other hand, felt like excelling in school served as a type of refuge. I had nowhere else to put all the grief and trauma and the frenetic energy of hypervigilance in my real life. School provided me with space where I could divert some of my constructive energy into something other than a problem, an illness, or an emergency. It gave me a chance to be someone other than what so many people in my life needed me to be for them. School served as one of my safe places. It was my getaway. It gave me a place to be when home was hard and going somewhere else was simply not an option.

As a Black woman in the academy, specifically as an older PhD student who also wears a few hats at a predominately White institution (PWI), I have had to navigate this pandemic from multiple lenses of embodiment and experience. The year 2020 was already proving to be challenging with rumors of an intrusive virus, the world mourning the death of Kobe Bryant while I lived with one of the biggest Lakers fans, and the overall viscosity of an upcoming presidential election. I was also coming out of a semester where I was dealing with the impact of the police-involved shooting death of Atatiana Carr-Jefferson in my childhood community, a community not far from the institution Kelli and I are both part of. I grappled with the need for justice and solidarity at a time when the trial for the murder of Botham Jean had wrapped up only weeks before Carr-Jefferson's murder. Somehow, 2020 was already foreshadowing the disruption that was coming.

So, imagine my chagrin when in Spring 2020, what was supposed to be the close out of me taking my last three classes and preparing my reading lists for my comprehensive exams, turned into the unforeseeable. After what I had been through since getting into the program, I struggled when the pandemic hit. What was supposed to be a semester where I had a chance to celebrate my dad's one-year cancer-free anniversary and teach part of a poetry class with one of my favorite poet/professors, I couldn't. I went from having a plan to get through my last semester to having to triage for the class I taught, navigating my office space since my husband was now working from home, dealing with my son having to transition to a virtual form of kindergarten, and finishing my own three courses. Triage took away the opportunity for me to teach in my directed study, and anxiety caved me in to where I had to negotiate extended incompletes for my other two classes. Whereas some may have struggled with loneliness or isolation, I struggled managing a household that required me to recalibrate my time to be "on" as a wife, mom, and a doctoral student. I simply couldn't manage everyone inside my house, outside my house, and myself. Anxiety took me from worrying primarily about school to worrying about if I was going to survive, be it the coronavirus or police brutality and anti-Black violence. There was still a semester to close out, a summer to come, and another school year. Somehow, I still had to think about getting through my exams with a growing pandemic and escalating racial hostility that I had to reckon with. How could I continue meeting deadlines and expectations of a program whose stipend my family depended on? How do I do all of this when I feel unsafe and fear for my family's safety on multiple fronts? How do I find the mental bandwidth to keep going when I am not okay? What was I supposed to do when I received an unexpected diagnosis that would compromise my ability to return to campus in a moderately functional way? How do I now manage this new development in my health that, coupled with my race and gender, could put me at greater risk of harm, discrimination, or alienation? What if I was not ready to confront the full implications of my new reality as I struggled with all of the other pressures piling on top of each other? What should I do? What could I do? What was safe for me to say? Would I have a choice in what I wanted to disclose because of the pressures of the institution for me to progress in my studies?

A week off was not enough time to grieve nor was a summer enough time to learn the rest of my discipline's field when we, as women, began to feel the pressure to continue to perform at peak academic acuity even when the world was shutting down around us. The pandemic tilted me over, and it did so in a way that meds and counseling and treatments and protests didn't address what our institution expected from me in terms of degree progress.

Centering *Vulnerability* Against the Myth of Productivity

We situate our stories to center our vulnerability in stark contrast to the expected progression towards our exams. The pandemic upended what we thought we could accomplish in the time given to us. It's not to say that others in our program didn't manage to complete and pass theirs without grappling with their own issues. Many of them did. But we are centering our vulnerability to demonstrate that every graduate student's experience is different, dispelling the myth of the dominant narrative that academic progress can move forward in one projected pathway at all times for all graduate students.

As universities continue to advocate for the inclusion of "marginalized" students, they must be prepared to create structures that support those students. Our situations are not unique, yet the university seemed shocked that we experienced them at all. Perhaps these attitudes are left over from a time when universities were only accessible to cisgender, heterosexual white men whose families could support them in their gap years or wives could free up their extra time for private medical treatment and leisure time. Perhaps these attitudes are wishful thinking on the part of departments who still rely on the "weed them out" strategy, that only the "fittest" can survive. As doctoral students, we should be evaluated on our critical thinking skills, and not our ability to suppress trauma in favor of timely graduation.

To acknowledge our experiences is to center vulnerability. In a roundtable discussion in *The American Historian,* graduate students echoed our call. One graduate student said, ". . . Our institutions want us to keep working as if nothing happened. The empty platitudes through town hall meetings are only lip service" (Student D, R1, "Graduate Students and COVID"). Another chimed, ". . . I felt like I had been set out to sea without a map in terms of advisement. I was in competition with Zoom meetings, undergraduates needing guidance through the shift to virtual instruction, and requests to historicize the events of the summer of 2020 for time on my advisors' calendars. At the same time, no one could help me shape a realistic set of goals for the next three, six, or even twelve months" (Student E, Private R1, "Graduate Students and COVID"). These issues are not new. How then can the university be reimagined for graduate students who often occupy a unique role of both student and instructor while handling their own life circumstances? We believe that articulating our stories resists and even subverts the normalization of a singular pathway to academic progress, thus reimagining a different systemic approach to graduate care.

Wouldn't it be great to get these exams over with? Are we done yet? What is really the hold up for us? The easier and less risky thing would be to remain silent. To shield others from our experiences may very well afford a particular type of safety, especially for us as women, and for Angela being a Black woman specifically. In *Presumed Incompetent,* Gutiérrez y Muhs et al., addresses the silences of their book by women academics of color who wanted to contribute and valued the efforts, but fear of retaliation and "professional ridicule" prevented them from doing so (11). We made the choice to share first for our friendship, for those around us who move through the academy visible or veiled, and to honor those whose silences are necessary for their survival.

Storying our experiences against what is perceived as the status quo in graduate/doctoral education is a vulnerable practice. Pushing against the dominant narrative of doctoral/graduate program progress above all else via a singular, timely pathway is risky for us as we are constantly reminded of our intersecting identities that exposes us to the threat of erasure or minimization since we are not single, nor white men, nor without children, nor completely able-bodied (as is Angela's case). There is a fear in being perceived as whiny, negative, or sympathy seeking. As a graduate student preparing for the job market, there is also the added stress of perception. Will my mentors consider me incompetent if I continually have delays? Am I deemed a liability to a potential employer because I have too many issues that can potentially impede my capacity to do my job and fulfill all of my obligations in the academy?

I (Kelli) recall when I finally reached out to my advisor at the time to explain that I had been avoiding my exams and was behind. In response to my admission, he emailed back: "You are doing great. I have no concerns about your professionalism, ability, work-habits, etc. This is a shitty time and grad school is already difficult." I cried after I read that email. I didn't realize how much my anxiety around my exam delay had been wrapped up in my fear of how others perceived me. I could never have anticipated how many emotions would flood me from just a simple interaction. Since that email I have actively repeated these same words to my students. I have told them about my own fears of being perceived and how our delays are not tied to our values or ability.

Part of dispelling productivity myths requires that we not only open ourselves up to other people, but that we model this behavior *with* others. As Hubrig et al. explain, "Rather than strengthening self-protection, vulnerability involves an open stance that acknowledges the interdependence of self and other, that allows the self to be changed by another" (295). Much work in the field of English is so focused on individual behavior, scholarship, and writing. However, relationality with one another allows us not to just see cracks in productivity maps but see ourselves.

I (Angela) remember when I had to speak to my advisor and explain, yet again, something else was wrong that I had to deal with and advocate for. What I worried about the most was being perceived as too much of a liability to handle the "rigors" of doctoral education. My problem was that my own vision was skewed. I wasn't just a PhD student. I was a Black woman, I was a wife, a mom of an elementary school kid, AND a PhD student. Every part of my identity and positionality hinged on the moment I found myself in. Whereas I was previously able to compartmentalize my various selves into their own separate silos, in my sista gurl vernacular, dis hit diff'rent. Andrea Hicks states: "One group that notably has been absent from most of the discussions is graduate students with young children, and in particular single or married female graduate student parents, who comprise an estimated 13% of graduate students in the United States (Mason, 2009). These women and their careers are at particularly vulnerable stages and will be greatly impacted by the pandemic, through loss of resources and research productivity, due to their parental responsibilities" (Hicks). I wasn't giving myself permission to not be okay. I wasn't giving myself permission to struggle with myself, my health, my household, and my circumstances in addition to my education. I wasn't giving myself a chance to wrestle through a vulnerability that exposed the inevitable fatigue of me constantly trying to fit my whole life into a system not designed to accommodate me fully. I finally had to take the permission not afforded me to lean into the discomfort and to reject the notion that somehow, I was dealing with too much for the academy. I believe the reality is that the academy was constructed too narrowly instead and remained that way for too long.

While we focus within this essay on our own vulnerabilities, we believe that truly dispelling productivity myths requires radically reshaping the structures of the academy through the concept of time. Crip time inspired us to reshape our understanding of productivity in the academy while also offering a model of expanding the reality of what progress actually looks like, not just more time, but the flexibility of it as well. As Alison Kafer explains, "Rather than bend disabled bodies and minds to meet the clock, crip time bends the clock to meet disabled bodies and minds" (27). Cripping time does not just accommodate disabled bodies but reorients our relation to time and the emotions connected to lost time—shifting from simply tolerating bodies and stories like ours to truly reimagining academic spaces and communities. As Ellen Samuels and Elizabeth Freeman explain, "Even as crip time is a space of frustration and often of loss, then, it is also a space that offers new kinds of connections and presence that are fundamental to imagining a new world into being" (250). Rather than moving past our feelings of grief, anger, and frustration, crip time allowed us to recognize that our own time does not work the same for others or all bodies, thus giving us a way to move through loss and towards new worlds.

Normalizing *Disruption*

The pandemic has not broken the academy—it has just revealed problems that always existed. Our goal should not be to return to "normal." Our lives, in all their complexities, disruptions, and unexpectedness, *are* normal. It is through our shared engagement in vulnerability that we seek to reframe the narrative of exceptionalism that creates hierarchies of indifference to struggle. It is through our experiences that we now ask you to imagine with us what sustainable graduate education looks like because our stories are not only for your reading, but it is for those with power to advocate for us, to act. In this imagining, we ask you to consider four takeaways: (1) creating space for grief, (2) increasing clarity and transparency, (3) developing relations, and (4) establishing actual material resources—more than just stipends—as interventions towards expansive graduate student care.

Create Space for Grief

Our stories demonstrate a deep need for graduate school policies to be updated to reflect the embodied and lived realities of contemporary graduate students. Crip time offers us the theoretical space that demands structural changes so that disruptions such as death, health problems, or traumatic events are not treated as hurdles we must overcome in order to be deemed worthy of academic progress or success. Those in power who work with graduate students should not only design their programs and courses with grief in mind, but they must invest in best grief practices. This change involves not just words of encouragement, but clear navigation of and access to resources, adjustable graduation timelines, and above all, guilt-free support to take the time needed. Grieving is not an anomaly to graduate students' experiences.

Increase Clarity and Transparency

Disruptions such as grief point towards another need in academic spaces: transparency of process. Normalizing disruption requires that we anticipate them by building clear systems and alternative paths for students to follow. Singular paths such as graduation timelines with no wiggle room, lack of policies or financial support (or financial support expires), lack of emergency semester leave, or no communication during times of crisis signal to students that their situation is abnormal or discouraged. This situation then places a burden on the graduate student, who already in crisis, now must also book additional advising appointments, request further information, and take on added stress that they may lose funding, might be denied extensions, or will be labeled unprofessional by their department. It also places labor upon individuals, rather than department collectives, to make "special exceptions" or advocate on behalf of singular students even though our stories demonstrate that disruptions are not unique nor unlikely. Clear processes normalize disruptions by shifting labor from individuals and onto academic collectives.

Develop Relations Through Empathy and Support

Within our stories we showed that our relations with both each other and our advisors provided support during a disruptive semester. Relations which provide empathy and support provide reassurance that we were not only capable but that our reactions were okay. We believe that individuals who interact with graduate students, particularly department chairs, directors of graduate studies, and professors, should recognize the role that relationality plays in education. Relationships allow us to be vulnerable, to seek help, and to accept sincere empathy—all of which provide necessary support in times of crisis. Whereas clear processes around disruption help to provide clarity, relationships provide the support that graduate students need when anxiety, depression, or crisis might be impacting their studies in very real ways. It also helps to reaffirm that a student's self-worth is not based on their productivity. Establishing relations creates trust which makes difficult conversations around delays and disruptions less stressful and more likely.

Establish Resources

Our narratives acknowledge the material nature of crisis. We both discussed how material conditions—bills, family support, housing, and death—impact a student's decision to push through even when they mentally cannot. In particular, for working-class students or students who provide financial support for their families, access to resources such as healthcare, a living wage, and emergency funds can be the difference between dropping out or continuing. Because departments often benefit from graduate student labor (as instructors, teaching assistants, tutors, or department aides), we believe they should invest in resources for students in times of need. Private healthcare, credit card debt, or semester leave without pay predictably encourage linear academic paths because they reward students who have access to private resources and punish those who do not. Because crises often stem from material conditions, we acknowledge that sustainable solutions be grounded in material resources as well.

By advocating for space, clarity and transparency, relations, and resources, we have put forth some key ideas to appeal for a graduate education experience that demonstrates that though our stories are unique to us, they are not exceptional. They are common. And stories like ours are often not shared because of fear, guilt, shame, or potential penalty. We challenge those in positions of authority to consider our lived experiences fully and to consider us as fully capable. We are not unusual or abnormal. We *are* graduate students.

Moving Forward in *Love, Survival,* and *Action*

We shared our stories to not only push against normative understandings of graduate/doctoral program progress, but we did so because our writing is an act of survival. When referencing Vincent Harding's naming of the Word as an articulation for Black liberation, Charles R. Lawrence III says that the "Word is an articulation and validation of our common experience. It is a vocation of struggle against dehumanization, a practice of raising questions about reasons for oppression, an inheritance of passion and hope . . . Within the Word we find two dimensions, reflection and action, in such radical interaction that if one is sacrificed—even in part—the other immediately suffers" (336–37).

We pay homage to the naming of the Word in the face of academic labor and expectation. We name our experiences so that graduate students, especially women, women of color, graduate student spouses and parents, can find liberation against the construct that somehow our disruptions make us unqualified for success. We name our struggles by raising questions of why we have felt excluded from educational pathways that did not originally have us in mind. We reflect on our stories, and we appeal to you, our readers, to act towards creating more holistic and inclusive graduate programs with grief support, material support, and overall care as the goal. We do so with love in mind.

Is there room for love in a PhD program? There must be. In Audre Lorde's speech, "The Transformation of Silence into Language and Action," she recalls the connection she made with other women who were learning to speak their truth and to face their fears and mortality, explaining that "for every real word spoken, for every attempt I had ever made to speak those truths for which I am still seeking, I had made contact with other women while we examined the words to fit a world in which we all believed, bridging our differences. And it was the concern and caring of all those women which gave me strength and enabled me to scrutinize the essentials of my living" (41).

If we truly believe in the power of language, then we must believe there is room for love in the academy. It is in caring for one another that we can survive but love alone cannot fuel the academic journey. Lorde's speech modeled vulnerability, but it also firmly connected love with action. Real love, for your students, your colleagues, and for language itself requires that we *do something* about the stories we read and hear. This is evidenced by Lorde's transition from speaking out to curriculum change. Just as Royster argued that storying is the first step to transformation, Lorde teaches us that breaking silence requires speaking out, listening, and action.

We have not only moved forward from our exams and the enduring throes of the pandemic, but we have since completed our PhDs, Angela in 2023 and Kelli in 2024. Angela's father, David Hemphill, Sr., died in December 2023, so he did not live to see this chapter come to print, though he was aware of its upcoming publication. Disruptions thus have continued as they always will. Even with the completion of our degrees, now as burgeoning scholars in the academy and in the field, we continue to empower ourselves through our vulnerability and advocacy to hope that one day we will experience the love we still seek through the manifestation of care, material resources, job security, and a recognition of our normalcy. We, Kelli and Angela, continue our friendship and support through this love across state lines and time zones as we transition from being PhD students to becoming an assistant professor and a public humanities researcher. We hope that you, dear readers, will one day support other graduate students who question if they will ever get done. Are we done yet? Yes, and no. However, through our love and the disruptions of time, one day we will be.

Bibliography

Ahmed, Sara. *Cultural Politics of Emotions.* Edinburgh University Press, 2004.

Cedillo, Christina V. "What Does It Mean to Move: Race, Disability, and Critical Embodiment Pedagogy." *Composition Forum* 39 (2018). https://compositionforum.com/issue/39/to-move.php.

Delgado, Richard. "Storytelling for Oppositionists and Others: A Plea for Narrative." *Michigan Law Review* 87, no. 8 (1989): 2411–41.

Delgado, Richard, Jean Stefancic, and Angela Harris. *Critical Race Theory: An Introduction, Second Edition.* New York University Press, 2012.

Dolmage, Jay. *Academic Ableism: Disability and Higher Education.* University of Michigan Press, 2017.

@Dr_Dix. "I Went to Class Because I Was Conditioned to Feel like My Education Was More Important than Anything Else, Even My Well-Being, Both Physical and Emotional. Part of That Was Because No One Had EVER Told Me Otherwise." Tweet. Twitter (now X), April 2021. https://twitter.com/Dr__Dix/status/1387822050648027138.

"Graduate Students and COVID: Experiences from a Difficult Year." *American Historian,* June 2021. https://www.oah.org/tah/the-state-of-graduate-education/.

Gutiérrez y Muhs, Gabriella, Yolanda Flores Niemann, Carmen G. González, and Angela P. Harris, eds. *Presumed Incompetent: The Intersections of Race and Class for Women in Academia.* University Press of Colorado, 2012.

Hicks, Andrea. "When the Leaky Pipeline Erodes: Female Graduate Student Parents and the Ramifications of the Pandemic." *Integrated Environmental Assessment and Management* 17, no. 4 (July 2021): 667–68. https://doi.org/10.1002/ieam.4423.

Hubrig, Ada, Jessica Masterson, Stevie Desjarlais, Shari Stenberg, and Brita Thielen. "Disrupting Diversity Management." *Pedagogy* 20, no. 2 (April 1, 2020): 279–301. https://doi.org/10.1215/15314200-8091903.

Jackson, Taylor M. "Putting Me First: Navigating Mental Health Challenges as a Black Woman Graduate Student." *Women, Gender, and Families of Color* 8, no. 2 (2020): 222–26. https://doi.org/10.5406/womgenfamcol.8.2.0222.

Kafer, Alison. *Feminist, Queer, Crip.* Indiana University Press, 2013.

Kerschbaum, Stephanie L. "Anecdotal Relations: On Orienting to Disability in the Composition Classroom." *Composition Forum* 32 (Fall 2015): n.p. https://composition forum.com/issue/32/anecdotal-relations.php.

Lawrence, Charles R., III. "The Word and the River: Pedagogy as Scholarship as Struggle." In *Critical Race Theory: The Key Writings That Formed the Movement,* edited by Kimberlé Crenshaw, Neil Gotanda, Gary Peller, and Kendall Thomas. New Press, 1995.

Lorde, Audre. "The Transformation of Silence into Language and Action." In *Sister Outsider: Essays and Speeches.* Crossing Press, 1984.

Martinez, Aja Y. "A Plea for Critical Race Theory Counterstory: Stock Story vs. Counterstory Dialogues Concerning Alejandra's 'Fit' in the Academy." In *Performing Antiracist Pedagogy in Rhetoric, Writing, and Communication,* edited by Frankie Condon and Vershawn A. Young. The WAC Clearinghouse. University Press of Colorado, 2016.

Martinez, Aja Y. *Counterstory: The Rhetoric and Writing of Critical Race Theory.* National Council of Teachers of English, 2020.

Pineault, Laura, and Siara Rouzer. "Even Ivory Towers Can't Protect Women from 'Bearing the Brunt' of the COVID-19 Pandemic." *American Psychological Association Online* (blog), n.d. https://www.apa.org/.

Royster, Jacqueline Jones. "When the First Voice You Hear Is Not Your Own." *College Composition and Communication* 47, no. 1 (1996): 29–40.

Royster, Jacqueline Jones, and Gesa E. Kirsch. *Feminist Rhetorical Practices: New Horizons for Rhetoric, Composition, and Literacy Studies.* Southern Illinois University Press, 2012.

Samuels, Ellen. "Six Ways of Looking at Crip Time." *Disability Studies Quarterly* 37, no. 3 (August 31, 2017). https://doi.org/10.18061/dsq.v37i3.5824.

Samuels, Ellen, and Elizabeth Freeman. "Introduction: Crip Temporalities." *South Atlantic Quarterly* 120, no. 2 (April 1, 2021): 245–54. https://doi.org/10.1215/00382876-8915937.

Titchkosky, Tanya. *The Question of Access: Disability, Space, Meaning.* University of Toronto Press, 2011.

Yergeau, M. Remi, Elizabeth Brewer, Stephanie Kerschbaum, et al. "Multimodality in Motion: Disability and Kairotic Space." *Kairos* 18, no. 1 (2013). https://kairos.technorhetoric.net/18.1/coverweb/yergeau-et-al/.

CHAPTER 15

Burnt Out Before I Began

Finding, and Failing to Find, a Work–Life Balance amid the Pandemic

C.C. Hendricks

I struggle to find the energy to write this narrative. I tell myself I'm just complaining. I turn to Sara Ahmed's words about complaint: "To share a story of complaint can be to make a connection" (9). I find the resolve to keep writing.

Ten days after my daughter turned five months old, I accepted my first tenure-track position to start August 2020. Absent from my new institution for the first year, I felt extra pressure to prove my worth. I misdirected questions, stepped on toes, and created more work for my immediate administrators (both women). I attended every meeting and volunteered for too many committees and initiatives. Luckily, my chair noticed my over involvement and wrote on my first-year review: "I worry that if C.C. is not given relief, her research will suffer, and more importantly, she will burn out." I didn't have the heart to tell her that I was worried I already had.

Now, one year before I go up for tenure, I feel less sure about my future as a professor and more overworked and under resourced than I did when I began my position. For the first time, I'm seriously considering leaving academia and giving up the job I earned multiple degrees for and the identity that I worked so hard to attain. Even almost five years later, I still feel the way Roxane Gay described she felt as a new assistant professor, "like the kid who gets to sit at the adult table for the first time at Thanksgiving . . . . not sure what fork to use. My feet can't reach the floor" (28). This feeling has grown into something more than imposter syndrome and different than traditional notions of "burnout." As reflected in recent studies on faculty mental health and well-being, I'm not alone in this feeling. In fact, between September 2022 and May 2023, 64 percent of women, and 69 percent of gender-minority faculty reported increased feelings of workplace stress (Vyletel et al.).

In this chapter, I reflect on pivotal experiences to capture how I balanced (or failed to balance) my roles as a new assistant professor, Writing Program Administrator (WPA), and mom since the pandemic began. I share snapshots of the moments in which I was most challenged by the conflicting demands of these roles. Interspersed throughout these moments, I identify methods, suggestions, resources, and questions that made, or might have made, my colleagues' and my labor easier. These suggestions are not meant to be a list of solutions, however, as they won't work for everyone. Instead, I offer these suggestions to "tack out" of my own experiences and move towards "viewpoints in anticipation of what might become more visible from a longer or broader view" (Royster and Kirsch, 72). I hope my narratives will add to the ongoing, critical conversations surrounding the inequities within gendered academic labor and women's well-being in academia.

Academic Motherhood

Since I joined the tenure track, one of my greatest challenges has been finding ways to balance my roles as a mom and new professor. Work–life balance is not a new problem for women faculty, or for mothers in virtually all professions. Yet, the pandemic exacerbated the caregiving demands of many women at work and home. These increased demands have resulted in women faculty falling further behind in publications, grant funding and promotions (Davis et al.; Kramer). When looking back at the last four years, these are the moments that stand out most in mind; just a few of the many moments when I've felt as though my profession, and academia in general, were incompatible with the mother I want to be.

Halloween 2020

We moved into our first house the day before Halloween and a few months after I accepted my first tenure-track job. Drowning in boxes, I insisted that River wear a costume (Wonder Woman), much to her and Kevin's dismay. This felt like a personal mission, like not commemorating Halloween in some way would signify my failure to follow the *code of motherhood* (Buchanan, 119). In the pictures, exhaustion is clear on all three of our faces. I vow to do better next year.

The Baby Monitors

I have a love/hate relationship with our baby monitors. As I'm teaching and writing, I can hear River and Kevin playing, laughing over the monitor in my home office. I try not to resent Kevin. I remind myself of how lucky and privileged we are that he can be with her. I fear that they're building a bond that she and I won't have. I feel guilty for having this fear. I push the button and as the green on light fades, I feel guilty. Focusing on work while at home lately feels next to impossible. The higher-tech monitors capture video and sound and can be accessed remotely. Watching the video feed from my campus office feels more obtrusive, as if I'm surveilling her. Yet, it also feels like a lifeline to the mother I think I should be. The boundary-less spaces of academic motherhood feel wrapped up in these two devices. Through them, I'm never fully present nor fully absent. I both dread and look forward to the day when River outgrows them.

Risk Tolerance

I've had to make impossible choices between my daughter's health and my students' best interests over the past four years. The emergence of new variants made these choices more visceral. Images of children struggling to breathe on Twitter early in the pandemic induced panic attacks that made sleep next to impossible. Yet, since I was asking adjunct instructors to teach face-to-face, at the behest of administration, I was determined to do so myself as well. As a junior faculty member, advocating for other instructors always feels like a risk. A necessary risk I will continue to take. I wonder how much risk tolerance I have left.

Risk tolerance has taken on new meanings for me now that many of the pandemic protections have been revoked. In addition, the threats that I contend with now seem more nebulous and less manageable than the virus at times. After contending with a "credible threat" of a mass shooting, continued threats of budget cuts and declining enrollments, and countless student crises over the past four years, my risk tolerance for both physical and mental stress is eroding. Today, I have less tolerance for the risks that our academic institutions expose both faculty and students to, less tolerance for the impossible position I feel my profession has put me in as a mother and teacher.

Formalizing institutional support for the labor, time, and care involved in academic motherhood is the most impactful way to move forward (Gaudet et al.). I have a lot of privilege as a white woman and more support as a mother than most. We must recognize how the challenges that I've reflected on here are compounded for single mothers and women of color, who are already the most burdened by inequitable labor conditions in academia. We must commit to creating more opportunities for these women to share their experiences, as seen in the critical narratives offered in *Presumed Incompetent*. It's also important to acknowledge the valuable work that is taking place in academia to support women's labor. In my own field of feminist rhetorical studies, for instance, the Coalition of Feminist Scholars in the History of Rhetoric and Composition offers mentorship programs focused on publication, service, and navigating the field, which provide junior and marginalized scholars spaces to collaborate and support one another (Eble and Gaillet, *Reinscribing*). The Feminist Caucus of the Conference of College Composition and Communication sponsors childcare grants and supports important works that chronicle women's experiences, such as The Women's Lives in the Profession Digital Literacy Narrative Project and the Service Mapping and Visibility Project.

Unequal Labor

While every faculty member's workload increased in some way since the beginning of the pandemic, women faculty have long been carrying heavier workloads. As such, women's engagement in academic service has become even more disproportionate when compared to their male colleagues since the pandemic began (Docka-Filipek and Stone; Mayo). Furthermore, according to the American Association of University Women, women hold most adjunct and non-tenure track positions, meaning they often take on higher teaching loads while having less protections and rights to combat the exploitation of their labor ("Fast Facts"). Even as a tenure-track assistant professor, there have been many times I felt as though the labor expectations placed upon me were untenable. The following snapshots are a few that may also resonate with the experiences of other women faculty and administrators.

Winter "Break"

I finished my first semester exhausted but satisfied. I had completely revamped the first-year writing curricula and felt good about my work as a teacher and administrator. I wasn't spending enough time with River, but the break felt like an opportunity to reset. Then, the email came. Without any preparation on how to assess enrollment needs, I was asked to staff an additional section of first-year writing weeks before classes began. No doubt the unpredictability of COVID on enrollment trends exacerbated this issue. And, yes, this was my job as a WPA; this is a common experience for many WPAs. Knowing all of this did not make this experience any less stressful. This was the moment I first realized how antithetical my new administrative position was with my role as a mother. Since then, I have worked hard to learn past enrollment trends but still have a sneaking suspicion that late December email may rear its ugly head again. Four years later, these dreaded administrative emails are not about the need for more sections but low enrollments. Even with decreased enrollments, the need to hire new adjuncts each semester has not dissipated, as many have left the institution or teaching in general due to the low pay, job precarity, and lack of institutional support they experienced as contingent labor.

The Union Meeting

I'm from a right-to-work state. So, I am simultaneously unfamiliar with and overenthusiastic about unions. Joining my institution's AAUP chapter was a no-brainer for me, particularly after I learned (*after* being hired) that our collective bargaining agreement had expired. The last Union meeting I attended was intense. Person after person aired grievances, some got emotional, and we all agreed that faculty morale was at an all-time low. I turned off my camera and began to cry, feeling despondent and like I became an academic at the wrong time. Yet, coming together in this moment was also comforting. If others felt this way, then it wasn't just my failure or ineptitude to manage it all; the system is set up to make me (and us) feel this way. I didn't work the rest of the day, determined not to give the institution one more second of my day that could've been spent with River. We played in the yard, and it was one of the first times since accepting this position that I felt really present, really okay with not thinking about work or what I *should* be doing, producing, accomplishing.

Self-Advocacy

One of the most necessary, yet illusive, strategies to contending with the unequal landscape of gendered academic labor is learning how to advocate for oneself. Even as a graduate of a doctoral program in Rhetorical Studies, I was not armed with the rhetorical strategies needed to effectively advocate for myself, nor was I prepared for how often I would need to do so.

Graduate students and junior faculty: Advocate for yourself, even (and especially) when you don't think you should or can. I am lucky to have supportive supervisors that argue on my behalf. Yet, it wasn't until I gathered the gumption to ask for an administrative course release at the end of my first year that I found my voice. After much lobbying from my Chair, the request was approved. It's not an annual release as I requested, but it's a start. Asking for this release not only made me feel like I could be a better professor and administrator but also like I was fulfilling one of my most important jobs as River's mom: to protect our time together. Even if it was denied, asking for it would've still been an important strategy for me. It gave the administration an opportunity to acknowledge my labor, or not. If they hadn't, I still would've learned how much they value my labor and would've been empowered to make more informed decisions about my workload and position moving forward. This course release has taken on a different weight over the past two years, as my Chair warns me that the Dean may take it away each semester, even though my administrative responsibilities for which I receive the release wouldn't disappear along with it.

How to advocate for oneself needs to be taught, however. Any rhetoric and composition program offering a course in WPA should cover methods for advocating for oneself and others rhetorically. More established faculty should share their own stories of self-advocacy: that time they were granted that release, that sabbatical, those funds. Sharing stories of failed self-advocacy can also be valuable. Yet, this sharing requires administrators that are willing to listen, to receive and act upon our efforts. As such, more women and faculty of color in positions of power in academia is paramount in providing junior scholars the space to feel empowered to advocate for themselves and others.

Data Collection

During my second year, my Chair suggested that I tally the number of hours I was working. I was horrified at the number. No wonder I wasn't spending enough time with River—there wasn't any time *left* to spend with her. This data became empowering. Every time I wanted to say no to something I felt I couldn't, I thought about that number. To all feminist faculty, junior or senior: *please quit saying yes to uncompensated labor!* I often feel that I can't say no because it will disadvantage my students or colleagues. Yet, oftentimes my overworking sets a precedent for other women to take on more labor. After surprising some of my new colleagues by not agreeing to what my predecessor did, I've come to realize that my willingness to overwork was an anti-feminist practice. Staying mindful of my workload and saying no to uncompensated labor wasn't just for me or River, but for future women in this position.

More broadly, programs, departments, and institutions should also regularly take stock of who is serving on what committee, who is advising how many students, and how many of those with the greatest workload are women and faculty of color. What would it mean to share this data at faculty meetings? To the dean and provost when asking for more support? As a rhetorician, I've always been suspicious of the pressure to quantify. Now, I see data as power. Collecting this data is also about collecting stories, like mine.

As feminist scholars from across the disciplines have long recognized, personal narrative and storytelling are vital forms of labor and resistance. Feminist rhetorical scholars have called for more critical attention to women's labor conditions in academia (e.g., Ballif, Davis, and Mountford; Flynn and Bourelle; Gold and Enoch; Miller; Schell). Building on this work, I offer my narratives to contribute to what Sara Ahmed identifies as the "shared project" of feminist storytelling as we "share the labor" of complaint and critique (Ahmed, *Feminist Killjoy*, 234–35). In centering my lived experiences within systemic problems, I aim to critique the inequities of gendered academic labor and model how our scholarship can expose how these inequities impact the physical and mental well-being of women faculty. Mostly, I hope my narratives can serve as a source of commiseration and perspective for other women graduate students and early career faculty, as they find ways to move through and thrive within academic institutions that have longed undervalued women's labor. Sharing how the academy forces impossible choices upon women, mothers, and caregivers for broader audiences is the most important step towards affecting change. I am honored to be a part of this step.

Collaboration

Collaborating with other women scholars, teachers, and administrators within my own institution, across the country, and internationally, has been a lifeline for me since the pandemic began. Quickly after accepting the position, I knew I wouldn't be able to teach the old curriculum. Hesitant to change everything about the program my first semester, I reached out to the only adjunct instructor at the time. Together, she and I built a first-year writing curriculum grounded in both her and previous students' experiences and my own vision for the program. Since then, several new instructors have joined us, and we've taken the same collaborative approach.

Since before I began this position, I've been a part of an intergenerational women's writing group sponsored by the Writing Across the Curriculum program of my alma mater. Writing, publishing, and presenting with these women has resulted in the scholarship that I am most proud of and invested in. However, collaboration, both with this group of women and my other women collaborators, has become increasingly difficult to manage over the last four years. Because I collaborate with mostly other women academics, they are also overburdened and under resourced, which can make our collaboration more labor intensive and time consuming. In addition, promotion guidelines often don't make room for collaborative projects that require more time and energy. For instance, two of my collaborators—also both academic moms—live in Western North Carolina, an area devastated by Hurricane Helene in September 2024. The damage sustained during the storm will rightfully require their labor and attention elsewhere for the foreseeable future. How do I capture the impact of a natural disaster that occurred states away on my own scholarly productivity or why a journal article that's been listed as in-progress in last year's annual review is still in-progress this year? Furthermore, such a consideration seems crass in the face of the death and devastation my collaborators and their communities are experiencing, but one that I must contend with given the pressure for productivity embedded in academic promotion.

Many feminist rhetorical scholars have recognized collaboration as a tool for feminist pedagogy, administration, and exposing and inciting change to unequal labor conditions (e.g., Buchanan; Lunsford and Ede). For instance, in *Widening Scripts,* interdisciplinary scholars share their experiences forming a "collective feminist survival kit" through the formation of a reading and writing group organized around Sara Ahmed's *Feminist Killjoy Handbook.* The authors point to collaborative reading and writing as a "feminist praxis . . . to regain autonomy and express solidarity in moments of extreme difficulty" (Assis et al., 37). Another potential model for collaboration as a tool for critical reflection and collective action is the feminist academic organization of gender scholars in Business, the Gender, Markets, and Consumers (GENMAC). GEN-MAC's mission is to "challenge hierarchies of knowledge, prioritize the care and support needed for the day-to-day survival of gender scholars in business schools, and spotlight and challenge structural inequalities and injustices in the academy" (Gurrieri et al., 2159–60). The issue is not that we know collaboration is a valuable approach, but how to actualize it in a way that doesn't further add to our workloads.

Academic institutions must formalize their support of collaboration in the form of compensated mentorships, programs, and opportunities. Mentorships are an important tool for supporting women's labor (Ballif, Davis, and Mountford; Bishop; Eble and Gaillet, *Stories* and *Reinscribing;* Lunsford and Ede). Most of the mentorship programs I've taken part in were uncompensated. Yet, mentoring and being mentored is still labor. The most successful experience I've had was when I was asked to mentor an instructor identified by the administration as "struggling." To compensate me and the instructor for this time, our WPA counted it as our required service. Organizations in the field with mentorship programs should provide platforms for participants to showcase their work in publications and conferences. Moreover, WPA positions should be collaborative. Many institutions rotate administrative positions, but what would it mean to have co-WPAs as a best practice? I would not have survived the last four years as a WPA without the generous collaboration of my colleagues, mentors, and friends, many of whom are women. If formal, compensated mentorship programs were in place, our collaboration could have lightened instead of added to their workloads.

When looking back over the moments I've shared in this chapter and the many, similar ones I haven't, a common thread emerges: the need for a reconsideration of how we recognize and value care work as academic labor, much of which is completed by women or gender minority faculty. Such a reconsideration requires commitment to "a feminist ethic of care" with particular consciousness of how labor conditions are experienced by those most likely to have their labor exploited (Naylor). Black feminists have long acknowledged self- and collective care as forms of activism (Finch). Audre Lorde, Angela Davis, bell hooks (*All About Love*), the Combahee River Collective, and Jennifer Nash recognize self-care as a political and radical act of resistance to the social and cultural institutions that marginalize. Centering care as a method for resisting the inequities of academic gendered labor involves critically reflecting on the rhetoric and standards by which labor is codified; revising promotion metrics to recognize care work, such as faculty-to-faculty mentoring and responding to increased rates of student mental health crises, as valid contributions to the university; and, implementing faculty well-being support systems grounded in collective care and institutional accountability and not individual responsibility.

Centering feminist care in this way also requires revisions to the rhetoric we use to discuss women's labor in the academy. Phrases like "work–life balance," "having it all," and "working mothers" are toxic and perpetuate unattainable ideals that are then used to devalue women's labor (Slaughter). In "The Double Standard of Work–life balance," Lahle Wolfe postulates that the term "was invented by a man because it suggests we can have careers, babies, and a clean house if we just prioritize and work harder at 'balancing' our lives." For me, the term "burnout" has been the hardest to accept. I hear it everywhere, but no one defines it. What I do know is that it doesn't come close to capturing how my colleagues and I feel. Even more, the term and its overuse erase the unequal burden of workplace stress, particularly on women of color, who experience higher rates of hostility, discrimination, and detrimental impacts on their health (Aya). The inequities ingrained in gendered academic labor make burnout inevitable for women in higher education, regardless of how much self-care they practice. Even more so, being told I'm burnt out doesn't feel particularly helpful or motivating. It makes me feel like a product that has passed its expiration date. How do you revive a burnt-out light bulb? You can't; you replace it if you can. Some of us only have one light bulb while others have too many.

The issues I've raised here are not new to women's labor. The pandemic has only brought them into sharper focus. When I began this project in 2021, I was hopeful. I clung to Sara Ahmed's recognition that the pandemic is "also a time that has taught us that, when necessary, we can organize worlds in other ways" (*Complaint!*, xi). Now, entering my ninth semester as an assistant professor, I am more exhausted and despondent than ever before. I'm grateful for what the pandemic has taught me about accessible teaching and assignment design. Yet, the challenges my colleagues, students, and I face rage on, as higher education and society at large has seemingly declared the pandemic over. Accommodations for online teaching, mandated masking, and other safety precautions are no longer guaranteed. Faculty and staff shortages from the pandemic remain unfilled, as we are all continually asked to do more with less.

I recently completed my third-year review file. While I should've been proud of all I accomplished, I was overwhelmed with anger at the unpaid hours of labor, the hours I missed with River. Still, the feminist in me clings to the unrelenting hope that things can be better. I think of bell hooks's assertion that hope is at the center of feminist teaching and community building (hooks, *Teaching*). I'm reminded of Cheryl Glenn's focus on hope as the operative effect of rhetorical feminism. For now, I will continue to focus on "the possibilities of struggling together toward something more beautiful, more humane" (Glenn, 206).

Bibliography

Ahmed, Sara. *Complaint!* Duke University Press, 2021.

Ahmed, Sara. *The Feminist Killjoy Handbook: The Radical Potential of Getting in the Way.* Seal Press, 2023.

Assis, Mariana P., Michelle Forrest, Angela Henderson, Lindsey MacCallum, Ian Reilly, Ellen Shaffner, and Scott Stoneman. *Widening Scripts: Cultivating Feminist Care in Academic Labor.* Punctum Books, 2023.

Aya, Ebony. "The Hostility Black Women Face in Higher Education Carries Dire Consequences." *The Conversation,* March 15, 2024. https://theconversation.com/.

Ballif, Michelle, Diane Davis, and Roxanne Mountford. *Women's Ways of Making It in Rhetoric and Composition*. Routledge, 2008.

Bishop, Wendy. "Against the Odds in Composition and Rhetoric." *College Composition and Communication* 53, no. 2 (2001): 322–35.

Buchanan, Lindal. *The Rhetoric of Motherhood*. Southern Illinois University Press, 2013.

Combahee River Collective. "A Black Feminist Statement." In *Words of Fire: An Anthology of African-American Feminist Thought*, edited by Beverly Guy-Sheftall. W. W. Norton, 1995.

Davis, Angela. "Radical Self-Care." AfroPunk. December 17, 2018. Video, 4:27 https://www.youtube.com/watch?v=Q1cHoL4vaBs.

Davis, Pamela B., Emma A. Meagher, Claire Pomeroy, et al. "Pandemic-related Barriers to the Success of Women in Research: A Framework for Action." *Nature Medicine* 28 (2022): 436–38.

Docka-Filipek, Danielle, and Lindsey B. Stone. "Twice a 'Housewife': On Academic Precarity, 'Hysterical' Women, Faculty Mental Health, and Service as Gendered Care Work for the 'University Family' in Pandemic Times." *Gender, Work, and Organization* 28, no. 6 (2021): 2158–79.

Eble, Michelle F., and Lynée Lewis Gaillet. "Reinscribing Mentoring." In *Retellings: Opportunities for Feminist Research in Rhetoric and Composition Studies*, edited by Jordynn Jack and Jessica Enoch. Parlor Press, 2019.

Eble, Michelle, F., and Lynée Lewis Gaillet, eds. *Stories of Mentoring: Theory and Praxis*. Parlor Press, 2008.

"Fast Facts: Women Working in Academia." American Association of University Women, https://www.aauw.org/resources/article/fast-facts-academia/. Accessed October 13, 2024.

Finch, Aisha K. "Introduction: Black Feminism and the Practice of Care." *Palimpsest: A Journal on Women, Gender, and the Black International* 11, no. 1 (2022): 1–41.

Flynn, Elizabeth A., and Tiffany Bourelle, eds. *Women's Professional Lives in Rhetoric and Composition: Choice, Chance, and Serendipity*. The Ohio State University Press, 2018.

Gaudet, Stéphanie, Isabelle Marchand, Merridee Bujakic, and Ivy Lynn Bourgeault. "Women and Gender Equity in Academia Through the Conceptual Lens of Care." *Journal of Gender Studies* 31, no. 1 (2022): 74–86.

Gay, Roxane. *Bad Feminist*. HarperCollins, 2014.

Glenn, Cheryl. *Rhetorical Feminism and This Thing Called Hope*. Southern Illinois University Press, 2018.

Gold, David, and Jessica Enoch, eds. *Women at Work: Rhetorics of Gender and Labor*. University of Pittsburgh Press, 2019.

Gurrieri, Lauren, Andrea Prothero, Shona Bettany, et al. "Feminist Academic Organizations: Challenging Sexism through Collective Mobilizing across Research, Support, and Advocacy." *Gender, Work, and Organization* 31 (2022): 2158–79.

Gutiérrez y Muhs, Gabriella, Yolanda F. Niemann, Carmen G. González, and Angela P. Harris, eds. *Presumed Incompetent: The Intersections of Race and Class for Women in Academia.* Utah State University Press, 2012.

hooks, bell. *Teaching Community: A Pedagogy of Hope.* Routledge, 2003.

hooks, bell. *All About Love: New Visions.* William Morrow, 2018.

Kramer, Jillian. "The Virus Moved Female Faculty to the Brink. Will Universities Help?" *New York Times,* October 6, 2020. https://www.nytimes.com/.

Lorde, Audre. "A Burst of Light." *Essence* 18, no. 9 (1988): 46–112.

Lunsford, Andrea A. *Writing Matters: Rhetoric in Public and Private Lives.* University of Georgia Press, 2007.

Lunsford, Andrea A., and Lisa Ede. *Writing Together: Collaboration in Theory and Practice.* Bedford/St. Martin's, 2011.

Mayo, Liz. "Women Do Higher Ed's Chores. That Must Change." *Chronicle of Higher Education,* February 13, 2023. https://www.chronicle.com/.

Miller, Susan. *Textual Carnivals: The Politics of Composition.* Southern Illinois University Press, 1993.

Nash, Jennifer C. "Practicing Love: Black Feminism, Love Politics, and Post-Intersectionality." *Meridians* 11, no. 2 (2011): 1–24.

Naylor, Lindsay. "A Feminist Ethic of Care in the Neoliberal University." *Society+Space,* October 2, 2023. https://www.societyandspace.org/.

Royster, Jacqueline Jones, and Gesa E. Kirsch. *Feminist Rhetorical Practices: New Horizons for Rhetoric, Composition, and Literacy Studies.* Southern Illinois University Press, 2012.

Schell, Eileen E. *Gypsy Academics and Mother-Teachers: Gender, Contingent Labor, and Writing Instruction.* Heinemann-Boynton/Cook, 1998.

Slaughter, Anne-Marie. "The Failure of the Phrase 'Work–life balance.'" *The Atlantic,* December 16, 2015. https://www.theatlantic.com/.

Vyletel, Brenda, Erin Voichoski, Sarah Lipson, and Justin Heinze. "Exploring Faculty Burnout Through the 2022–23 HMS Faculty/Staff Survey." *American Psychological Association,* August 31, 2023, https://www.apa.org/.

Wolfe, Lahle. "The Double Standard of Work–Life Balance." *LiveAbout.com,* October 4, 2019, https://www.liveabout.com/.

My Shame Story

Gendered Ethnic Inequities of
Student Evaluation of Teaching

Mary Lourdes Silva

At the beginning of the pandemic, in the most ironic unexpected twist, I could finally be myself again. Administration placed student evaluation of teaching (SET) on hold. In March 2020, I worked in academic triage, laboring twelve hours a day from the first spring break of the pandemic to the second. The labor was typical, a mad scramble to online teaching; attending webinars in Zoom and *about* Zoom; organizing professional development workshops for colleagues; calling truant students, praying they were alive and well; and conferencing with the dozens struggling with anxiety and depression. Studies about the gender inequalities of academic labor during the pandemic find that women had work disrupted more often than men due to gendered expectations to engage in emotional care for students, colleagues, and family members (Altan-Olcay and Bergeron; Berheide et al.; Docka and Stone). For me, the additional emotional and academic labor was a welcome distraction from my anxiety of SETs. For the first time in a long time, I was free again.

Shame Is the Hand That Silences Us

Researcher and best-selling author Brené Brown writes, "Shame loves secrecy. The most dangerous thing to do after a shaming experience is hide or bury our story" (10). After years of hiding from colleagues, it was no longer a secret that some students did not want me in the classroom. Forced to review our official SETs in our annual teacher reports, I could count on reading cruel comments about my poor pronunciation of words, occasional grammar mistakes in assignment directions or marginal comments, and lack of general competence. Without fail, I could count on white male colleagues, whom I previously mentored, repeatedly outperforming me on SETs, even though they lacked my pedagogical expertise and often had students unengaged or distracted by their mobile devices.

Brown states that shame is the fear of not being enough, not worthy of connection or community. I was not enough. I did not share my students' privileged past. I don't know what it is like to be raised by American-born, college-educated parents who spoke good English; who fraternized with other college-educated relatives and friends; who sent kids off to summer camp; paid for tutors and nannies; and filled their shelves with books rather than canned food and couponed cereal boxes. As a first-generation white Latina, I learned quickly that belonging was a transactional relationship: my homework and immigrant work ethic for straight A's. Teachers adored me. School was my sanctuary. Years later, when I taught at Hispanic-Serving Institutions, my students adored me. I knew then that education was my calling because students learned to believe that they belonged as well. However, true belonging, as Brown states, doesn't ask us to change who we are; it demands we be who we are. For the past seventeen years, working at predominantly white institutions (PWI), each year (not counting the pandemic) a handful of student evaluations stung, like a slap to my cheek.

Gender Bias in Student Evaluation of Teaching

My story is a familiar one, an ember from a much larger blaze. On Facebook, a constellation of articles from *Inside Higher Education* about SETs reappear on my feed—"Bias Against Female Instructors"; "Gender Bias in TA Evals"; "The Skinny on Teaching Evals and Bias"; and "Colleges Must Change to Retain BIPOC Women Faculty." The satirical blog post, "Reviewing Course Evaluations: The Drinking Game" by Steph Jeffries, poignantly describes the first rule of the drinking game: "If you are female, drink one shot immediately. From an underrepresented community: one shot. Both: three shots, because intersectionality. Each shot will help you lower your expectations for fairness before you read through the comments." The articles made their rounds via progressive academic circles and enough *Likes, Shares,* and *Retweets* temporarily validated the voices of educators harmed or humiliated by an institutional assessment based on a white supremacist system that privileges certain bodies, discursive practices, ideologies, and epistemologies.

In 2020, the pandemic disrupted institutional assessments altogether. A "new normal" emerged regarding assessment of student learning. Working entirely online for three consecutive semesters, we were asked to be flexible regarding late work, deadlines, and assignment expectations. Moreover, college administrators acknowledged the additional labor imposed on faculty unqualified to teach online courses and waived SETs for two consecutive semesters. And just like that, like a magic wand waved over my head, the anxiety and trauma of being forced to read SETs disappeared. I enjoyed teaching once again, experimenting with online writing instruction, adapting my courses based on a hybrid-flexible course design, and working with students struggling with anxiety and depression due to the pandemic. As a technologist at a small liberal arts college famous for its music, theater, and creative writing programs, my pandemic-ready course design offered something that students' Luddite professors could not offer. After losing my father and older sister in 2020, I also understood their loss and grief.

In spring 2021, administrators warned us that SETs would return. As if it were another pending wave of COVID, I set out to protect myself from emotional harm. The research on the gender, racial, and ethnic biases of SETs is quite compelling. Developed in the 1920s by two independent educational psychologists, SET was initially limited to classroom use to improve instruction. In 1953, one of the developers, Edwin Guthrie warned against the misuse of SET "as ultimate measure of merit" (802, qtd. in Stroebe, "Student Evaluations"). Today, a great majority of universities and colleges use SET to base their decisions regarding hiring, promotion, merit pay, funding opportunities, awards, and more (Stroebe, "Student Evaluations"), despite the copious studies that question the validity and reliability of SET as a measurement of teaching effectiveness (Beran and Rokosh; Boring et al.; Clayson; Galbraith et al.; Shevlin et al.; Spooren et al.; Uttl et al.). Problems of validity and reliability are exacerbated for many female faculty and female faculty of color who receive statistically significant lower SET scores (Baslow; Boring et al.) and inherit the additional labor and emotional work to navigate intersectional systems of gender, race, ethnic bias, and sexuality in various professional roles (e.g., colleague, instructor, researcher/writer, and administrator).

Female professors are expected to be more available outside of class (Bennett; El-Alayli et al.; Rideau and Robbins) and are held to a different gendered metric system (Sprague and Massoni), a sliding scale between two variables—very nurturing or cold-stone bitch. Even when SETs are positive for females and raise no red flags for administration, female faculty must contend with sexist discourse about being "nice" but seldom "brilliant" or "intelligent" (Burke et al.; MacNell et al.; Mitchell and Martin; Rivera and Tilcsik; Rubin; Storage et al.). To "satisfy" students, female faculty must decide whether to invest more time and energy in comparison to their male counterparts to receive equivalent SET scores (Owen), or compromise their research, publication agenda, and/or self-care. However, increased investment in course design and student learning does not guarantee positive results. In several studies, researchers found that highly qualified experienced faculty received lower SET scores (Stroebe, "Why Good Teaching"; Uttl et al.). In sum, SET is an institutional assessment that privileges white men and harms women and BIPOC faculty.

For tenure, I did whatever it took to improve my SETs:

Participate in multiple professional development institutes, workshops, and seminars; CHECK!

Rather than conferencing the standard 1–2 times a semester with students, heed white colleague's advice and conference 3 times; CHECK!

When 30 minutes of conferencing didn't make a difference on my SETs, make it 45 minutes; CHECK!

Write longer, more cordial emails; CHECK!

Pay $150 out of pocket for video software and spend 50% more time providing video feedback on student work to appear more nurturing; CHECK!

When one white colleague commented that I spoke too loudly in the classroom, mute my tenor voice to appear less threatening; CHECK!

Enunciate syllables to hide any imperfections; CHECK!

When I struggle to pronounce a word correctly, insert a self-deprecating joke; CHECK!

Script and self-correct my English in real-time; CHECK!

Whatever it took, it didn't matter. It didn't matter that I was Director of First-Year Composition, training new faculty; it didn't matter that I coordinated an annual technology writing institute at a major R1 university, coordinated tango events in my community, presented papers at international conferences, published research in writing studies, and attended various professional development workshops merely for the love of learning. As a white Latina in higher education where only 3% of full-time faculty are Hispanic females ("Fast Facts: Race/Ethnicity of College Faculty"), no amount of "self-improvement" could alter the implicit biases embedded in my SETs.

Teaching in Predominantly White Institutions

At PWIs, I stood in the way of privileged students who had never received anything lower than an A–. Frequent absences and homework extensions were expected and normalized in their literacy education. Accountability was always negotiable. It took me years to realize that privileged students lived by a different set of rules, and it was my job to adapt to them. Rideau and Robbins report that women of color are more likely to have their expertise challenged by students and more likely to experience the classroom as a hostile work environment. Without a support network, Latina faculty have reported feelings of loneliness, isolation, and marginalization (Gonzales et al.; Saldaña et al.; Vasquez-Guignard). Sanchez-Peña et al. note how "white-passing" Latinas may not experience racism in the same way as Black or mixed-race Latinas, yet still share similar feelings of racism, isolation, and exclusion. Latina faculty must navigate cultural "borderlands," traversing professional and personal spaces, while maintaining and negotiating their identities as scholars, colleagues, community members, and family members, leaving some Latina faculty to feel self-doubt and incompetent (Saldaña et al.). In their testimony about self-doubt, Saldaña et al. explains that "as Chicana/Latina academics, we fear that if we were to offer an authentic testimony of what our spirit, body, minds experience in the academy, we will be exposed, judged, and rejected by our peers and made into outcasts by the larger institution" (42).

When I reported experiences of hostility in the classroom to my department chair, the default presumption was that I must have done something wrong. I shared the data about gender and race bias in SET, which he renounced, arguing it could not possibly be gender/race bias because the majority of female faculty and female faculty of color in our department had few issues with SET. Based on his logic, racism and sexism do not exist if most in our small academic community do not experience racism and sexism. Without a single visit to my classroom or a review of my curricular materials, this administrator concluded that I was the problem, the department outlier. In my varied professional roles as Director of Composition, member of the Personnel and Writing Intensive Committees, and the Humanities and Sciences Curriculum Committee, I had observed dozens of contingent faculty and reviewed syllabi and curricular materials from multiple disciplines; and without fail, the worst faculty were white males, sages on the stage, with far less education and pedagogical training, while disengaged students chatted online or surfed the web.

And still . . . .and still, they received better SET scores than me. They flew under the radar, adopting a passive learning, current traditional rhetorical approach to writing instruction, while my department chair flagged me as the problem, going out of his way to reject a research grant proposal so that I could "focus on my teaching" and deny me the chance to be Director of the Writing

Center due to some problematic SETs. Not only did my department tenure committee know about my history of SET, which fortunately, did not factor into the All-College Committee's 7–0 vote of approval for tenure, the Executive Committee was recently alerted of my SETs, which means nearly one-third of my department now knows *I am the problem.*

Gonzales et al. make clear that Latina faculty strive for institutional legitimacy. According to Riva-Holly, "Latinas who embrace and accept their designated roles in the academy, become grateful outsiders" while those who resist are excluded and vilified (qtd. In Pizarro). We often feel pressured to code switch, which can be exhausting to manage and assess which colleagues are "safe" for sharing your authentic self. After sixteen years of code-switching to survive a toxic institutional review process, I no longer recognized myself.

Yes, with tenure, I have a twig of power, but it is a myth that tenured faculty no longer have to worry about their SETs. It was with tenure when I was denied merit pay, a research grant, and an administrative position due to my SETs. And no, there is no "innovative" way to revise SET questions or procedures to eliminate implicit biases. At best, SET designers can reduce *evidence* of bias. In other words, rather than being reminded by 5 students per class that I don't belong, I should be grateful that only 1–2 students will find pleasure in mocking me. And yes, heeding the advice, "Don't let the opinions of 18-year-olds get to you," ignores the central issue in which university administrators subject faculty of color and female faculty to institutional bullying. Although few universities like the University of Southern California and Ryerson University in Canada have disentangled SETs from tenure and promotion, faculty are still expected to read prejudiced anonymous comments (Flaherty, "Teaching Eval Shake-Up."; Flaherty, "Arbitrating the Use of Student Evaluations").

Ethical and Equitable Changes to Faculty Evaluations

What could this pandemic teach us about labor and the gendered ethnic/racial inequities of SET? How could academic labor be improved to better align with our intersectional identities and personal lives? First, faculty don't need SETs. Female faculty and faculty of color can thrive and innovate under the worst conditions without the pending doubts of administration. Allow faculty to generate their own systems of course review where students participate non-anonymously in the process throughout the semester. An open dialogic exchange between faculty, administrators, and students allows faculty to make real-time changes to their courses to improve student learning outcomes. Furthermore, evidence-based assessment that includes course materials; course-management system analytics, such as student time on tasks; student work; student reflections; and instructor reflections allows faculty to generate quantitative and qualitative data that serves their pedagogical curricular needs and the needs of administrators.

The Price of Shame

Since 2003, I have written with a ceramic figure on my desk gifted by "Mary Lourdes' Girls": a red apple inscribed with the grade *A+* atop a book of *English* and *Writing*. "Mary Lourdes' Girls" was a group of three students of color who repeatedly enrolled in my writing group at the writing center throughout their undergraduate education. They gifted me the ceramic figure at my MFA graduation ceremony after I was awarded the President's Medal, the highest honor for a graduate student. This ceramic student evaluation reminds me that at one time I worked in learning spaces where students valued my expertise, empathy, and ethnic roots. They saw themselves in me, and how could I ever forget myself in them?

Shame is internalized sedimented blame, one element of wet clay pressed against the next by the hands of institutionalized oppression and individual childhood traumas. I know now that higher education is built on white language supremacy that privileges the literacy habits and values of upper middle-class white male heteronormative able-bodied academics and punishes the rest of us (Inoue). But knowing better and doing better has nothing to do with shame; it is about belonging and knowing that belonging isn't always up to you to decide. Maya Angelou would disagree, "You are only free when you realize you belong no place—you belong every place—no place at all. The price is high. The reward is great" (22). For now, the price is pain. The reward pending.

This is my shame story . . . an abrupt end to the silence, followed by more silence. Given how few faculty of color are in higher education, even fewer come forward to share their shame story about student evaluation of teaching. I write this story in secrecy, my silent protest. My colleagues and administrators will most likely never read it. I don't write this story for them. I write it for the faculty oppressed by SETs who shout into pillows and cry in the shadows.

Bibliography

Altan-Olcay, Özlem, and Suzanne Bergeron. "Care in Times of the Pandemic: Rethinking Meanings of Work in the University." *Gender, Work, and Organization* (2022): https://doi.org/10.1111/gwao.12871.

Angelou, Maya. "A Conversation with Maya Angelou: Bill Moyers/1973." *Conversations with Maya Angelou,* edited by Jeffrey M. Elliot, 18–28. University Press of Mississippi, 1989.

Baslow, Susan A. "Student Evaluations of College Professors: When Gender Matters." *Journal of Educational Psychology* 87, no. 4 (1995): 656–65.

Bennett, Sheila K. "Student Perceptions of and Expectations for Male and Female Instructors: Evidence Relating to the Question of Gender Bias in Teaching Evaluation." *Journal of Educational Psychology* 74, no. 2 (1982):170–79. https://doi.org/10.1037/0022-0663.74.2.170.

Beran, Tanya N., and Jennifer L. Rokosh. "The Consequential Validity of Student Ratings: What Do Instructors Really Think?" *Alberta Journal of Educational Research* 55, no. 4 (2009): 497–511.

Berheide, Catherine White, Megan A. Carpenter, and David A. Cotter. "Teaching College in the Time of COVID-19: Gender and Race Differences in Faculty Emotional Labor." *Sex Roles* 86, no. 7–8 (2022): 441–55, https://doi.org/10.1007/s11199-021-01271-0.

Boring, Anne, Kellie Ottoboni, and Philip B. Stark. "Student Evaluations of Teaching (Mostly) Do Not Measure Teaching Effectiveness." *ScienceOpen Research* (2016): https://doi.org/10.14293/S2199-1006.1.SOR-EDU.AETBZC.v1.

Brown, Brené. *The Gifts of Imperfection: Letting Go of Who We Think We Should Be and Embracing Who We Are.* Hazelden Publishing, 2010.

Burke, Alison S., Whitney Head-Burgess, and Mark Siders. "He's Smart and She's Nice: Student Perceptions of Male and Female Faculty." *International Journal of Gender and Women's Studies* 5, no. 1 (2017): 1–6.

Buser, Whitney, Cassondra Batz-Barbarich, and Jill Kearns Hayter. "Evaluation of Women in Economics: Evidence of Gender Bias Following Behavioral Role Violations." *Sex Roles* 86, no. 11–12 (2022): 695–710.

Clayson, Dennis E., and Debra A. Haley. "Are Students Telling Us the Truth? A Critical Look at the Student Evaluation of Teaching." *Marketing Education Review* 21, no. 2 (2011): 101–12.

Docka-Filipek, Danielle, and Lindsey B. Stone. "Twice a 'Housewife': On Academic Precarity, 'Hysterical' Women, Faculty Mental Health, and Service as Gendered Care Work for the 'University Family' in Pandemic Times." *Gender, Work & Organization* 28, no. 6 (Nov. 2021): 2158–79. https://doi.org/10.1111/gwao.12723.

El-Alayli, Amani, Ashley A. Hansen-Brown, and Michelle Ceynar. "Dancing Backwards in High Heels: Female Professors Experience More Work Demands and Special Favor Requests, Particularly from Academically Entitled Students." *Sex Roles* 79, no. 3–4 (2018): 136–50. https://doi.org/10.1007/s11199-017-0872-6.

"Fast Facts: Race/Ethnicity of College Faculty." *National Center for Education Statistics,* https://nces.ed.gov/fastfacts/display.asp?id=61. Accessed February 28, 2022.

Flaherty, Colleen. "Teaching Eval Shake-Up." *Inside Higher Ed,* May 21, 2018. https://www.insidehighered.com/.

Flaherty, Colleen. "Arbitrating the Use of Student Evaluations of Teaching." *Inside Higher Ed,* August 30, 2018. https://www.insidehighered.com/.

Galbraith, Craig S., Gregory B. Merrill, and Doug M. Kline. "Are Student Evaluations of Teaching Effectiveness Valid for Measuring Student Learning Outcomes in Business Related Classes? A Neural Network and Bayesian Analyses." *Research in Higher Education* 53, no. 3 (2012): 353–74.

Gonzales, Leslie D., Elizabeth Murakami, and Anne-Marie Núñez. "Latina Faculty in the Labyrinth: Constructing and Contesting Legitimacy in Hispanic Serving Institutions." *The Journal of Educational Foundations* 27, no. 1 (2013): 65–89.

Inoue, Asao B. *Above the Well: An Antiracist Literacy Argument from A Boy of Color.* The WAC Clearinghouse. Utah State University Press, 2021.

Jeffries, Steph. "Reviewing Course Evaluations: The Drinking Game." *McSweeney's Internet Tendency,* May 19, 2019, https://www.mcsweeneys.net/.

MacNell, Lillian, Adam Driscoll, and Andrea N. Hunt. "What's in a Name: Exposing Gender Bias in Student Ratings of Teaching." *Journal of Collective Bargaining in the Academy* 0, article 52 (2015). http://thekeep.eiu.edu/jcba/vol0/iss10/52.

Mitchell, Kristina M. W., and Jonathan Martin. "Gender Bias in Student Evaluations." *PS: Political Science & Politics* 51, no. 3 (2018): 648–52.

Owen, Ann. "The Next Lawsuits to Hit Higher Education." *Inside Higher Ed,* June 24, 2019, https://www.insidehighered.com/.

Pizarro, Jesenia M. "The Uncivil Latina." *Race and Justice* 7, no. 2, 2017, pp. 160–78. https://doi.org/10.1177/2153368717690790.

Rideau, Ryan, and Claire K. Robbins. "The Experiences of Non-Tenure-Track Faculty Members of Color with Racism in the Classroom." *To Improve the Academy: A Journal of Educational Development* 39, no. 2 (2020): 129–60.

Rivera, Lauren A., and András Tilcsik. "Scaling Down Inequality: Rating Scales, Gender Bias, and the Architecture of Evaluation." *American Sociological Review* 84, no. 2 (2019): 248–74.

Rubin, Rebecca B. "Ideal Traits and Terms of Address for Male and Female College Professors." *Journal of Personality and Social Psychology* 41, no 5 (1981): 966–74.

Saldaña, Lilliana Patricia, Felicia Castro-Villarreal, and Erica Sosa. "Testimonios of Latina Junior Faculty: Bridging Academia, Family, and Community Lives in the Academy." *The Journal of Educational Foundations* 27, no. 1 (2013): 31–48.

Sanchez-Peña, Matilde, Joyce Main, Nikitha Sambamurthy, Monica Cox, and Ebony McGee. "The Factors Affecting the Persistence of Latina Faculty: A Literature Review Using the Intersectionality of Race, Gender, and Class." *2016 IEEE Frontiers in Education Conference (FIE).* IEEE (2016). https://doi.org/10.1109/FIE.2016.7757519.

Shevlin, Mark, Philip Banyard, Mark Davies, and Mark Griffiths. "The Validity of Student Evaluation of Teaching in Higher Education: Love Me, Love My Lectures?" *Assessment and Evaluation in Higher Education* 25, no. 4 (2000): 397–405.

Spooren, Pieter, Bert Brockx, and Dimitri Mortelmans. "On the Validity of Student Evaluation of Teaching: The State of the Art." *Review of Educational Research* 83, no. 4 (2013): 598–642.

Sprague, Joey, and Kelley Massoni. "Student Evaluations and Gendered Expectations: What We Can't Count Can Hurt Us." *Sex Roles* 53, no. 11–12 (2005): 779–93.

Storage, Daniel, Zachary Horne, Andrei Cimpian, and Sarah-Jane Leslie. "The Frequency of 'Brilliant' and 'Genius' in Teaching Evaluations Predicts the Representation of Women and African Americans across Fields." *PLOS One* 11, no. 3 (2016): https://doi.org/10.1371/journal.pone.0150194.

Stroebe, Wolfgang. "Why Good Teaching Evaluations May Reward Bad Teaching: On Grade Inflation and Other Unintended Consequences of Student Evaluations." *Perspectives on Psychological Science* 11, no. 6 (2016): 800–16.

Stroebe, Wolfgang. "Student Evaluations of Teaching Encourages Poor Teaching and Contributes to Grade Inflation: A Theoretical and Empirical Analysis." *Basic and Applied Social Psychology* 42, no. 4 (2020): 276–94.

Uttl, Bob, Carmela A. White, and Daniela Wong Gonzalez. "Meta-Analysis of Faculty's Teaching Effectiveness: Student Evaluation of Teaching Ratings and Student Learning Are Not Related." *Studies in Educational Evaluation* 54 (2017): 22–42.

Vasquez-Guignard, Sandra. "Latina University Professors, Insights into the Journeys of Those who Strive to Leadership within Academia." PhD diss., Pepperdine University, 2010.

CHAPTER 17

Pursuing 20/20 Vision

Learning the Labor of Activist Editors

Nancy Myers and Heather Brook Adams

A pandemic implicates human bodies—individually, in family or kinship networks, in community, and, notably, on a worldwide scale. Rather than only introducing the novel (e.g., a virus), a pandemic can reintroduce material realities of bodies—those that were already apparent and those taken for granted. These realities include each body's health, illness, and possible death. COVID-19 put into stark relief across 2020 what Melinda Gates aptly explains: "This pandemic has magnified every existing inequality in our society—like systemic racism, gender inequality, and poverty. And it's impossible to pick one issue as more serious because so many people live at the intersection of all those challenges" (Ford). Gates's intersection evokes the body and calls attention to material effects of pandemic life—lost income, risk of eviction, exhaustion and despair of frontline workers, risk of exposure, illness of self, family or friends, and death. No one has fully escaped fear, anxiety, or loss of some kind.

The *gravitas* of the pandemic is the context during which, we, Nancy and Heather, coedited a collection on the rhetorics of reproductive politics. Thus, the material bodies of the chapter writers and the editors, the metaphorical body of the collection, and the human bodies addressed throughout the content of the collection were salient to us over the last four years. In discussing the work of journal editors, Melissa Ianetta points to this relationship among scholarship, editing, and material bodies, "between the body of the editor and the body of a journal. That is, editors are often invisible figures in the scholarship of our field, rarely discernible in our scholarly conversation" (267). For editors and for writers, scholarly concerns about bodies may inform an intellectual stance, but the creators' toil remains invisible. As editors of a collection on rhetorics of reproduction, we embarked on our project knowing that injustices directed toward bodies would be central to each chapter. Soon thereafter, we found ourselves reconsidering our responsibilities as editors given our burgeoning understanding that unseen labor, exacerbated during a pandemic, directly affects the body as it challenges, exhausts, and frustrates.

In August 2019, we began facilitating a rhetorical collection that engages a coalitional social justice framework,[1] intentionally incorporated a wide range of contributors into the project and explicitly bound the purposes of the project to the various and extreme contingencies of 2020 and 2021 (e.g., politics/policy, public/personal health, economic turbulence, social/racial injustices). Now in 2024, we have published our coedited collection, *Inclusive Aims: Rhetoric's Role in Reproductive Justice,* and it is the process of collaborating on that collection from 2020 into 2022 that we are reflecting on as we consider the value of collection editing, collaboration, and collectives outside our field. The collection as well as this reflection on our editing suggests the interminable needs and opportunities for more equitable and continually responsive publishing and for more visibility as to the value of edited collections. These dual aims would increase the likelihood that our editing practices might be more of a norm than an exception.

Based on this process of editing and deliberate reflection, we argue that *activism*—one aspect of Cheryl Glenn's "rhetorical feminism" and what Rebecca Jones refers to as "rhetorical activism"—should be recognized as a feminist inventive art of the edited collection (4, 34). As feminist scholars committed to pursuing social justice by addressing varied and interlocking systems of oppression, we reflect on having labored as activist editors creating space and offering individualized support to a range of emerging, seasoned, and non-academic writers. Addressing tensions that arose in this editing process, this chapter foregrounds our experiences with activist editing that involved recalibrating our editorial responsibilities with attention to inclusivity and labor, accommodating individuals, and supporting a collective. "Recalibrating responsibilities" refers to our sense of duty in proactively and reactively responding to exigences outside and within the project given the material, social, and political context in which it developed. This process involved rethinking what we assumed about scholarly writing and editing to pursue our vision while taking seriously burgeoning opportunities and needs related to the world-changing events of 2020 and later. "Accommodating individuals" means listening to, honoring, and responding to contributors' varied ways of knowing while creating editorial coherence. After all, a collection—no matter how inclusive and capacious it may be—must have an arc and focus to be of legitimate value to scholarly discussions as well as public-facing ones. We extend the goal of "supporting a collective" by advocating for the public-facing edited collection as an intellectual and epistemic collaboration. As editors we learned just as the contributors learned how to re/generate a vision for the collection and each chapter within it. The collection arc and introduction could not have been written without this give and take.

Recalibrating Responsibilities

Looking back on the year 2020—the year that our project transformed from a vision to a real work in progress—enables us to better recognize and consider what became intertwined, heightened responsibilities—assuring the inclusivity of the collaborative project and accounting for the labor conditions of contributors. Prior to the World Health Organization declaring COVID-19 a global pandemic in March 2020, we already felt a responsibility to strive toward an inclusive project (thus upholding the reproductive justice practice of centering marginalized voices and experiences) and to make editorial choices that would counter the typical differential labor conditions of academic writing that so frequently reinforce, if not produce, gendered and racialized inequalities. In other words, we wanted our project to reflect various experiences, to function as a gathering of a variously diverse group of writers, and to provide a humane, supportive writing opportunity for each contributor. As a result, the final collection included chapters drawing from many fields such as rhetoric, feminist and gender studies, history, law, critical race studies, communication, health, as well as reproductive justice activism. As our first collaborative project together, we were eager to avail ourselves of our prior experiences and to learn from each other in these regards. The events of 2020 would make these concerns all the more pressing and would come to encourage our renewed sense of editorial responsibility. More than just responding to the COVID-19-specific context, it is important to note, we experienced 2020 as a time when racial equity, personal and communal health and wellness, and labor conditions were yoked concerns. As we considered these concerns in conversation with one another, we realized not only the value of pressing forward with the collection but also our need for a comprehensive and responsive editorial vision and subsequent set of practices that would support all contributors and the project.

An example of our earlier and revised approach to thinking about inclusivity relates to our sense of contributor and readerly audiences. Our initial draft of the call for proposals (CFP) provided us the opportunity to discern what we wanted the rhetorical purpose(s) of the collection to be and what audience(s) it would invite. We agreed that actively engaging with the ideas of reproductive justice thought leaders was a crucial step in striving to shape a collection that supported rights and justice for all—a decision that would help us avoid inadvertently advancing feminist concerns that, for instance, prioritize abortion rights over the more varied and interlacing concerns that disparate communities identify. The final collection's topics range from discourse practices related to telehealth, birthing doula care, and negligence due to systemic racism and transphobia to representations of vasectomy, strategies for political solidarity, and considerations for navigating the challenges of activist interventions. Early in our process we recognized that centering the theory of change articulated by activists and engaging it alongside rhetorical theory and analysis was doing a different type of work than we had undertaken previously. Thus, we adopted an attitude of openness toward learning what rhetorical functions an academic project might gain by following models of activism, what Jonathan Alexander and Susan C. Jarratt define (along with protest) as "a complex mix of bodies, technologies, discourses, and even histories that need to be considered collectively so as to guide a new understanding of contemporary rhetorical interventions within and across numerous spheres" (4).

We later engaged with contributors' drafts and reflected on the emerging shape of the collection in light of the grave racial and health injustices provoking public outcry, calls for justice amid longstanding patterns of racial violence and dehumanization of non-white people, and new forms of concord and discord. Increasingly we found convergences between the unsatisfying conditions related to the various crises of 2020 and the reproductive injustices that were made salient in contributors' chapters. We agreed that our priority would be to support a collection that would be accessible and of interest to a generally educated and public readership—an audience of people inside and outside the academy who might encounter the collection in classrooms and libraries and through online searching and not just through the literate networks of scholars in one field. This anticipated audience heightened our enthusiasm about the timeliness of the collection and the necessity of unlearning our understanding of scholarly writing and editing. However, we still needed to attend to the second major audience, our contributors, who potentially faced constraints on their ability to write. In hindsight, we agree with Maria do Mar Pereira,[2] who configures the pandemic as "a widespread disruption of academic labor and profound upheaval in living and working conditions, physical and mental health, and professional and personal relationships" (2). Initially, we needed to gauge the feasibility of continuing with a project at a time when most people were experiencing upheavals in their labor (whether in remunerated or unremunerated work). Specific to the labor of writing, data from the early months of the pandemic evidenced a dip in research productivity for many; various academic journals reported fewer or a smaller proportion of articles written by "women" (3).

Buoyed by contributors who remained committed to the collection, we realized a responsibility for facilitating the development of a quality manuscript at a time when disruptions were affecting particular people acutely and in ways that exacerbated existing labor injustices. We then reconsidered our processes for such support based on a wider set of labor concerns—ones that Pereira articulates as the "qualitative, collective, slow, and reproductive dimensions" of labor (5) that are distinct from scholarly writing but that nevertheless can have an impact on it. We asked ourselves what might be necessary to show grace and support to the range of contributors to our project—each with their own unique lived context and with differing levels of experience as academic writers—all while supporting the group's investment in time, energy, and intellectual labor. Importantly, we strove to anticipate the likelihood of various disruptions to productivity that the contributors would need to navigate as they attended to disparate and important parts of their daily lives. Pushing against a neoliberal fetishization of academic productivity reflected in the unique valuation of certain forms of academic publishing, Pereira claims that labor disruptions should not only be measured by how they result in fewer research "outputs," but rather be understood as complex interferences that affect "other aspects of our experience as human beings with multiple interests, limited capacities, fluctuating energies, overwhelming emotions, vulnerable bodies, and fallible brains" (5). We now understand that our sense of the pandemic context did provide us the ability to recalibrate our editorial vision and subsequent processes. We took on this challenge based on our feeling of responsibility for developing an inclusive, public-facing project that was responsive to heightened issues around labor and to the diverse forms of "disruption"—some of which would positively shape our and contributors' sense of exigency for the collection—related to writing during a pandemic.

Accommodating Minds and Bodies

The responsibilities of editing during a pandemic include accommodating others on many, and on unexpected, fronts. The contributors and editors found themselves housebound and became homeschool teachers and daycare workers of children and parents in the same space and time as being professionals whether academics, graduate students, high school teachers, lawyers, or activists. We sent out the chapter acceptances and calendar for June drafts in February 2020; then the covid-19 lockdown happened in March. By June we had extended the chapter draft deadline to mid-August and lost two of our contributors, one because of closed archives and one because of other deadlines compromised by the shutdown. The pandemic made apparent the need for us to shift from responsive to preemptive accommodation in order for our coedited collection to move forward. Over that summer, the two of us made a commitment to each other to dedicate the next year to this project by recognizing that our contributors, and we as editors, needed not only intellectual support but also emotional understanding and flexibility. Accommodation, thus, manifested in especially proactive communication strategies such as consistent and regular communication to each other and to contributors and coherent responses to chapter drafts that unified our commentary instead of replicating the practice of reviews delivering incompatible feedback. We deepened our commitment to proactive communication by providing explicit yet invitational revision explanations. Further, we revamped our timeline for responding to work, adopting a rolling, six-week revision window for each of the first three chapter revisions. We hoped this new cadence would provide flexibility to each contributor, and we found that it resulted in regular, rich editorial sessions over Zoom. Overall, this multipart structure provided supportive guiderails for the labor of the project through explicit and intentional processes that responded to the varied needs of writers and, usefully, enabled other forms of responsiveness. What echoed in our ears was Karma R. Chávez's challenge—"we cannot nor should we try to reduce actual bodies to abstract conceptualizations of 'the body' because that at once reductive and totalizing move, like all such moves, enforces and animates systemic oppressions" (248). Although we are most familiar with Chávez's ideas in relation to rhetorical theory building and analysis, we found them to be particularly apt for what became the embodied work of activist editing.

A disposition of preemptive, rather than reactive, accommodation required many discussions and plans of action on our parts. Accommodation means negotiating with people about their situations, their communications with us, and their writing, and we needed this coordination with each other as well as with our contributors and afterword writers. Our ways to address this tension ties to the linguistic understanding of accommodation in what Colleen Donnelly refers to as an "interactive process" (164). We wanted to be as transparent in our interactions with each other and the contributors as possible, so it was important to us to provide supportive, and, as far as possible, noncontradictory lines of communication between us and each contributor. Our attempts to leverage our communication in cultivating what we now recognize as a collective are supported by Donnelly, who concludes that "participants' attitudes toward each other and the rapport they develop, or lack thereof, have a direct effect on the outcome of the communication" (164). During a pandemic and with cross-disciplinary writers, both theories of rhetoric and tenets of reproductive justice needed to be highlighted in the chapters, so multiple revision rounds seemed appropriate. As instances of interaction, our revision requests could then also include resource sharing. For even the first chapter drafts we suggested and/or sent related scholarship for consideration to make our invitations for revision that much more concrete and actionable—all while remaining open as the writers developed their analyses. The first three revision rounds were focused on fine-tuning the arguments, supporting them with relevant theories, and working toward content organization that seemed appropriate for the arc of each chapter.

As Richard Nordquist claims, "accommodation most often takes the form of *convergence,* when a speaker chooses a language variety that seems to fit the style of the other speaker." Working toward that convergence was, for us, an act of process and languaging; we responded to three to four chapters every two weeks with cowritten, detailed letters for each of the four drafts, only sending chapter drafts with tracked changes and comment boxes in the later revision rounds. Throughout this process, we read and took notes on each chapter then met to discuss the chapters' strengths and next revisions. While we distributed the drafting of the letters between us, we met virtually to make changes and additions to each letter before sending. By taking on this labor-heavy, synchronous collaboration we were working toward responses that made visible that we were likeminded in the development of both the chapters and the collection arc, committed to providing the contributors praise, points for invention or development, and clear revision requests. The process rooted us in the project in development far more than a divide and conquer approach would have enabled. The six-week revision windows worked smoothly for most contributors with only a few extensions needed across the fall 2020 and winter 2021 months—a fact that illustrates the commitment and enthusiasm of our contributors despite the numerous ways we all were adapting to ongoing COVID-19-related realties. We made ourselves available through email, virtual meetings, and phone calls as our contributors requested, and they did. Even with this support of time and attention, we lost two more chapter authors due to pandemic stressors.

Accommodation is never a neutral term; our commitment to the contributors and their arguments required our flexibility. While working toward a collective and convergence with our contributors, we quickly learned that we had to allow for contributors' divergence as well, what Nordquist relates as a speaker's signaling "social distance or disapproval by using a language variety that differs from the style of the other speaker." For example, we met with one contributor both virtually and via email regularly, and the chapter developed both to the author's and our satisfactions; however, ultimately, the contributor decided that specific wording, which we asked to be changed to highlight the systemic nature of the issue being addressed, could not be revised. We honored this decision. Our communications also allowed for other types of compromises from identifying overarching themes, to discussing the value of the chapter arguments and analysis for rhetoric and reproductive justice, to supporting changes in or fine-tuning the arguments.

What truly astonished us early in this revision process was the personal bodily connections that the writers had with their subjects, arguments, examples, and analysis. Arguments about giving birth, assisting births, managing fertility, and being activists were sometimes explicitly connected to the positionality of an author but always implicitly linked to authors' care and concern as people writing with the embodied experiences of self and others in mind. Situating ourselves as reproductive justice advocates and as professional academics, we wanted to help shape these emotional and ethical arguments into viable scholarship to honor those lived experiences and to once again promote our belief in the need for scholarship to be more publicly accessible. While we had responsibilities that our contributors did not have, we appreciated and tried to honor the contributors' material, intellectual, and emotional responsibilities as committed writers in this collective. Since February of 2020, we have seen yet again that material circumstances matter just as much as intellectual ones and that they can work together to generate more powerful and potent scholarship for rhetoric and reproductive justice. The discipline of rhetoric and writing studies focuses on and supports "the importance of including multiple voices in research topics and projects" (Eble et al., 344). This inclusivity and the discipline's broad and varied research trajectory that is often "linked to contemporary social and institutional situations and needs" also requires a more proactive form of accommodation (361). In terms of activist editing, such inclusivity is the unglamorous but necessary work of making a project plan and using communication strategies that bridge the social and the institutional—realms that are frequently removed from each other and that can reproduce—or refigure—hierarchies of academe. By embracing both goals, our collaborative editing undercuts the scholarly hierarchy of an elite and rarified reading audience as well as the hierarchy of editors over contributors. In addition, it makes more visible and more valuable the labor of collection editing in academic circles.

Supporting the Collective

Our goal of "supporting a collective" is one that has also been shaped by the specific contingencies of the global pandemic. Although many of us in the US continue to lament a failure of a polarized electorate to fully come together in support of the life, dignity, and needs of all, many of us have grappled with the embodied ways we already live in interconnected systems of care and the responsibilities we might feel to protect ourselves and others. These responsibilities manifest as physical acts such as wearing masks, practicing social distancing, getting vaccines as well as adjacent actions such as renegotiating how we behave when we rely on essential service providers who are so often underpaid, yet integral to systems of collective living. As feminists, we—like so many people—recognized in new and newly profound ways how extant inequities in power and privilege resulted in greater chasms due to this emergency. As Lauren McKeon explains about the pandemic—while "many people's worlds were getting smaller, scarier, more uncertain" it "was arguably women who felt this most keenly—women who balanced barefoot on the razor's edge" (6). McKeon draws from firsthand accounts of Canadian women who share their experiences living through the first year of the global pandemic and implores readers to "pause and pay attention" to this "exceptional" time and to "unflinchingly examine its darkest truths" by considering what enduring lessons exist among these stories (15).

We in no way wish to draw a one-to-one correlation between editing a book and working in a COVID-19 hospital ward, working a job that did not afford the luxury of remote labor, working with and/or through a diagnosis of COVID-19, or any of the innumerable and harsh realities of the pandemic. We do, however, take up the spirit of McKeon's invitation to listen, reflect, and learn—enacting an attitude during the ongoing process of collection editing and now, through this reflective assessment on our work. From our early visioning and through the seemingly mundane, if important, work of creating a schedule, workflow, and revision feedback plan, we labored to not only create an edited collection but to support a collective (that is, the contributors and us as editors). Supporting a collective is, for us two, an effort of "inclusion activism," what Kelly

Blewett, Christina M. LaVecchia, Laura R. Micciche, and Janine Morris define as "an intentional effort to ensure participation and access as well as leadership opportunities to people of all backgrounds, at all career stages" (275). Writing about their experience as editorial team members of *Composition Studies,* these scholars articulate the specific editorial practices (internal and external) that can support greater inclusion, access, and varied experiences and perspectives within disciplinary journals. Editing a stand-alone collection—one that engages with knowledge from our field but that is, unlike a journal issue, not so tightly bound to the disciplinary contours of "field knowledge" (Blewett et al., 275)—means that our sense of collective could, and did, shift from being informed by orientations *to* a field (and related scholarly conversations) to enabling the collection to have its own center of gravity. In other words, in distinction from Blewett et al.'s helpful metaphor of making a seat at "the table" as a way to describe inclusive activism in journal editing, we liken our activity to building another table altogether—an activity that is shaped by those contributors who signed on to the project and centered around the mostly non-scholarly exigencies of a reproductive justice-informed project. As we communicated with contributors during months of great global hardship, we grew into the realization that the people around the table and the reason for gathering were becoming the primary factors shaping our editorial activity. Instead of inviting others to our table, we were inviting others to collaboratively build a table unlike one we had seen before.

A key illustration of the collective visioning and of the give-and-take of this commitment to support a collection is our openness to considering what centering reproductive justice could and would mean for this project thematically and organizationally. As an extension of our willingness to recruit widely for contributors, we also enacted a disposition of true openness to how those proposing chapters were interpreting our call for abstracts. In centering reproductive justice theory, we encouraged proposal writers to consider three commonly acknowledged realms of reproductive justice activism and knowledge production—rights, health, and justice. We invited proposals that addressed how one or more of these terms shape the discursive/material landscapes of reproductive politics and that explored the implications of those shapings. Indeed, the earliest working title for the project included these three realms.

The breadth of this call, while in some ways typical for the genre, enabled us as editors to remain open to what we anticipated would become a recursive process of coming to know what the collective imagined the collection could be. Choosing this approach amplified our editorial roles—coordinating contributors, being responsible for managing the project (in terms of creating timelines and the like), leveraging our extensive experience with teaching/ mentoring academic writers, and drawing upon our experiences with academic editing and publishing. What this approach explicitly avoided was naming or claiming the specific stakes of the project and the interpretation of what rhetorics of reproductive justice should include. While we did make editorial choices among the many strong proposals that we received (one of the most significant traditional sites of editorial gatekeeping), we eschewed the comfort or assuredness of accepting (or further inviting) projects that felt familiar to our lived and scholarly experiences as feminists. Instead, we leaned toward selecting as many projects as possible that could contribute to a broad and multifaceted engagement with the idea of rhetorics of reproductive justice. In other words, we relied on contributors to help us identify what our primary term—rhetorics of reproductive justice—could mean, quickly realizing that the heuristics of rights, health, and justice were useful entry points that would no longer suffice as an organizing frame.

A tangible manifestation of this (productive) "trouble" with arrangement was the table of contents—the organizing and grouping schema of the collective that aids in navigating readers through the project. Simply put, it would have been more efficient to organize the table of contents and to create sections for the project based on our editorial vision, but it was more crucial to supporting a collective vision to take a recursive approach. By supporting a collective in this way, we attempted to reckon with the tension between (1) our positionality as white, cisgender, mostly able-bodied, feminist scholar-teachers and (2) our goal of addressing reproductive politics (which we greatly care about) while listening carefully and collaboratively to those working in and on reproductive justice in the past, present, and (hopefully) the future. In this way we enacted a sort of "letting go," what Jennifer C. Nash conceptualizes (in the context of black feminist theory) as the divestment of the notion of property as knowledge that is defensively guarded (3). This paradox—of leading a group of collaborators while also actively letting go of our role as (primary) shapers of the project itself—is one that pushed us into unfamiliar territory. As a consequence of the world-remaking activity of so many people throughout the turbulence of 2020 and 2021, it seemed that letting go for the sake of the collective was the only realistic and ethical way to move forward.

We reflectively consider these ethical commitments to be an example of "ethics in praxis," or the ethics that are "characterized by situational, embodied, and reflexive orientations rather than by attributes more common in virtue ethics" (Melonçon et al., 430). Perhaps most significantly to the two of us is the resulting way that supporting a collective continually delayed (again, in a productive manner) our ability to write the introduction to the collection. While the two of us have come to appreciate our slightly different approaches to invention, we both anticipated being able to create an early working draft of the introduction in time to solicit feedback on our work in progress from other academics. Our early writing, however, was especially challenging as we tried to extend from the CFP and respond to a working table of contents (which we continued to rearrange as we better understood how the project was transforming). We were still learning from our contributors; we were still building our table collectively. We as editors needed and wanted to reciprocate the time, care, and attention being given by the collaborators as we considered how the scope and contours of the collection/collective were emerging. Heather began to set aside the notes she had taken from her reading of other introductions to collections as a practice of genre knowledge-building, and Nancy verbalized how this instance of introduction writing differed in some ways from previous approaches, enabling her to think in new ways about the genre. As an ethical practice of supporting the collective, our writing, we realized, needed to be "kairos-driven," "attuned" to the crisis scenario presented by an unfolding pandemic, and anticipatory of "opportunities [that such strained conditions offer] to 'play' at various imagined futures" (Melonçon et al., 430). We waited and thought, we listened and responded, and—eventually—we wrote. In shattering our own expectations of the timing, pacing, and approach to introducing the collection, we worked to undercut the hierarchy of the editorial introduction and to allow the collective's vision to guide us.

A 20/20 Vision

Our title's invocation of 20/20 vision reflects what we learned during the years 2020 through 2022. In hindsight, we see that some of our activist editing decisions were in our vision for the original collection and that others were responsive, emerging from our continual interaction with contributors. We return to Ianetta's call to appreciate editing—in her case of journals and in our case of collections—as an activity that performs activism through deep listening and accommodation toward convergence. She writes that "editing involves hearing carefully what a writer is saying, responding to it in a manner that seems to best suit the writer's goals in this exigency and helping the writer with development" (268). While we agree that these goals of writerly convergence are needed for activist editing, we now realize the extent to which activism through editing demands attention to writers as whole people who operate in material and social contexts that matter. In other words, a project's most significant tensions might lie not in realizing editorial goals, but in the reality of the day-to-day situation of editing collections as humans (with bodies) and with humans (also mind-bodies) who embrace various agendas, experiences, and needs. Also important to consider in light of activist editors' aims, the gendered and racialized division of vital but discounted work for academics carries unseen burdens and expectations internal to academe and compounded by that same imbalance external to it.

Our experiences with such tensions in our own deeply collaborative editing practice have taught us to be more mindful of those we are laboring with and of those who may read our work. In both our collaboration with each other and with the contributors as well as in the emergence of this collective group of contributors focused on a reproductive framework, we continually recognized that bodies are, as Simone de Beauvoir contends, "the instrument[s] of our hold on the world" (44). We have labored with the formulation and composition of this collection and this chapter on editing to make visible bodies, first, as they interminably generate physical, emotional, and intellectual insights on the rhetorics of reproductive justice and, second, as they negotiate this complicated labor by collaborating in visible ways. Our newfound understanding of this "invisible" work suggests how these efforts function as activism and offers a rationale for what might be the sustainable and durable effects of this activity.

Our vision is much clearer now in 2024, and we are humbled by this experience of learning from others in order to broaden the disciplinary value of collection editing and of audience potential. We consider ourselves more fully able to appreciate our emerging understanding of activist editing as a feminist art and to better grapple with Ianetta's assertion that "as a field we [can] collectively lose an understanding of what the real work of editing involves and means" (268). We also recognize how this work will continue to change, materially, due to the ongoing economic impacts of this unprecedented time. With universities cutting budgets, libraries subscribing to prominent journal and ebook services, textbook sales waning, and open access publishing flourishing, university and academic presses, in order to survive, will—if they have not already—require subvention monies, collaborate by joining forces with other presses and journals, move to print on demand, and compete for sales with primarily commercial presses with academic publishing departments. The changing landscape of higher education and the ongoing economic and labor-related concerns since the pandemic offer university publishing an opportunity to pause, rethink, and readdress the way it does business. For instance, several presses are promoting public-facing scholarly manuscripts to attract varied audiences. Yet, universities remain an obstacle to change as they overwhelmingly continue to privilege particular forms of scholarly production over the other demands of academic life, thus reinforcing the gender and racial inequities that existed before the pandemic (Pereira, 7–8). Consider, too, that our co-edited collection represents some of the (traditionally) least prestigious forms of academic activity—editing (rather than authorship) and collaboration (rather than individual work) that is aimed at a broad (rather than only scholarly) audience. Of course, this chapter has provided us with the room to explore all the reasons why this traditionally less-privileged approach to making knowledge is the very reason we have gleaned these insights and retain a sense of hopeful possibility.

To be clear, in this academic environment and if scholarly edited collections continue, more will be asked of collection editors. The pandemic has brought into stark relief this imbalance between institutional publication expectations and university press marketing pressures and its impact on bodies. Several university presses we approached explained that they were no longer publishing edited collections, meaning that there may be simply less opportunity for such collective meaning-making in our field than there once was. Quality, for those collections that are produced, will continue to be tied to invisible labor, given that some academic presses accept book publication based on the editor's proposal. In such cases an editor verifies the quality of the chapters. Some well-funded and tier-one university presses do not accept manuscripts from academics who have not already published a scholarly peer-reviewed book, narrowing avenues of access. In so doing, they discount material realities and uphold ongoing systems of hierarchy that devalue certain bodies and the laboring of those bodies. If this imbalance and inequity across academic publishing continues, editors will need to more forcefully advocate for the value of the inclusive edited collection.

Rhetorical activism is an act of leadership that requires open, responsive engagement with actual body-minds to better envision and argue for a collective's and a collection's scholarly and societal potential. Our experience practicing activism through the feminist inventive art of the edited collection has revealed to us one example of what Carly Woods refers to as a "rhetorical paradox" (267)—that while scholarly communities outwardly and verbally value efforts toward inclusion and equity, the actual rhetorical possibilities of moving toward this more just scholarly future remain unmet. By continually and consistently advocating for the importance of scholarly editing to tenure committees, to presses, to professional organizations, and to the public, we make the case that "perceived" deficits (writers with fewer or no academic publications, the edited collection as a genre, the public-facing and action-oriented publication) are strengths in its ever-expanding focus on alternative bodies, contexts, perspectives, and life situations.

As we reflect on our experiences from a later vantage point, our 20/20 vision enables an increasingly encompassing view. Most of our everyday experiences—and certainly those related to scholarship and publication—seemed to slow during and after the height of COVID-19. While the pace of publishing seems to have largely "rebounded," the material conditions of scholarly production continue to hinder marginalized people's "productivity." Accordingly, as collection editors, our rhetorical activism now includes a humbling understanding of perseverance and patience. We found hope in our contributors' persistence and in our own ability to renegotiate our sense of how a collection can be both timely and conversant with longer, less immediate arcs of injustice. We moved toward publication with a project that anchors hope through a steadfast commitment to widening the aims of feminist rhetorical coalition through academic writing. To cultivate feminist hope, as Glenn reminds us, we "support our friends, colleagues, and students as they come to voice, feel empowered in critical discussions, and write, speak, and teach the words that reshape (and repair) the world and pave our future" (212).

One of our central commitments—to center the work of intellectuals, experienced and emergent, with topics not yet examined in reproductive justice rhetorics—continues to feel, at times, out of step with pre-pandemic notions of scholarly production. For instance, investing in this commitment means creating "liabilities" according to the logics of hyper productivity and the sanctity of speed and efficiency. Working responsively with writers means adopting a flexible and engaging approach to finding ways of moving toward "yes" instead of engaging in tactics that aim to "protect" one's time. Being collectively accountable to the possibilities of making knowledge together can mean lessening one's attachment to the logics of individualism that have long shaped so much of intellectual life.

Simultaneously, institutional factors limit the possibilities of activities such as feminist activist editing, even for those who are committed to this pursuit. Academic publication expectations have yet to catch up with the effects of the pandemic in a postsecondary education landscape that continues to experience seismic shifts (e.g., lower student enrollments, dwindling numbers of tenure-stream academic positions, public hostility toward higher education, and other budget-constricting factors). In order for emerging academics to have credentials to attain a more stable position, tenured or not, and to move forward toward promotion in their new academic homes, both institutions and scholarly venues need to structurally reconsider their publishing expectations—moving from a call for more inclusivity and public work to evidence of the promise of academics' truly inclusive aims.

We return to familiar questions, considering them through our 20/20 vision and with a renewed sense of collective accountability. How do timelines hinder innovative scholarly production rather than encourage it? How do professional organizations tangibly demonstrate the value of edited collections? How do peer review questions and editorial board discussions truly reckon with the myriad forms of inclusion in scholarship and support its contributors? How do reappointment, tenure, and promotion guidelines recognize scholars' investments in student and community engagement?

While we are advocating for the importance of the edited collection, of activist editorial work, and for a collaborative and reflective approach to the future of academe, as individuals, we can only do so much. Our questions, our reflections, and our earlier acknowledgments of changes being made slowly in academic publishing and professional organizations are the activist work of this chapter, as they offer others, including other collectives, the opportunity of revisiting the actions and requirements tied to their values. Rhetorical activism may be limited when embraced by individual academics; however, a community working for change may not only envision a more just, diverse, and inclusive future for academe, but also realize their aims, however audacious and crucial they may be.

Notes

1. Loretta J. Ross and Rickie Solinger's articulation of this framework has animated this project.

2. Maria do Mar Pereira surveys research on gender inequalities in academic labor during the pandemic, concluding that scholarship illuminates legitimate gender disparities particular to the COVID-19 context and obscures the pervasiveness of such disparities, which existed—albeit differently—before the pandemic.

Bibliography

Adams, Heather Brook, and Nancy Myers, eds. *Inclusive Aims: Rhetoric's Role in Reproductive Justice.* Parlor Press, 2024.

Alexander, Jonathan, and Susan C. Jarratt. Introduction to *Unruly Rhetorics: Protest, Persuasion, and Publics.* Edited by Jonathan Alexander, Susan C. Jarratt, and Nancy Welsh. University of Pittsburgh Press, 2018.

Beauvoir, Simone de. *The Second Sex.* Translated by Constance Borde and Sheila Malovany-Chevallier. Alfred A. Knopf, 2010.

Blewett, Kelly, Christina M. LaVecchia, Laura R. Micciche, and Janine Morris. "Editing as Inclusion Activism." *College English* 81, no. 4 (2019): 273–96.

Chávez, Karma R. "The Body: An Abstract and Actual Rhetorical Concept." *Rhetoric Society Quarterly* 48, no. 3 (2018): 242–50.

Donnelly, Colleen Elaine. *Linguistics for Writers.* State University of New York Press, 1994.

Eble, Michelle F., Tracy Ann Morse, Wendy Sharer, and William P. Banks. "Valuing Editorial Collaborations as Scholarship: A Survey of Tenure and Promotion Documents." *College English* 81, no. 4 (2019): 339–66.

Ford, Liz. "Pandemic Could Result in a 'Lost Decade' for Developing Countries Says Co-Chair of Bill and Melinda Gates Foundation in Stark Report." *The Guardian,* September 15, 2020. https://www.theguardian.com/.

Glenn, Cheryl. *Rhetorical Feminism and This Thing Called Hope.* Southern Illinois University Press, 2018.

Ianetta, Melissa. "Scholarly Editing: History, Performance Future." *College English* 81, no. 4 (2019): 267–72.

Jones, Rebecca. "Rhetorical Activism: Responsibility in the Ivory Tower." In *Activism and Rhetoric: Theories and Contexts for Political Engagement,* 2nd ed., edited by Jong Hwa Lee and Seth Kahn. Routledge, 2020.

McKeon, Lauren. *Women of the Pandemic: Stories from the Front Lines of COVID-19.* McClelland & Stewart, 2021.

Melonçon, Lisa, Cathryn Molloy, and J. Blake Scott. "Ethics in Praxis: Situational, Embodied, Relational." *Rhetoric of Health and Medicine* 3, no. 4 (2020): 430–36.

Nash, Jennifer C. *Black Feminism Reimagined: After Intersectionality.* Duke University Press, 2019.

Nordquist, Richard. "Definition and Examples of Linguistic Accommodation." *ThoughtCo.,* updated April 30, 2025, https://www.thoughtco.com/what-is-accommodation-speech-1688964.

Pereira, Maria do Mar. "Researching Gender Inequalities in Academic Labor During the COVID-19 Pandemic: Avoiding Common Problems and Asking Different Questions." *Gender Work Organ* 28, no. 2 (2021): 1–12.

Ross, Loretta J., and Rickie Solinger. *Reproductive Justice: An Introduction.* University of California Press, 2017.

Woods, Carly S. "Repunctuated Feminism" *Women's Studies in Communication* 36, no. 3 (2013): 267–87.

CHAPTER 18

Empowering Rhetorics

Writing and Reading Stories as a Feminist, Spiritual Tool

Taylor Paige Winfield

I founded an emotional and spiritual support organization during the COVID-19 pandemic before hitting my limits and stepping back from the volunteer work. As I will explore in this narrative, I had become entangled in expectations about what it means to be a socially responsive scholar, leader, and woman. I was caught between a neoliberal academy that tells scholars that their research and writing must come first and feminist rhetoric that celebrates scholar-activism. I fell short on both ends—for ignoring my scholarship for months, and then for taking a step back from the activism to concentrate on my academic career. I was also stuck between traditional views of leaders as undaunted and visionary—stopping at nothing to accomplish their goals—and feminist theories that emphasize accepting vulnerabilities and prioritizing self-care as a sign of strength. Again, I fell short—I was not able to keep powering through endlessly, and by the time I was starting to pay attention to my own needs, I was burnt out.

Furthermore, I was enmeshed in gendered norms that frame care as a feminine capacity wherein 'good,' 'moral' women are willing to sacrifice themselves and their well-being to serve others (Klostermann). Although the position of women as caregivers is most tightly bound to familial roles, society also relies on us to fill gaps in the public service infrastructure's ability to meet care demands. Through this lens, I was a 'good' woman by caring for others and creating a resource that compensated for under-resourced public mental and spiritual health services. But, in pulling back from leading the organization, I rejected the gendered labor that society demanded from me as a 'caring' woman. At first, it was hard to swallow that I had become so entrenched in these roles, but in the process of (re)writing and (re)reading my story for this volume, I was able to find meaning in the experience. I discovered that my story was similar to those of many women who engaged in additional gendered labor during the pandemic and saw their careers diverted; I was not alone in my challenges. The act of composing the narrative offered a spiritual pathway toward healing and self-understanding.

Writing this chapter has been a way to process my experience, and it echoes the narratives throughout this collection in its call to listen to and sit with the personal experiences of women laboring through/in times of crisis. Narrating our experience as evidence is a central feminist rhetorical practice (hooks "Teaching"; Glenn; Spigelman). Despite our progress expanding the concept of evidence, "with experience and emotion given full consideration," these practices remain secondary to the discipline at large (Glenn, 74). But personal testimony is "fertile ground" for advancing "the production of liberatory feminist theory because it usually forms the basis of our theory-making" (hooks, "Teaching," 70). The tension I felt between societal expectations of 'goodness' as a woman and my own professional and mental health provide generative space for theory-making, and for processing collective experiences of women during this particular crisis. Narrativizing my experience thus forms scholarly evidence for how we might reform practices and expectations for labor in and beyond the academy.

The World Was Calling on Me

As the world realized we were on the brink of an emotional and spiritual crisis in addition to a public health crisis in March of 2020, I felt a strong urge to do *something, anything,* to take *action.* March was also the month I finished my first unit of training in spiritually integrated psychotherapy. I was a doctoral student in sociology, but I started this training to learn skills to be a trauma-informed researcher when working with people in highly vulnerable circumstances. Through this work, I learned more about the range of vulnerabilities people may experience (e.g., physical, psychological, spiritual/existential, and structural), and how these vulnerabilities overlap and intersect (Winfield). This understanding helped me appreciate the various ways in which people were struggling with the COVID-19 pandemic, as well as the heightened need for support. I knew that other people and organizations were better suited to handle the physical health components of the crisis, but I sensed I might be able to help people cope with some of the social, emotional, and spiritual elements.

So, in March 2020, I asked myself—*How can I use my training in sociology and spiritually integrated psychotherapy to help ease some of the current and upcoming suffering?* I started with social media. I said if anyone needed someone to talk to, I was there. Several people responded. I decided to reach out to my networks to see if other emotional or spiritual care providers would be willing to offer free support. Within ten days, I had gathered a team of twenty providers, including licensed therapists and social workers, board-certified chaplains, and clergy with clinical experience, who were willing to volunteer their time to help those who were struggling with the pandemic.

Together, we created an online system, wherein individuals could sign up to be matched with a provider for six sessions and referred to longer-term support if necessary. Our goal was to address gaps in the public and social support network, including the need for accessible and inclusive mental health care and spiritual/existential care that was free from evangelism and proselytization. We aimed to offer support that bridged emotional and spiritual care to help people cultivate their sense of worth and resilience while exploring meaning *on their own terms.* This meaning—or what I call spirituality—may come from nature, art, relationships, or the sense that there is something bigger than oneself (whether it is a community or a higher power).

Within a month, my life was transformed. Instead of working on my dissertation, I was managing our growing pool of volunteers. Instead of reading scholarship, I was reading about how to set up a nonprofit. Instead of unwinding after dinner, my evenings were filled with team meetings and one-on-one support sessions with clients. I knew I was neglecting my scholarship, my husband, and myself—but I let those concerns fall away into the intoxicating mix of adrenaline, endorphins, and purpose. Each time I met with someone and spoke with them about their fears and hopes, I too experienced hope and a sense of spiritual connection in the face of this enormous global challenge.

The organization soon grew to over one hundred providers who were supporting more than 200 clients. I woke up each morning eager to check our system for new sign-ups, make sure they were matched, and follow up with existing clients. We put together a justice task force to help us engage in equitable practices to serve individuals from diverse backgrounds. We arranged trainings for volunteers on crisis care, bridging emotional and spiritual support, and justice and trauma-informed practices. I moved through each day in a euphoric state, relishing in media attention and praise from family, friends, and community members. There was something seductive and energizing about feeling like I was making a difference. The world was calling on me, and I answered.

Yet, as the pandemic raged on month after month, wave after wave, my adrenaline started to fade. I became increasingly exhausted. I missed my scholarship. I missed watching funny television programs in the evenings with my husband. I missed time to myself. When I reached out to other volunteers to invite them to take over as director so I could rest, I found they were also hitting their limits. Our project was entirely run by people generously donating their time and skills; people who could not work for free indefinitely. Although we were able to secure minor funding to help with logistics, larger and more sustainable funding to compensate providers was not available because we were not a registered non-profit.

I looked for larger organizations that could adopt the project, but each effort fell through. I tried to carry on. I was proud of what we had created and could not imagine letting it fall apart simply because I was tired. It felt as if stepping back from the work would be to admit failure on multiple fronts— failure as a leader for letting the project fall apart, as a care provider for not being able to provide support to clients any longer, and failure as an academic and as a scholar-activist—all those months spent away from my scholarship without generating lasting change. And underneath it all, I felt a failure as a woman who had been socialized to believe she *should* be able to do it all, that she *should* be able to put others before herself, and whose worth was entangled with being a caregiver (daughter, wife). My failure to set boundaries to protect myself from this situation was another admission of defeat—I *should* have known better.

Eventually, I accepted that someone else would have to take the reins or that we would have to shut down the endeavor. I carved out time for myself, my family, and my scholarship. Yet, the shadow of the *should* remained. On the one-year anniversary of the project, we had served over 500 people. By all accounts, it was a huge success and far surpassed what I could have imagined in early March 2020. Still, I felt that I had let our future clients and team down by not finding a sustainable solution—and had let myself down by continuing to neglect my own needs for so long.

The Healing Power of Stories

When I first sat down to write my narrative for this volume, it was painful. Like many women in academia and other professions, I saw clearly how deeply entrenched I had become in dominant expectations about who I was *supposed* to be. Yet, in the process of (re)writing and (re)reading, I was able to recognize the agency and courage it took to step back, and the power of feminist rhetoric in understanding and finding meaning in my experience. As I wrote, I found my-self entering my own profoundly emotionally and spiritually healing process. I had spent so many months working with clients to use their own stories to recognize their strength and resilience without realizing that I might be able to do the same for myself.

By working through my own narrative, I found meaning in the chaos of memory and could move through the lingering difficult emotions. Writing reconnected me with my creative life force and a larger community of women struggling with similar challenges during the pandemic. Within feminist rhetorics literature, the role of language in meaning making and connection is central; yet, these rhetorical acts are less often framed as spiritual practices (Browdy). In a world enveloped in (ongoing) crises, I came to recognize femi-nist rhetorics as empowering social, emotional, *and spiritual* tools that might help women find collective healing. These rhetorics can help us disentangle ourselves from who we think we *ought* to be or what we think we *should* be able to do, and (re)connect with our inner worth and hope (Glenn; hooks "Feminism"; Gold and Enoch; Hersey).

When we write and share our individual stories, the systemic natures of our seemingly personal experiences are revealed (Glenn; Gold and Enoch). My story shows the symptoms of a society that under-invests in public goods and services, with the expectation that individual citizens (in particular women) will fill the gaps (Fraser). This is a society that expects women to have the bandwidth for both fulfilling professional careers *and* personal lives, without recognizing the burden of trying to 'do it all.' These dynamics go hand in hand with academic cultures that require scholars to continue to produce during personal and global crises, all while contributing to the public good in their *free* time (Spooner). And tropes persist within leadership about how to act quickly, create sustainable change, and care for others (all while making sure you do not get burnt out). Any failure is a personal, not public problem. These condi-tions have existed long before the COVID-19 pandemic. However, the pandemic brought to the surface the absurdity of the expectations and burdens put on women.

As we move past the pandemic towards a new normal, we can continue to use stories to draw attention to issues of gendered labor and create spaces for healing. Stories are a way to focus on womens' lived experiences and to illustrate larger discursive and material conditions that shape our lives (Klos-termann). Stories create empowering rhetorics that invite emotion, dialogue, poetry, and openness into conversations among scholars, leaders, and women

(Glenn). As I learned through my own experience, composing and sharing stories are also powerful spiritual practices for meaning making and self-healing. In finding the words and structure for my narrative, I found words and structure for my experience. I realized the extent to which I was placed in an impossible situation and the nature of the discourses that had made me feel stuck, but knew I was not alone in these challenges. The sentences, repetition, and metaphors stirred emotions within me and created movement toward peace and closure.

Within academia, scholars can use stories in their writing, teaching, and research to highlight systemic inequalities and bring coherence to their experiences across spheres of life. Indeed, this collection illustrates the value of personal experience as scholarly evidence. Instructors can also apply the power of stories in the classroom—inviting students to compose narratives about how their lived experience relates to course materials or to analyze others' narratives to identify larger social dynamics. These practices will encourage further reflexivity in academia and offer opportunities to support faculty, staff, and students as they negotiate between multiple roles, expectations, and identifications. Because scholars must contend with "blurred boundaries" between areas of our lives, stories help us find coherence and clarity on how to move forward and ways to create more livable conditions in academia.

Bibliography

Browdy, Ronisha Witlee. "Rhetorical Spirits: Spirituality as Rhetorical Device in New Age Womanist of Color Texts." Graduate Theses and Dissertations, University of South Florida, 2013.

Fraser, Nancy. "Contradictions of Capital and Care." *New Left Review,* no. 100 (August 1, 2016): 99–117.

Glenn, Cheryl. *Rhetorical Feminism and This Thing Called Hope.* Southern Illinois Press, 2018.

Gold, David, and Jessica Enoch, eds. *Women at Work: Rhetorics of Gender and Labor.* University of Pittsburgh Press, 2019.

Hersey, Tricia. *Rest Is Resistance.* Hachette, 2022.

hooks, bell. *Teaching to Transgress: Education as the Practice of Freedom.* Routledge, 1994.

hooks, bell. *Feminism Is for Everybody: Passionate Politics.* South End Press, 2000.

Klostermann, Janna. "Care Has Limits: Women's Moral Lives and Revised Meanings of Care Work." PhD diss., Carleton University, 2020.

Spigelman, Candace. *Personally Speaking: Experience as Evidence in Academic Discourse.* Southern Illinois University Press, 2004.

Spooner, Marc. "Qualitative Research and Global Audit Culture: The Politics of Productivity, Accountability, and Possibility." In *The SAGE Handbook of Qualitative Research,* edited by Norman K. Denzin and Yvonna S. Lincoln. Sage, 2017.

Winfield, Taylor Paige. "Vulnerable Research: Competencies for Trauma and Justice-Informed Ethnography." *Journal of Contemporary Ethnography* 51, no. 2 (2022): 135–70. https://doi.org/10.1177/08912416211017254.

Afterword
Archive, Heuristic, Argument

Jessica Enoch

Blurred Boundaries is not only a collection of essays or a conversation among scholars. It is an *archive,* a *heuristic,* and an *argument.* At each rhetorical level of purpose, it invites and indeed compels readers to remember and meditate on how the COVID-19 pandemic, along with other critical factors in operation during that period—racial violence and protest along with an excruciatingly stressful presidential election—so distinctly affected gendered work experiences within the academy. In processing the significance of *Blurred Boundaries'* chapters to compose this afterword, I want to dwell on this tripartite function of the collection.

Archive

The chapters of *Blurred Boundaries* demonstrate the absolute necessity for recording and remembering the variety and diversity of women's COVID-19 experiences, especially as the pandemic radically recast the kinds, amount, and distribution of work in the academy (and at home). Through each unique chapter, the authors recount differing gendered pandemic experiences, critically considering how these experiences were inflected by race, culture, age, familial situation, academic rank, and even academic project. The chapters reveal how dramatically and devastatingly the pandemic remade the ways the contributors understood themselves as academics, parents, administrators, colleagues, teachers, collaborators, and activists; how it revised and often collapsed spaces of work and home; how it disrupted and redefined the work of writing, parenting, teaching, learning, administering writing programs, and, indeed, editing collections.

The collection's chapters put on display the rich and diverse ways to populate an archive that reckons with and remembers the pandemic and its consequentialities. Personal narrative pervades the volume—and the power of story (and counterstory) is clear—but the authors also show how COVID-19 memory and the COVID archive relies on qualitative research practices, autoethnography, data collection, inquiry, interviews, and analysis of diverse sources, from social media postings to parenting newsletters. Readers cannot close this volume without a deep sense of the methodological diversity at play in *Blurred Boundaries* and the ways these varied approaches lead to understandings of how the pandemic created and exacerbated lasting inequities for women academics and how they, in turn, have attempted to address these inequities and argue for redress.

This is an archive of telling and disturbing pandemic details that recall that harrowing, stress-filled, and frustrating experience. The authors recount how they created offices in their homes, administrated virtual kindergarten from the couch, created detailed schedules to move them and their children through the day, put together tenure dossiers amongst children's toys, endured endless Zoom meetings, contended with hostile colleagues, managed an overwhelming and ever-increasing workload, and deliberated about how and when to teach in person or stay online as well as whether and when to take comprehensive exams. The authors' experiences make clear how they wrestled with myths of productivity, with parenting decisions, with demands and expectations for earning tenure, with deliberations about whether to stay on the job or to resign. Through these chapters, readers come to know the nuanced and subtle rhetoricity of space and time, as the collection's writers detail how neither are experienced objectively and how both transformed during the pandemic. Home spaces became work and teaching spaces. Time was "stretched tight" for many of these authors who were working around the clock as parents, teachers, administrators, and researchers (Walters), while their (often male) colleagues without familial or administrative duties were experiencing "extra" time and getting *more* work done.

But this is also, of course, an archive of emotion. One cannot read this collection without noting how the pandemic wrecked emotional havoc. The chapters brim over with descriptions of disorientation, anxiety, burnout, fear, guilt, fatigue, and the "quiet terror of uncertainty" (Matravers). The authors make known their intentions to extend care, compassion, and empathy, and they articulate their deep (and basic) needs for safety, physical and mental health, and indeed rest. Along with such articulations of emotions is the authors' attention to their intersectional positionalities, as the contributors engage with questions of power, marginalization, and privilege.

Heuristic

Readers, like me, will not only take in and witness these stories and this archive, but they will also use the chapters as heuristics that they can connect to and invent from. There is, thus, an implicit invitation within this volume to respond to this archive, to blur the boundaries between this text and our own experiences and to tell our own COVID stories by asking—Where did we connect with the experiences in these chapters? How was our experience different? Where is the resonance and dissonance? Here is a quick demonstration of the collection's heuristic power.

At the end of 2019 my book *Domestic Occupations* came out—a book in which I examine the gendered rhetoricity of home spaces and work spaces, exploring women's changing, historical ties to the home and their varied occupation of work spaces and investigating how these two spaces can gain new meaning due, in large part, to women's occupation (or evacuation) of them. Personally, and professionally, *Domestic Occupations* was a difficult book to write. I composed it while I was, with my partner, raising three very small children, and as I researched women's spatial experiences in the nineteenth and twentieth centuries, I was also contending with my own tense relationships to home and work. I wanted to be a "good mother" at home with my children, and I wanted to work—to research, write, and teach. *Domestic Occupations* is feminist historiographic research, but it was also deeply personal for me, and when I was finished writing it, I wanted a break from thinking at every turn about women's spatial obligations (including my own).

Just as my book was feeling "done"—in print and off my desk—the pandemic hit and, understandably, close colleagues asked if I was going to write about how the pandemic was recasting women's work and collapsing their home and work spaces. The home was, once again, gaining new rhetorical and gendered meaning in this pandemic moment. While I knew there was so much to say, I just couldn't do it. I felt overwhelmed with my own domestic occupations. With three children at home, I was trying to navigate their virtual learning in first, fourth, and sixth grade. I was running a writing program in which I had to support 60+ faculty taking their 120+ sections of English 101 online. I was teaching graduate and undergraduate classes with my youngest child on my lap. I was mentoring graduate students who were developing dissertation projects and negotiating the job market in the face of a harrowing and unpredictable academic and economic climate. I was deeply worried about my aging parents, visiting them in their driveway and waving through their windows. I was in Zoom meetings around the clock. In many ways I was lucky. My family and I were relatively safe. I could continue working. I could assist my children with their learning. I had a partner who would share this work. But it was also clear to me that every burner was on high and in front; everything felt like a top priority. Oh, how I wish I had known about the "Primal Scream Line" that Shannon Walters writes about in her chapter. I was, to put it lightly, overworked, exhausted, and afraid. I was (and maybe still am) burnt out. Even though I knew I was living the subject matter of my book in a way that invited and deserved my scholarly attention, I could not write about it. It was too close and too much. Until, I guess, now.

Argument

Inviting even more COVID-19 experiences into the archive is not all this collection accomplishes. An explicit and implicit claim in many of the collection's chapters is that the pandemic that began in 2020 did not call into being a wholly new reality for these authors (and their readers). As crises often do, the pandemic exacerbated, highlighted, and deepened already existing inequities. That is, our experiences with the coronavirus (and its [mis]management) only underscore the ever-present inequities that women workers confront and reveal the structures that should be in place to address these inequities and support them. The chapters in *Blurred Boundaries* thus embolden us to understand the continued exigence for compassionate communities and care work without forgetting the very real (and often gendered) labor that undergirds these commitments. They prompt us to discern when institutional "not thinking" is in play and to call out its effects on marginalized populations within our institutional communities (Nickoson and Sheridan). The chapters stress the absolute need for accessible childcare and mental health supports for both faculty and graduate students. They shine light on how ageism operates within university settings and offer examples of better ways to support adult learners. The chapters remind us of the problematic nature of student evaluations that often offer evidence of student prejudice and discrimination rather than effective or ineffective pedagogy. The chapters challenge readers to interrogate work norms and to explore greater and more varied paths for women's academic leadership. They also assert the need for greater transparency when it comes to leave and raises, and they articulate the need for universities to mine both the positive and negative effects of stop-the-clock policies. The volume's arguments abound.

The collection's codas provide a different and particularly compelling form of argument. They remind readers that memory is always processual, always changing given time and context. As Barbie Zelizer writes, remembering is not a "finite activity with an identifiable beginning and end. Rather it is seen as a process that is constantly unfolding, changing, and transforming" (218). The authors' returns to their writing and their memories through their codas make legible the processual nature of memory. Their codas underscore the point that this collection does not put an end to COVID remembrance. Instead, *Blurred Boundaries* invites more returns, continual engagement and rethinking. Over time and experience, our engagements with this collection—its archive, its heuristics, and its arguments—will change and transform, and we should embrace and make use of the rhetorical and commemorative value it holds for us now and in the future.

Bibliography

Zelizer, Barbie. "Reading the Past Against the Grain: The Shape of Memory Studies." *Critical Studies in Mass Communication* 12, no. 2 (1995): 214–39.

ACKNOWLEDGMENTS

For us, editing *Blurred Boundaries* represents a labor of love, as we addressed (ironically) a set of interminable gendered labor issues. During a time when work, for us, was not only unbearably challenging but also served as a panacea during the confusion of the pandemic, we found shelter, comfort, and communion in the routine of engaging in work we understood with contributors whom we admired. Our authors—representing faculty from across institutions, rank, and personal circumstances—patiently partnered with us while we tried to figure out collective ways to continue researching and writing with little material or emotional support, as we negotiated ways to structure an academic collection whose contents patterned the unpredictability of a pandemic, and as we sought infrastructure post-pandemic to unite the eclectic contributions. We are eternally grateful to our project collaborators for sticking with us this through this enterprise.

We wish to thank Aurora Bell, Acquisitions Editor at University of South Carolina Press, for her enthusiastic support of this project, her timely correspondence with us regarding the long series of next steps that always accompany production of an edited collection, and her unwavering optimism and understanding of the connections among rhetorical issues, cultural practices, and feminist issues. We also appreciate the advice of our astute external reviewers. Although their identities are unknown to us, throughout the stages of the editing process they became not only honest advisors but also friendly advocates. We found hope and vindication of our messy structure in their recognition of the value and timeliness of our topic, while we also took to heart and mind their shrewd advice for improving this volume. Collectively, Jill Porco's eagle eyes, Kerri Tolan's production editing, Dianne Wade's marketing prowess, Tiffany Gray's keen indexing skills, Ashley Mathias's book-design skills, and Emily Weigel's artistic vision breathed life into this collection. We thank you all.

Jessie

This collection exists because when I mentioned to Lynée that this felt like an important era to document, she embraced and encouraged the idea. I am so grateful to have her as a mentor and co-editor throughout this (long!) process. I am grateful for the many important mentors and advocates, whose support has encouraged me to pursue projects that felt wild—Ashley Holmes, Michael Harker, Lara Smith-Sitton, Jennifer Dickey, David Parker, and Tom Keene. Jessica Enoch's work deeply inspired the premise of *Blurred Boundaries* and having her read and respond to the collection affirms its value in the field, and in our work. What an honor to have been mentored by all of you.

Deepest thanks to my parents for supporting my early and continued learning. Thank you to Olivia August for being the most supportive outside reader and pushing me to be a better writer. And thank you Ben, for your unwavering support. Finally, I hold deep gratitude for the many personal and professional friends I know who did impossible things during a global pandemic—you inspired this project, and you inspire me daily.

Lynée

First and foremost, I want to thank Jessie for her vision for this project, her rigorous research commitment, and her mad editorial skills. Her yeoman's work brought this project to fruition. I also wish to thank over three decades of students for teaching me, by example, how to blend the personal and professional; their dedication to education (sometimes against unbelievable odds) continues to humble and awe me. Contributors who have become valued friends and colleagues along the way represent the silver lining of academic partnering. And, finally, every day I send up thanks for my daughters, who have attended conferences with me since their childhoods, coauthored with me, and continue to serve as sounding boards for every project I undertake; they have grown into beautiful, successful working women in their own right.

CONTRIBUTORS

Abby Arnold-Patti is associate professor of communication and media studies at Lees-McRae College in Banner Elk, North Carolina. Her award-winning research uses ethnography, autoethnography, and critical rhetoric to study the intersection of identity, history, and place. Her work can be found in international, national, and regional academic journals such as the *Journal for the History of Rhetoric*, the *Southern Communication Journal*, and the *Journal of Autoethnography*. She lives in the heart of the beautiful Blue Ridge Mountains with her husband, three children, and all their pets.

Heather Brook Adams is associate professor of English and cross-appointed faculty in women's, gender, and sexuality studies at the University of North Carolina Greensboro. A feminist historiographer of the recent past, Adams's scholarship investigates themes such as health and wellness through a focus on rhetorics of reproduction, advocacy, and emotion. She is the author of *Enduring Shame: A Recent History of Unwed Pregnancy and Righteous Reproduction* (2022) and coeditor of *Inclusive Aims: Rhetoric's Role in Reproductive Justice* (2024). Extending her experience with community-engaged research and teaching, Adams is also a principal investigator for and director of Humanities at Work, an Andrew W. Mellon Foundation-funded, paid internship program at UNC Greensboro.

Meaghan Brewer is associate professor at Pace University, where she teaches courses in rhetoric, composition, and literacy theory and directs the writing across the curriculum program. Her research interests include literacy theory, writing pedagogy, and disciplinarity. Her work has appeared in various journals and collections including *College Composition and Communication, Composition Forum, Composition Studies, Journal of Second Language Writing,* and *Peitho.* Her book, *Conceptions of Literacy: Graduate Instructors and the Teaching of First-Year Composition,* was published with Utah State University Press (2020).

Keri Carter is assistant professor in university studies at Middle Tennessee State University (MTSU). She primarily teaches courses in professional and integrated studies programs in University College at MTSU, and she also teaches assessment, learning, and student success higher education courses as affiliate faculty with the College of Education. Prior to this role, Carter spent six years serving in writing center administration and teaching English. Her current research focuses on many facets of student success and academic support as well as higher education teaching, leadership, and culture.

Sara Cooper is associate professor of English at Murray State University in western Kentucky, where she teaches graduate courses in the Doctor of Arts in English Pedagogy program. Her research interests include multimodal composition, embodiment, commonplace writing, and feminist rhetorics. She is the author of "Radcliffe's Strongest Woman: The Bricolaged Body in One Progressive Era Women's College Scrapbook" (*Rhetoric Review,* 2002), which received a Theresa J. Enos Anniversary Award (honorable mention). In 2020 she was named College Teacher of the Year by the Kentucky Council of Teachers of English (KCTE). She is also mom to a vibrant nine-year-old, Ayla.

Danielle De Arment-Donohue is associate professor of English at Laurel Ridge Community College and earned her PhD in writing and rhetoric from George Mason University in 2025. She began her career as a high school English teacher and has also taught at Northern Virginia Community College and Shenandoah University. Danielle holds master's degrees from George Mason University and the University of Virginia and is a National Board-Certified Teacher. She is committed to studying composition pedagogy, with a focus on writing transfer in two-year colleges. Her research primarily focuses on rhetoric related to teacher well-being and workplace lactation experiences, and she has published work in this area in the Society for Technical Communication's journal, *Technical Communication.* De Arment-Donohue hopes her research contributions in these areas lead to more equitable working conditions.

Nandini Deo is associate professor of political science at Lehigh University. She spent 2023–2024 as a Fulbright Nehru Scholar at SNDT Women's University in Mumbai. Deo is moving to Georgetown University in Qatar in 2026 with her spouse and three unschooled children. She is the founder of Democracy Days, a self-directed education organization. Currently she is researching the politics of unschooling. Deo is the author of *Corporate Social Responsibility and Civil Society in India* (2024) and *Mobilizing Gender and Religion in India* (2016), co-author of *The Politics of Collective Advocacy* (2011) with Duncan McDuie Ra, and the editor of *Postsecular Feminisms in Transnational Context* (2018).

Jessica Enoch is professor of English and director of the Academic Writing Program at the University of Maryland. Her recent publications include *Domestic Occupations:*

Spatial Rhetorics and Women's Work (2019); *Mestiza Rhetorics: An Anthology of Mexicana Activism in the Spanish-Language Press, 1887–1922* (coedited with Cristina Ramírez, 2019), and *Women at Work: Rhetorics of Gender and Labor* (coedited with David Gold, 2019). *Domestic Occupations* won the Winifred Bryan Horner Outstanding Book Award in 2020. Her work has appeared in such outlets as *Rhetoric Society Quarterly, Rhetoric Review, Quarterly Journal of Speech, College English,* and *College Composition and Communication.*

Lynée Lewis Gaillet, Distinguished University Professor of English at Georgia State University, researches rhetorical history and composition pedagogy, mentoring issues, feminist activism, and archival research methodologies. Her thirteen book projects include *Stories of Mentoring* (2008), *The Present State of Scholarship in the History of Rhetoric* (2010), *Scholarly Publication in a Changing Academic Landscape* (2014), *Primary Research and Writing* (2015), and *Remembering Women Differently: Refiguring Rhetorical Work* (2019). She is recipient of an NEH Award and an International Society for the History of Rhetoric Fellowship. Gaillet has served as English department chair, president of the National Coalition of Feminist Scholars, and executive director of the South Atlantic Modern Language Association.

Kelli R. Gill (she/her) is a rhetoric and composition scholar currently serving as a Marion L. Brittain Postdoctoral Fellow at The Georgia Institute of Technology. She received her PhD at Texas Christian University in rhetoric and composition in 2024. From a disciplinary perspective in digital and cultural rhetorics, her research centers storytelling as a methodology with focuses in community writing, social justice, and food studies. Her work has been featured in journals such as *Across the Disciplines, Double Helix,* and *Trace: A Journal of Writing, Media, and Ecology.* She is also the creator and manager of the scholarly website foodrhetoric.com, an open-access resource for learning and teaching at the intersection of food and writing.

Rebecca Hallman Martini is associate professor of English and director of the Jill and Marvin Willis Center for Writing at the University of Georgia where she specializes in writing center studies, writing across the disciplines, ethnographic research methods, and composition pedagogy. Her book, *Disrupting the Center: A Partnership-Based Approach to Writing in the University* (Utah State University Press, 2022), won the 2024 Conference on College Composition and Communication (CCCC) Advancement of Knowledge Award. Her work has been published in *WPA, Across the Disciplines, WCJ,* and *Computers and Composition.* She is also the founding editor of the International Writing Center Association's newest journal, *The Peer Review: A Journal for Writing Center Practitioners,* and is working to establish writing center partnerships in Germany and Brazil. Her most cherished work, however, is being mom to Esme (seven) and Maya (four).

Michael Harker is professor of English at Georgia State University, where he serves as senior writing program director and co-director of the Digital Archives of Literacy Narratives (DALN). His scholarship engages the history and theory of rhetoric, composition, and literacy studies, with a sustained commitment to advancing literacy education and research through academic leadership and archival work.

C.C. Hendricks is assistant professor in the communication arts and sciences department and core faculty member of the women's and gender studies department at the University of New Hampshire. She is a mom and feminist rhetorician. She has held writing program administrative positions and teaches undergraduate and graduate courses in composition, women's and gender studies, professional and technical writing, and English education. Her work has appeared in *Ms. Magazine, Women in Higher Education, Peitho, The WAC Journal, Across the Disciplines, Composition Studies,* and edited collections. She is currently working on a book project on Diane di Prima.

Ashley J. Holmes is Associate Vice Provost for Teaching and Learning at Oregon State University (OSU), where she leads the Center for Teaching and Learning. Holmes's research focuses on place-based learning, high-impact practices, and the scholarship of teaching and learning. She recently published the monograph *Learning on Location: Place-Based Approaches for Diverse Learners in Higher Education* (2023) and co-edited the collection *Learning from the Mess: Method/ological Praxis in Rhetoric and Writing Studies* (2024). Prior to joining OSU in July 2024, Ashley was faculty in English at Georgia State University for twelve years, where she taught undergraduate and graduate classes in rhetoric and composition. She also served as Interim Director of Teaching Effectiveness in the Center for Teaching, Learning, and Online Education (2023–24) and as Director of the Writing Across the Curriculum Program (2018–23).

Jessica Jorgenson Borchert is associate teaching professor at Iowa State University where she teaches technical communication courses. Her research interests include motherhood/postpartum rhetoric, inclusive teaching practices, and user experience (UX) design. Along with teaching at Iowa State, she also works to grow initiatives within the English department that focus on technical communication and user experience.

Angela D. Mack, PhD (she/her) is a rhetoric and composition scholar whose work focuses on community engagement and care and racialized cartographies of the Black lived experience. With a background in performance poetry, storytelling, and creative writing, her research areas include African American and Afro-diasporic rhetorics and composition, popular culture, poetry, public and digital humanities, and memorial activism. She is the 2024 recipient of the Conference on College

Composition & Communication's James Berlin Memorial Outstanding Dissertation Award; an inaugural cohort fellow of Modern Language Association's Public Humanities Incubator; and the 2024 recipient of the Computers and Composition Hugh Burns Distinguished Dissertation Award. Her work can be found in *constellations: a cultural rhetorics publishing space*; *Women, Gender, and Families of Color*; and *Dialogue: The Interdisciplinary Journal of Popular Culture and Pedagogy*.

Molly E. MacLachlan is associate professor of rhetoric and composition at the University of North Georgia and the director of composition. She teaches within the Writing and Publication major as well as first year composition courses. Outside of the academy, she is both a stepmom to Bruce and a mom to Arwen. Work–life balance is still a focus of her research and daily life, and she is continuing her research on stepparenting and the intersection of being both mom and stepmom. Somehow, she also manages to practice yoga, strength train, and dance (sometimes while wearing Arwen to ballet class).

Laura Sceniak Matravers is a teacher-scholar who currently works part-time as an adjunct instructor of English at a community college in the US Southeast. Prior to this post, she was an associate professor of English. She earned her PhD in rhetoric and composition from the University of Louisville in 2018. Other published work of hers has appeared in *Kairos* and the collection *Mobility Work in Composition*, which she coedited.

Jessica Edens McCrary is associate director of Emory University's National Scholarships & Fellowships Program, where she works with students and alumni on their writing and career self-efficacy through the process of applying to nationally competitive awards. Her dissertation research employed methods from history, archival studies, and feminist rhetorical theory to analyze the rhetorical nature of acts of remembrance and documentation of the Equal Rights Amendment battle in Georgia. McCrary's research foci include archival methods, women and labor, feminist rhetoric, writing program administration, and undergraduate scholar development. Her work has been published in *College English, Written Communication,* and the *Journal of the Georgia Association of Historians.*

Michelle Miley is associate professor of English, rhetoric and writing studies at Montana State University. Her current research interests include rhetorics of mothering and nurture, and retheorizing WAC/WID with the advent of generative AI. Her publications include "Bringing Feminist Theory Home" (*Theories and Methods of Writing Center Studies*), "Writing Center as Homeplace (A Site for Radical Resistance)" (*The Peer Review*), and "Feminist Mothering: A Theory/Practice for Writing Center Administration," (*WLN: A Journal of Writing Center Scholarship*). She is loving learning what it means to be mother to two adult children, Abby and Matt.

Elizabeth Ellis Miller is associate professor of English at Mississippi State University, where she teaches courses in rhetorics of social change, first-year and professional writing, and theories of composition. Her work appears in *College Communication and Composition, College English, Rhetoric Review, Journal for the History of Rhetoric, Rhetoric & Public Affairs,* and edited collections. She is the author of *Liturgy of Change: Rhetorics of the Civil Rights Mass Meeting* (University of South Carolina, 2023).

Nancy Myers is associate professor emerita in the Department of English at the University of North Carolina Greensboro, where she was also cross-appointed faculty in the women's, gender, and sexuality studies program. Her more recent feminist rhetorical scholarship includes essays in *Nineteenth-Century American Activist Rhetorics; Women at Work: Rhetorics of Gender and Labor; Remembering Women Differently: Refiguring Rhetorical Work; In the Archives of Composition;* and *Rhetoric, History, and Women's Oratorical Education.* She is coeditor with Heather Brook Adams of *Inclusive Aims: Rhetoric's Role in Reproductive Justice* (2024), with Kathleen J. Ryan and Rebecca Jones of *Rethinking Ethos* (2016), and with Edward P. J. Corbett and Gary Tate of the third and fourth editions of *The Writing Teacher's Sourcebook.* Myers served from 2010 to 2012 as president of the Coalition of Feminist Scholars in the History of Rhetoric and Composition.

Lee Nickoson, professor of rhetoric and composition, directs the rhetoric and writing studies program at Bowling Green State University where she researches and teaches courses on writing program administration, writing research, and composition pedagogies. With Kelly A. Moreland, she co-chairs Teacher-to-Teacher, an annual half-day teaching network forum as part of the CCCC and learns from colleagues' innovative scholarship as an associate publisher of the WAC Clearinghouse and the coeditor (with Lindsey Harding) of the WAC Clearinghouse Repository. Nickoson continues to learn from her students and collaborators about meaningful ways to affect change through writing.

Ceceilia Parnther is associate professor of executive leadership at Le Moyne College. Her research develops and implements qualitatively dominant research designs to explore equity and integrity in leadership and practice. Parnther's career path as a scholar-practitioner includes serving in leadership and teaching roles in higher education administration for fifteen years. She co-edited the volume *Voices from Women Leaders in Higher Education: Pipelines, Pathways, and Promotion* (2022). She is editor-in-chief of *Academic Integrity and Referencing for SAGE Student Success.* She has recently published in the *Journal of Mentoring and Coaching in Higher Education, The Journal of College and Character,* and *Innovative Higher Education.*

Laura Seroka is associate professor of communication at Berea College. Her research and teaching focuses on strategic communication, specifically applied toward improving healthcare and environmental activism outcomes. With ties to the Appalachian region and a passion for undergraduate research, she and students recently conducted a study to better understand the diverse health needs and behaviors of co-cultural Appalachians. She and her family can often be found hiking the trails within the Blue Ridge Mountains and Red River Gorge, with their homeschooling nature journals tucked into backpacks.

Mary P. Sheridan is professor of English and director of the Commonwealth Center for Humanities and Society at the University of Louisville. She researches and teaches questions at the intersection of community engagement, feminist methodologies, and higher education. Currently, Sheridan is exploring both contemporary changes within higher education and how these interact with public rhetoric belittling higher education in general and the humanities in particular. For her academic scholarship, she has been awarded the Winifred Bryan Horner Outstanding Book Award from Coalition of Women Scholars in the History of Rhetoric and Composition; the Civic Scholarship/Book of the Year Award from *Reflections: A Journal of Writing, Service-Learning, and Community Literacy*; and, as part of a collaborative group, the Computers and Composition Michelle Kendrick Outstanding Digital Production/Scholarship Award.

Mary Lourdes Silva (she/her) is full professor of writing and director of first-year writing at Ithaca College. Her past and current research examines the citation practices of first-year college writing students; pedagogical use of multimodal and multimedia technologies and practices; implementation of institutional ePortfolio assessment; gender/race bias in education; movement-touch literacy as a modality to teach reflective thinking in first-year writing; the psychological and financial implications of faculty compelled to review biased student evaluations of teaching; and critical AI literacy in first-year writing. She is also a community organizer and teaches Argentine tango at Cornell University.

Shannon Walters is Associate Professor of English at Temple University where she researches and teaches in rhetoric and composition, disability studies and gender studies. She is the author of *Rhetorical Touch: Disability, Identification, Haptics* (University of South Carolina Press, 2014). Her work has appeared recently in *College Composition and Communication, Composition Forum, Feminist Media Studies* and *The Journal of Literary & Cultural Disability Studies*. Her current project argues for a conceptual approach to disability studies and crip theory based in rhetorics of the paranormal.

Heidi M. Williams is associate professor specializing in rhetoric and composition at Tennessee State University and has almost twenty years of experience teaching in higher education. She has dedicated her career to cultivating classroom spaces that enhance experiential educational opportunities through active learning environments that are dynamic, practical, and have larger civic implications. She has taught at three colleges and in Zhejiang, China. Williams is deeply committed to education in multiple capacities. Outside of the institution, she homeschools her two daughters and is heavily involved in the Tennessee homeschool community.

Taylor Paige Winfield is assistant professor in the School of Sociology at the University of Arizona. Her research investigates how people from diverse backgrounds navigate military and correctional institutions and push these institutions to change. As a feminist scholar and community-engaged researcher, she has over a decade of experience conducting research in global settings with restrictive access. Her work has appeared in journals such as *Ethnography, Journal of Contemporary Ethnography, Sociological Theory,* and *Theory & Society.* She has training in Spiritually-Integrated Psychotherapy from the Canadian Association for Spiritual Care.